6000198062

D1826684

N

Representations of Gender from Prehistory to the Present

Studies in Gender and Material Culture

This series, edited by Moira Donald and Linda Hurcombe of the University of Exeter, is a pioneering project consisting of three books which focus on different aspects of the relationship between gender and material culture from prehistory to the present. Incorporating the work of archaeologists, classicists, art historians and social historians, these volumes form a unique interdisciplinary collection written by leading scholars in the field from many countries. This project stems from an exciting interdisciplinary conference on *Gender and Material Culture* which was the first of a series of regular gender and history conferences organized by the University of Exeter.

GENDER AND MATERIAL CULTURE IN ARCHAEOLOGICAL PERSPECTIVE

GENDER AND MATERIAL CULTURE IN HISTORICAL PERSPECTIVE

REPRESENTATIONS OF GENDER FROM PREHISTORY TO THE PRESENT

Studies in Gender and Material Culture
Standing Order ISBN 0–333–64322–4 (three volume set)
(*outside North America only*)

You can receive future titles in this series as they are published by placing a standing order. Please contact your bookseller or, in case of difficulty, write to us at the address below with your name and address, the title of the series and the ISBN quoted above.

Customer Services Department, Macmillan Distribution Ltd, Houndmills, Basingstoke, Hampshire RG21 6XS, England

Representations of Gender from Prehistory to the Present

Edited by

Moira Donald
Senior Lecturer in History
University of Exeter

and

Linda Hurcombe
Lecturer in Prehistory
University of Exeter

First published in Great Britain 2000 by
MACMILLAN PRESS LTD
Houndmills, Basingstoke, Hampshire RG21 6XS and London
Companies and representatives throughout the world

A catalogue record for this book is available from the British Library.

ISBN 0–333–64331–3

 First published in the United States of America 2000 by
ST. MARTIN'S PRESS, INC.,
Scholarly and Reference Division,
175 Fifth Avenue, New York, N.Y. 10010

ISBN 0–312–22397–8

Library of Congress Cataloging-in-Publication Data
Representations of gender from prehistory to the present / edited by
Moira Donald and Linda Hurcombe.
p.   cm. — (Studies in gender and material culture)
Includes bibliographical references and index.
ISBN 0–312–22397–8 (cloth)
1. Women—History.   2. Sex role—History.   3. Feminist
archaeology.   4. Material culture.   I. Donald, Moira.
II. Hurcombe, Linda.   III. Series.

HQ1121.R45   1999
305.3'09—dc21   99–33851
                                                          CIP

This book is printed on paper suitable for recycling and made from fully managed and sustained
forest sources.

10   9   8   7   6   5   4   3   2   1
09   08   07   06   05   04   03   02   01   00

Printed and bound in Great Britain by
Antony Rowe Ltd, Chippenham, Wiltshire

Contents

List of Figures and Tables

Figures

Tables

Preface

This volume is one of a series originating from an international conference held at the University of Exeter in July 1994. The idea for the conference and the volumes developed out of discussions between a modern historian and an archaeologist about their work which, despite being separated by thousands of years chronologically, was thematically linked. Moira Donald was teaching a course on the material culture of the home and had just embarked on a research project on households in nineteenth-century Exeter.[1] Linda Hurcombe was teaching a course on material culture in pre-history and was examining the problem of engendering the archaeological past from human evolution onwards.[2] Our discussions led to the organization of a multi-disciplinary conference, *Gender and Material Culture from Prehistory to the Present*. This conference attracted speakers from around the world and has culminated in the publication of the present series of which this volume forms a part. The other volumes are entitled *Gender and Material Culture in Historical Perspective* and *Gender and Material Culture in Archaeological Perspective*.

Gender studies has emerged as a significant and exciting new field, but individual researchers can sometimes feel isolated within their discipline or their academic department. With the conference and these volumes it was our aim to open up debate to a wide audience in a variety of fields. The series will, we hope, be accessible to students and academics alike and will encourage the breaking down of traditional discipline boundaries, incorporating work from archaeologists, classicists, historians and art historians. The key objectives of the three-volume series are to bring a gendered approach to interpretations of material culture and to place material culture at the centre of the study of the past, irrespective of period.

We are grateful to all the participants in the *Gender and Material Culture, especially Barbara Bender, our keynote speaker, who also wrote the introduction to the volume Representations of Gender from Prehistory to the Present*. Our thanks go also to our past and present colleagues of the University of Exeter who gave papers: Sandra Cavallo, Julia Crick, Tia DeNora, Anne Duffin,

---

1. Di Cooper and Moira Donald (1995) 'Household and "Hidden" Kin in Early Nineteenth-century England: four case studies in suburban Exeter, 1821–61', *Continuity and Change*, 10(2), pp. 257–77.
2. Linda Hurcombe (1995) 'Our Own Engendered Species', *Antiquity*, 69, pp. 87–100.

Helen Sims, Karen Stears, Tina Tuohy and John Wilkins. Many other colleagues from Archaeology and History at Exeter participated in other ways and they also deserve our thanks, particularly John Critchley, who as Head of Department at that time facilitated our administrative efforts. The University of Exeter gave us a grant towards the initial organization of the conference and towards some of the editorial work on the volumes. The technicians in the Archaeology drawing office all contributed in various ways during the preparation of the conference and at the event itself. Sue Rouillard was responsible for much of the artwork and some of the images on the conference material. Seán Goddard took the photographs which were used in the poster and jacket design under Sue's direction. Sue also oversaw the complex business of illustrations and figures for all three volumes, for which we give our warm thanks. Sean Hawken, Cathy Pink and Jim Williams aided Linda Hurcombe in the final stages of the archaeology volume. Aruna Vasudevan and Keith Povey for Macmillan succeeded in keeping the three-volume series on track. Our thanks go above all to Di Cooper, co-researcher with Moira Donald on the Exeter households project. Di was the lynchpin of the conference administration and contributed a great deal of the spadework on the editing of the volumes and correspondence with the contributors. Her role was invaluable in the successful completion of this project. Finally, thanks are also deserved by our patient contributors and those close to us who have lived with this project for some time.

MOIRA DONALD
LINDA HURCOMBE

Acknowledgements

The publisher and editors also wish to thank the following for their kind permission to reproduce copyright material: Desmond Morris; Professor P.J. Ucko; Glasgow Museum Art Gallery; Museum Kelvingrove; Dr Stuart Swiny; Carnegie Institute of Washington; Dr John Parkington; Rock Art Research Unit, University of Witwatersrand; Boston Museum of Fine Art; Marlin von Wagner Museum, Wurzburg; Trustees of the British Museum; Hermitage Museum, Petersburg; Sotheby's; Manchester City Art Gallery; Victoria and Albert Museum, London; Mrs Marion Sharples; Blackburn City Museum; Imperial War Museum, London; Science Museum, Science and Society Picture Library, London; *The Tatler*; Bodleian Library, Oxford. Every effort has been made to contact all the copyright-holders, but if any have been inadvertently omitted the publishers will be pleased to make the necessary arrangement at the earliest opportunity.

Notes on the Contributors

Tim Barringer is Assistant Professor in the Department of the History of Art at Yale University, having formerly taught in the Universities of London (Birkbeck College) and Birmingham in Britain. He has published widely on Victorian visual culture and is the author of *Reading the Pre-Raphaelites* (1999) and is the co-editor with Tom Flynn of *Colonialism and the Object: Empire, Material Culture and the Museum* (1998) and with Elizabeth Prettejohn of *Frederic Leighton: Antiquity, Renaissance, Modernity* (1999).

Barbara Bender is Profesor in Heritage Anthropology, University College London. She is the author of *Stonehenge: Making Space* (1998), The editor of *Landscape: Politics and Perspective* (1993) and the co-editor of *Contested Landscapes and Landscapes of Movement and Exile (2000)*. She is working on a joint anthro/archaeological project on Bodmin Moor, as well as on the politics and recreation of the past aat Emain Mach. armagh, Northern Ireland and on a community project, 'Where Memory meets History', in East Devon.

Christopher Breward is Reader in Historical and Cultural Studies at the London College of Fashion, London Institute. He is the author of *The Culture of Fashion: A New History of Fashionable Dress* (1995) and *The Hidden Consumer: Masculinities, Fashion and City Life 1860–1914* (1999) and is joint editor with Marius Kwint and Jeremy Aynsley of *Material Memories: Design and Evocation* (1999). He is on the editorial board of the journal *Fashion Theory* and is working on the cultural history of fashion in London in the modern period.

Moira Donald is Senior Lecturer in History at the University of Exeter. She has published on various subjects, including women in the Russian Revolution, kin in nineteenth-century Exeter, the home as workplace, and the European socialist movement. As well as co-editing with Linda Hurcombe this three-volume series on *Gender and Material Culture*, she is the author of *Marxism and Revolution: Karl Kautsky and the Russian Marxists 1900–1924* (1993) and the co-editor with Tim Rees of *Reinterpreting Revolution in Twentieth-Century Europe* (2000). She is writing a history of the Second International and developing a research project on nineteenth-century households.

Matthew Fox is Lecturer in Classics at the University of Birmingham. He studied in Oxford and Berlin, and is the author of *Roman Historical Myths*

(1996). His work on gender has focused on masculinity and its representation, and he has been continuing to develop his interest in psychoanalytical approaches. He has written on transvestite Hercules, on masculinity in classical Athens and on satyrs. He is currently working on a large-scale study of the hermeneutics of ancient historical writing.

Naomi Hamilton studied at Cambridge and the Institute of Archaeology, London, and is currently completing her PhD at Edinburgh on gender in the prehistoric cultures of Central Anatolia. She worked for several years as a field archaeologist with the Museum of London and since 1993 she has been a member of the excavation team at Catalhoyuk, Turkey. Her main interests are in gender, society, nationalism, Cyprus, Turkey and the Phoenecians. Her publications include contributions to the *Cambridge Journal of Archaeology* and a chapter on figurines and burials in M. Hodder (ed.), *On the Surface: Catalhoyuk 1993–5* (1996).

Kelley Hays-Gilpin is Assistant Professor of Anthropology at Northern Arizona University, where she teaches archaeological theory, prehistory, ceramic analysis, and gender archaeology. She received her PhD at the University of Arizona in 1992, then worked until 1997 for the Navajo Nation Archaeology Program. Recent publications include *Reader in Gender Archaeology* with David S. Whitley, and *Prehistoric Sandals from Northeastern Arizona* with Ann C. Deegan and Elizabeth A. Morris. She is presently analysing Hopi painted pottery and mural paintings in a multidisciplinary project involving Hopi elders, linguists and art historians.

Virginia Hewitt is curator of paper money in the Department of Coins and Medals at the British Museum. Much of her research focuses on the imagery and symbolism on paper currency. Recent publications include *The Banker's Art* (1995), which she edited, 'Beware of imitations: the campaign for a new Bank of England note, 1797–1821' *The Numismatic Chronicle* (158, 1998), and 'A distant view – imagery and imagination in the paper money of the British Empire, 1800–1960' in *National-States and Money*, (1999). She is currently working on a catalogue of English provincial banknotes in the British Museum.

Louise A. Hitchcock received her PhD in Art History from UCLA in 1998, and is now a Research Associate of the Cotsen Institute of Archaeology at UCLA. Her research interests are in Aegean architecture, archaeological theory and gender. She has excavated in California, Crete and Syria and, as a Fulbright Fellow, has investigated Aegean influences on Cypriot architecture. She is the co-author of *Aegean Art and Architecture* with Donald Preziosi, and has published several articles on Minoan architecture and gender.

Linda Hurcombe is Lecturer in Archaeology at the University of Exeter. As well as co-editing with Moira Donald this three-volume series on *Gender and Material Culture*, she is the author of a book on obsidian usewear analysis and of numerous articles on palaeolithic stone tools from Pakistan, issues of artefact function and gender, including an article on the gender bias of archaeology published in *Antiquity* in 1995. Her research interests are focused on prehistoric stone tools, materials and gender and the exploitation of plants for craftwork.

Claire L. Lyons is Collections Curator at the Getty Research Institute for the History of Art and the Humanities, Los Angeles, California. She has a PhD in classical archaeology from Bryn Mawr College and has published numerous articles on ancient funerary practice, colonial–indigenous contact, the history of archaeology and the history of collecting. Major recent publications include *Morgantina: The Archaic Cemeteries* (1996) and a volume co-edited with A. Koloski-Ostrow, *Naked Truths: Women, Sexuality and Gender in Classical Art and Archaeology* (1997).

Helen Sims has an MA in women's studies from the University of Exeter. She went on to train in social work and is now employed by the Children's Society and also works at a resource centre for young people with disabilities. She recently spent time in Greece researching the subject of deinstitutionalization in southern Europe and is preparing her findings for publication.

Judith Stevenson is working at UCLA on her PhD in sociocultural anthropology. She is examining South Africa's nation-building process through a gender-sensitive analysis in which she investigates women's networks and activisms at grassroots level. The study is based on oral testimonies from Tswana women in a small township near Johannesburg. She previously worked on South African rock art, and her contribution to the present book is based on her earlier work.

Lauren E. Talalay is Associate Director and Associate Curator at the Kelsey Museum of Archaeology and Adjunct Associate Professor in the Department of Classical Studies, University of Michigan. Her main areas of interest includes the Greek neolithic, particularly figurines and gender in prehistory. She is the author of *Deities, Dolls and Devices: Neolithic figurines from Franchthi Cave, Greece* (1993) and of articles on prehistoric figurines and body symbolism in the Mediterranean.

John Wilkins is Senior Lecturer in Classics at the University of Exeter. He has published several books on food, including *Food in Antiquity* (edited with D. Harvey, 1995), *Food in European Literature* (edited, 1996) and *The*

Boastful Chef: the Discourse of Food in Ancient Greek Comedy (forthcoming). Other works include a commentary on Euripides (*Euripides: Heraclidae*, 1993), a book on ancient comedy co-edited with David Harvey, *The Rivals of Aristophanes* (forthcoming) and a book co-edited with David Braund on the food-writer Athenaeus of Naucratis, *Athenaeus and his Philosophers at Dinner*.

Angela Woollacott is Associate Professor of History at Case Western Reserve University, Cleveland, Ohio. Her publications include *On Her Their Lives Depend: Munitions Workers in the Great War* (1994), co-edited Miriam Cooke, *Gendering War Talk* (1993), and co-edited with Mrinalini Sinha and Donna Guy, *Feminisms and Internationalism* (1999). She is currently completing a book entitled *White Colonials, Modernity and Metropolis: Australian Women in London 1870–1940*, and is also working on another project, *Gender and the Politics of Empire*.

Ina Zweiniger-Bargielowska is Lecturer in Modern British Social and Economic History at the University of Wales, Aberystwyth. Her publications include *The Conservatives and British Society, 1880–1990* (1996) edited with M. Francis, and *Austerity in Britain: Rationing, Controls and Consumption, 1939–1955* (2000). She is editing a textbook on women in twentieth-century Britain.

Introduction

Barbara Bender

This volume is about *representations* of gender. It is difficult to know where 'representations' begin and end. Representations, images, symbols, and icons stand in for objects, people, or emotions in ways that may or may not reflect the 'realities' of lived social relations.[1] They can be powerful or mute, available or hidden. In this volume representations take the form of figurines, frescoes, pottery decoration, rock art, Victorian pictures, fashion ... But why stop there? Aren't all material items in some sense representational? A fridge, a three-piece suite, jewellery, weaponry, tools, architecture are all symbolically loaded. They stand in for ideals or desires, carry messages, promote or discourage thought and action.[2] The question is, therefore, not so much whether artefacts are representational or not, but rather what approach we take. The same object may be considered in terms of representation, or of production, consumption, ownership, or use ...

The chapters in this volume are stimulating in their *cumulative* working through of gender issues, in the deconstructions they offer of biases (usually male) in contemporary strategies and agendas that have blinded us to other ways of approaching the material record, and in their wide-ranging theoretical and comparative referencing. Archaeologists have been more reluctant to discuss issues of gender than have – many – historians. I assume that this is because historians have for far longer accepted the subjectivity and reflexive nature of their enterprise and have, therefore been more open to ideas developed in cultural studies, philosophy, linguistics, etc. Archaeologists working within a positivist, so-called 'scientific' framework have been more resistant.[3] It was the Post Processual backlash in the 1980s that created a space for feminist intervention.[4]

Gender theory is complex, disputed, changing and often obscure and difficult. But, rather than by-passing or oversimplifying, we should, I think, be trying to make the theory (theories) more accessible, more available. Otherwise there remains the risk that gender still gets confused with simply allowing women more prominence in the record. One of the important things about feminist or critical theory is that it forces us to politicize our debates. We need a gendered theoretical *and* practical understanding of an interwoven past and present in order to confront *both* the present political and academic configurations *and* the constructions of the past – or, rather, of many different pasts. As Conkey (1993) puts it, the (belated) recognition that

> archaeology is more interpretative than positivist, more committed to the development of theory, more committed to 'empirical depth' than to 'empiricism' means that our knowledge must still be close to the ground and honed to the case in hand.[5]

Indeed, as we recognize the cultural specificity of gendered practices our work needs to be more than ever locally nuanced.

I want, briefly, to touch first on issues of gender, and then on issues of gendered material culture, and in so doing I shall mention some anthropological literature which may be useful to archaeologists and historians alike.

Questions of gender

We used to think that gender was a cultural elaboration of biological sex differences, and that biological sex was a given, a universal. We are now beginning to recognize that fixed binary sexes, with fixed categorizations, are an historically late western cultural construction. *We* instantly categorize babies, but there are plenty of societies in which sex is not so much given at birth as accreted. Tim Yates (1993), in his discussion of the rock art of Bohusland in Sweden, noted that the sketchy human figures were given many and varied attributes – long hair, penises, sheathed swords, helmets, enlarged hands and enlarged calf-muscles. Archaeologists assumed that those figures without penises were women, although these images did not necessarily correlate with long hair or a lack of weapons, and that two figures joined at the waist by a line were a married couple, although on closer inspection one had a penis, the other had enlarged calf-muscles.[6] Yates suggested that *none* of these figures were women, they were all *sort of* men, and that in this society masculine identity was not fixed but acquired. What the figures show is an *accumulation* of male identity. Naomi Hamilton, in Chapter 2 this volume, suggests something rather similar for the Neolithic figurines of Europe and the Near East. If biological sex is not a given, it follows that it is not necessarily binary.

As for gender, we have recognized for some time now that binary gender divisions are part of a western normative male discourse. Several chapters pick up on the possibility of other, more fluid categorisations (Talalay, Hamilton, Stevenson, Hitchcock, Barringer, Woolacott – Chapters 1, 2, 4, 5, 10, 13 respectively). Gendered identities need not be stable; they may be negotiated throughout people's life-cycles and associated activities. Marilyn

Strathern, in *The Gender of the Gift* (1988), notes that in Melanesia gender is one of the ways of signalling that something has been created. The child makes the mother, and out of the complementary work of men and women in the gardens appears the 'relationship of husband and wife'.[7] Whilst Sandra Harding (1983) suggests that 'the sex/gender system limits and creates opportunities within which are constructed the social practices of daily life, the characteristics of social institutions and all our patterns of thought',[8] Strathern reverses this order.

Gendered identities are performative, contextual and relational.[9] Moreover, as Moore (1993) points out, they may be refracted, submerged or negated by cross-cutting divisions of age, status or ranking.

> If gender makes a difference, then so too do race, class, sexuality, religion and other forms of difference ... [We] have to question the primacy of gender difference ... [It] is not the stable concept the anthropologist assumes it to be.[10]

Questions of gendered material culture

What of material culture? There is still a tendency to see material culture as a *reflection* of gendered relationships. And there is still a tendency to separate out people and things: people *do* things, people *make* things, people *own* things (or don't). But we've already seen that, in Melanesia, work is creative of gender.[11] And so is material culture. Annette Weiner, in *Inalienable Wealth* (1985), discusses the inalienability of objects, the way in which 'things' are part of, and creative of, identity.[12] Maureen MacKenzie in her extraordinary book, *Androgynous Objects* (1991), focuses on Papua New Guinean 'bag people', on the fluid gendering of their string bags in different contexts. As the bag moves through different social contexts and transactions in an ongoing round of production and consumption it acquires – and negotiates – new forms, new function, new meanings. The story of the gendered bag is a wonderful metaphor for the story of gendered human beings. Bags (and people) are things-in-motion. Bags are multi-authored: the women make the basic net bag, and some are used by women, some are adorned by men, thus hiding the women's work. At one level the men appropriate and mask the women's labour, and in the male account of things (recounted to male ethnographers) *their* decorated bags used in *their* rituals are part of *their* superiority over women. But MacKenzie points out that the ethnographers have accepted this reading at face value. And the reason they accept it is because of one of our many naturalized binary oppositions correlates public *with* male *with* important, and private (domestic) *with* female *with* unimportant. The men and their bird-feathered netbags operate in the public arena. But – and this is the important point – the women do not subscribe to the western devaluation of domestic labour, nor to the notion that the worlds of women and men are autonomous. The men boast of their superiority but they also acknowledge their dependency on women. The netbag contains, amongst other things, ceremonial red paint that contains menstrual blood.

MacKenzie suggests that the women are complacent about their exclusion from male rituals because they are aware of their productive and reproductive contributions to the joint enterprise of collective well-being. She stresses the complementarity of these processes and questions the entrenched notion that exclusion (of women by men in rituals) equals inequality.[13] She emphasizes, as does Diane Bell (1984),[14] that women not only have their own rituals, but also understand their own importance within the apparently exclusive male rituals. Nonetheless, I would suggest that in many societies there may be complementarity *and*, in some contexts, inequality. MacKenzie notes, for example, that if the women are not 'correctly' covered, the men will punish them. But women cannot punish men.

This notion that gendered activities are often more complementary than they appear at first glance, and that public/domestic, male/female divisions are to some extent illusory is shown again in a study of Alaskan Inupiat by Barbara Bodenhorn (1993).[15] Whale hunting, one of the mainstays of subsistence, is (at least in recent years) an exclusively male reserve, and the beached whales are divided amid great public acclaim. And yet the female-centred hearth is neither considered 'private' nor unimportant. When Bodenhorn said to a male hunter 'Only men hunt', he replied, 'the whale comes to the woman'. It is the generosity of her work that attracts the whale. 'The woman is the soul of the whale, her lamp is its heart. It is the woman of the hearth that gives the whale life.'[16]

Thus we need to be clear that 'culture/nature, public/private and production/reproduction are all transformations of one another ... all part of [a] western folk model'.[17] And, in a gendered world of people/things, there are many other taken-for-granted binaries that we need to question, such as (practical) technology versus ritual practice;[18] clock versus seasonal/personal understandings of time;[19] indexical (apparently objective) versus non-indexical (subjective, lived, person-centred) representations of spaces and places.[20] We have to try to understand and (re)-constitute the self, gender, knowledge, social relations and culture without resorting to linear, teleological, hierarchical, holistic, or binary ways of thinking or being.[21]

*   *   *

In Part I of the book, four writers discuss gendered representations in prehistory. Lauren Talalay and Naomi Hamilton in Chapters 1 and 2 consider the ways in which figurines have been used to promote a matriarchal 'Golden Age'. Talalay, working with Mediterranean evidence, notes that very few of the figurines can be sexed, but of those that can, the large majority are female and these ones are more carefully made and more often adorned. In considering the apparently sexless or androgynous images, Talalay urges us 'to contemplate gender ascriptions that include more than the traditional male/female, either/or dichotomies', and the possibility of a dynamic classification that moves in and out of sexual or gendered identities, or of gradations of gendered identity. With regards to the significance of the female figurines, she stresses that even if some of them represented goddesses, that tells us nothing about the socio–political status of women, and that the popular (Gimbutas-led) notion of a nurturing, sensitive, pacific female leadership simply essentializes women's reproductive abilities. Moving beyond the simple discovery of female (or other) figurines to the wider archaeological contextualisation of gendered relations, Talalay notes that women are often more visible than men in the mortuary record and have more grave goods, and that, at least in some instances, female burials are associated with domestic activities. All of which suggests that the relative value given to different spheres of labour may have been quite unlike our own.

Naomi Hamilton is primarily concerned with deconstructing interpretations of Near Eastern and European figurines, exposing underlying attitudes to gender roles and the frequent elision of sex and gender. She invokes ethnographic analogies to suggest, like Talalay, that we need to think about sex–gender dissonance, fluidity and difference. The relative paucity of male figurines may suggest either that 'figurines were not associated with males, or that maleness was not an important concept at the time'.

Whilst Talalay touches on the work of American feminist archaeologists, and Hamilton uses ethnographic analogy, Hays-Gilpin, in Chapter 3 on Anasazi farmers in north-eastern Arizona, turns briefly to Post-Processual debates on the nature of material culture. She notes that objects are not just passive reflections of cognitive, social or utilitarian norms, 'but [are] actively modified and reinterpreted in ongoing processes of cultural change'. She could, perhaps, have taken this discussion further and suggested that the objects themselves, or the representations, actively *affect* ongoing social relationships. Hays-Gilpin considers the archaeological and later ethnographic evidence, and notes changes in attitudes and in the use of material culture. One might wish that the assumed links between a greater commitment to farming, a more settled way of life and greater specialization, and between intensification in decoration and social tension, be more critically considered. Equally, the suggestion that if women did most of the farm work, residence was likely to be matrilocal and descent matrilineal, and that women would therefore have a great deal of sexual and economic autonomy, is not necessarily true. There are plenty of case studies that show that it's not what you do, but the way that it's valued that counts.

Judith Stevenson, in her account in Chapter 4 of shaman images in San rock art, finds an interesting discrepancy between the ethnographic accounts which suggest that 30 per cent of shamans were female, and the rock-art representations of shamans, very few of which appear to be female. But, as Stevenson points out, we should perhaps not look for a straightforward gendering of ritual practitioners. Both women and men may have been shamans, but the shaman may have been envisaged as something 'contradictory, subjective, decentred [and] dynamic'. The images are metaphors which 'overlap and mix up themes and motifs, creating a richly complex layering of meanings about social processes'. She cites Biesele (1993): 'womanly power and manly power and the power of shamans ... are really one power, a power in turn coterminous with the identical powers of creation and healing'.[22] This emphasis on the power of metaphor, and on the potential for representations to address powers that are both male and female (or something that is neither, or more) may have wider implications.

Part II of the book focuses on Minoan, Greek and Roman representations where archaeological and historical evidence play off each other. The use of contemporary written evidence may seem less problematic than the use of more general ethnographic analogy but actually requires rather similar probing: who wrote the histories, for what purposes, in what contexts? And what assumptions and biases do our readings of these histories involve?

Louise Hitchcock in Chapter 5, discussing ambiguity in fresco paintings from Knossos, draws on literary sources from Assyria and Egypt without too much discussion of what agendas such sources might ascribe to. She shows that in a world in which bronze figurines and figures in frescoes are for the most part clearly designated as female or male, there are occasions on which male and female elements are combined. Having unpicked the unwarranted assumption that somehow these ambiguous figures must be read as either female or male, she suggests that in Minoan Crete, as in Assyria or Egypt, there were times and places where 'sexual ambiguity, multiple genders, plurality and difference played a sanctioned role'. Intriguingly, she also mentions that representations of the passing of time may cross-cut conventional gendered imaging. Pale skin colour may *usually* denote female, and ruddy skin male gendering, but pale skin colour on an otherwise male figure might indicate past or future time.

With Claire Lyons' Chapter 6 we move to early colonial Sicily. If, instead of the more usual focus on trade and exchange and on imported pottery – i.e. on the public sphere which is frequently male-dominated – we attend to domestic pottery found in graves and settlement sites, we can begin to consider the relationship between indigenous people and colonizers and uncover 'a lively, dynamic process of transculturation in which indigenous women are active agents'. Lyons draws on the limited historical sources – skewed, of course, towards accounts of colonization rather than indigenous reception, resistance or negotiation – and on New World historical and ethnographic accounts which, in the hand of feminist historians, have yielded comparable stories of subtle, changing and gendered transculturation.

French feminist writers receive little attention in this volume but Matthew Fox, in his Chapter 7 on Satyrs and Hetaerae, uses the work of Irigaray as a springboard to emphasize first, that over and over again representations of women have reinforced the definition of women as not-man, and that this definition has constantly to be reiterated in order to maintain the edifice of patriarchal values and, second, that we need to consider not so much what is represented, as what conditions the gaze. Fox suggests, in the context of Hetaerae representations on Greek vases, that the aim is amusement, diversion and the reaffirmation of the male viewer's sense of identity. The question arises as to whether, in Greek representations, there is any room for a female gaze. Fox proposes that the Maenads – women who worship Dionysus and are linked to religious rituals – appear to have had a certain autonomy and are sometimes portrayed enjoying their own society. In the context of ritual and festival, women had a public presence and, as so often, there is perhaps a tension between women's involvement and men's need to monopolize the discourse.

Finally, John Wilkins in Chapter 8 discusses the – limited – literary evidence for food preparation. Limited because food preparation is frequently the domain of low status women or of slaves and is thus marginalized if not totally ignored. Brecht's poem springs to mind:

Even in fabulous Atlantis the very night the ocean engulfed it,
the drowning still roared for their slaves.
Young Alexander conquered India,
was he alone?
Caesar defeated the Gauls,
did he not have a cook at least in his service?

... Every page a victory,
who cooked the feast for the victors?
Every ten years a great man,
who paid the bill?
So many accounts, so many questions. (excerpt from *Questions of a Studious Working Man*, by Bertold Brecht)

Part III moves to the modern historical period, and to the historical analysis of gendered representations. Virginia Hewitt in Chapter 9 offers a generalized account of the symbolic imagery of women on paper money. The frequent employment of conservative and idealised images of women underlines the general point that images are metaphors, and that the portrayal of women may have very little to do with either their social status, or the reality of their lived lives. The tropes that are reiterated – security, fertility, labour, docility – form an interesting and conservative counterweight to the world of commodity exchange in which these pieces of paper circulate.

Next there is Tim Barringer's Chapter 10 on the gendering of artistic labour in mid-Victorian Britain. Barringer recognizes that not just the images but the contemporary literary texts provide cultural constructions of separate gendered spheres of sexuality that are not an adequate, or even necessarily a useful, device for an historical understanding of the social functioning of gender in the nineteenth century.

The texts and representations have to be thought of as 'discursive strategies' and analyzed in terms of how they shape and reinforce (changing) rhetorical constructions of gender. Barringer's chapter addresses mid-Victorian male anxieties surrounding the distinction between manual (muscular, active, open-air) and mental labour (ambiguous, effete, even effeminate), and the re-assertion of the masculine gendering of artistic production through professionalization and the creation of all-male institutions.

Helen Sims, in Chapter 11, writing about women and posters of the Great War, shows how posters attempted to represent women's participation in 'the reassuring mode of service, support, and sacrifice' and focused on aspects of work that were associated with caring, food, nature and health. In pushing women into production, there are attempts to prescribe both the type of work and the type of woman who should enlist.

Part IV addresses the role of clothing in shaping gender identity. Christopher Breward's Chapter 12 on Men, Fashion and Luxury, 1870–1914 complements Barringer's Chapter 10. Most of the studies of nineteenth-century commodification and the growth of new department stores have focused on the definition of femininity. But what of men and fashion? Breward discovers that whilst it is possible to prise open a notion of self conscious, popular masculine fashionality ... of organized, indeed commodified working-class and lower middle-class culture, there was, for the middle classes, a more 'problematic discourse-[which focused on] ... external healthiness and physical glory of the male body, demanded a rigorous attention to structures of self-denial'. This discourse was difficult to maintain in an arena of expanded consumer choice. Self-denial sat uneasily with 'an almost fetishistic attention to detail' and rigorous notions of context-specific clothing. Again, as in so many chapters, the warning is that the literary rhetoric of 'clerics, headmasters and editors' *is* rhetorical, and is subverted by the material culture evidence and by other, less mainstream trade or magazine literature.

In Chapter 13 we return to the First World War. Angela Woollacott, discussing female munitions workers' uniforms, explores the threatened subversion of this masculine/work coupling. What happens when women are brought into the production process? When their participation threatens their (perceived) role as home-makers and supporters? Woollacott shows that working-class women, employed in munitions, undermined the prescribed images. Working-class women had always been seen as a problem because of their undesirable autonomy but now, as they moved into male preserves, wore trousers, and subverted their uniforms by personal adornment, they threatened not just men, but fashionable middle-class women. Woollacott suggests that these munitions uniforms are polyvalent: they hold different meanings for the women themselves, for those that observe them, and for British wartime culture. She effectively uses Judith Butler's notion of gender as performative, consisting of 'articulated and enacted desires'. She also sums up nicely many of the aspirations behind the different chapters in this volume. Slightly amended, her brief is to consider:

> on a systematic cultural level ... clothing as related to political economy and class structure, to communication, ritual, performance and art; on an individual level ... related to pleasure, to fantasy, to self-expression and artistic expression.

The final Chapter 14, by Ina Zweiniger-Bargielowska, takes the story a stage further, to the 1940s, and emphasizes the link between gendered material culture and politics. In the inter-war period, with mass consumption and rising living standards for those in work, magazines and cinemas, 'the body [became] a vehicle for pleasure and display'. After the rigours of wartime rationing, women fought against the continued post-war austerity and in the election of 1951 the Conservatives' consumer agenda was voted for by many more women than men.

Notes

1. Moira Gatens (1991), suggests that representations may be metaphoric or metonymic. They may involve the construction of images which act as models or metaphors, or, and here 'metaphor slides into metonymy', that stand in for something else. In the first case the concern is with the way in which the image affects who is represented, whilst in the second, the concern is with who the image represents.
2. Miller (1988), pp. 353–72.
3. Du Cros and Smith (1993).
4. Wylie (1990).
5. Conkey (1993).
6. Yates (1993).
7. Strathern (1988); Weiner (1993), pp. 285–301.

8. Harding (1983), p. 312, cited in Wylie (1990).
9. Butler (1993).
10. Moore (1993).
11. Strathern (1988).
12. Weiner (1985), pp. 210–27.
13. Strathern (1988) points out that we often equate notions of equality and inequality with a person's ability or otherwise to control the fruits of their work. The western assumption is that we should have the right to, and be given full credit for, the fruits of our labour. This suggests that the objects produced are gendered according to the producer. But, in Melanesia, just as gender is a process, so is the affiliation of objects. They are not gendered in terms of the producer but in terms of their destination. Moreover they are not categorized once and for all, but rather their meaning is transformed through the dynamics of exchange.
14. Bell (1984).
15. Bodenhorn (1993).
16. Bodenhorn (1993), p. 187.
17. Moore (1993).
18. Gell (1988), pp. 6–9.
19. Gell (1992).
20. Gell (1985), pp. 271–86; Turnbull (1993).
21. Flax (1987), pp. 621–3.
22. Biesele (1993).

Bibliography

Bell, D. (1984) *Daughters of the Dreaming* (London).

Biesele, M. (1993) *Women Like Meat* (Bloomington and Indianapolis).

Bodenhorn, B. (1993) 'Gendered Spaces, Public Places: Public and private revisited on the north slope of Alaska', in B. Bender (ed.), *Landscape: Politics and perspectives* (Oxford).

Butler, J. (1993) *Bodies that Matter* (New York).

Conkey, M. (1993) 'Making the Connections: Feminist theory and archaeologies of gender', in H. Du Cros and L. Smith (eds), *Women in Archaeology* (Canberra).

Du Cros, H. and L. Smith (eds) (1993) *Women in Archaeology* (Canberra).

Flax, J. (1987) 'Postmodernism and Gender Relations in Feminist Theory', *Signs*, 12, pp. 621-43.

Gatens, M. (1991), in R. Diprose and R. Ferrell (eds), *Cartographies: Post-structuralism and the mapping of bodies and spaces* (London).

Gell, A. (1985) 'How to Read a Map: Remarks on the practical logic of navigation', *Man*, 20, pp. 271–86.

Gell, A. (1988) 'Technology and Magic', *Anthropology Today*, 4, pp. 6–9.

Gell, A. (1992) *The Anthropology of Time* (Oxford).

Harding, S. and M.B. Hintikka (eds) (1983) *Discovering Feminist Perspectives on Epistemology, Metaphysics, Methodology and Philosophy*

MacKenzie, M. (1991) *Androgynous Objects: String bags and gender in central New Guinea* (Chur).

Miller, D. (1988) 'Appropriating the State on the Council Estate', *Man*, 23, pp. 353–72.

Moore, H. (1993) 'The Differences within and the Differences between', in del T. del Valle (ed.), *Gendered Anthropology* (London).

Strathern, M. (1988) *The Gender of the Gift* (Berkeley).

Turnbull, D. (1993) *Maps are Territories. Science is an Atlas* (Chicago).

Weiner, A. (1985) 'Inalienable Wealth', *American Ethnologist*, 12, pp. 210–27.

Weiner, J. (1993) 'Anthropology contra Heidegger Part II: The limit of relationship', *Critique of Anthropology*, 13, pp. 285–301.

Wylie, A. (1990) 'Feminist Critiques and Archaeological Challenges', in D. Walde and N. Willows (eds), *The Archaeology of Gender* (Calgary).

Yates, T. (1993) 'Frameworks for an Archaeology of the Body', in C. Tilley (ed.), *Interpretative Archaeology* (Oxford).

Part I

Engendering Images in Archaeology

1

Archaeological Ms.conceptions: Contemplating Gender and Power in the Greek Neolithic*

Lauren E. Talalay

During the last few decades feminist scholarship has sought to destabilize mainstream thinking across diverse disciplines by re-examining the issues of women, gender relations and gender ideologies. While the resulting publications embrace disparate theoretical stances, all of them ultimately question the way knowledge is constituted. As one writer has observed, feminist theorists have called upon scholars

> to unpack the processes that select and preserve evidence; to decenter narrative to interrogate categories of analysis within each discipline; [and] to demonstrate the way that gender works to legitimize structures of power.[1]

Archaeology – a discipline conventionally defined as empirical – has only recently adopted a gendered approach to its data.[2] Gender-driven scholarship of preliterate societies in the New World has animated the field, sparking important debate. Old World prehistorians, however, have barely begun to grapple with questions raised by feminist agendas. And while this failure is not surprising, given the positivist bent of the discipline, Old World prehistorians have not traditionally ignored the role of women in early European and Mediterranean societies. Much of that research, though, was unidimensional and religiocentric, especially in the case of Stone Age studies. The questions asked were not always fully developed and scholars based their inferences almost exclusively on the seeming abundance of female images and figurines from Neolithic and Upper Palaeolithic archaeological context.[3] Discussions often revealed as much about modern discourse on women as they did about antiquity.[4] The legacy of earlier investigations can be found in the still popular belief (despite compelling arguments to the contrary)[5] that female figurines in the Mediterranean Stone Age bespeak a 'Golden Age', a primordial paradise, a time when women ruled supreme.

As this chapter suggests, not only are such conclusions unwarranted but they subtly undermine the definition of women's power. Equally important, the long-term focus on figurines and Mother Goddesses has sidetracked scholars, limiting them to restricted concepts of gender in Stone Age cultures. In the ensuing pages I examine the implications of this traditional focus, seeking to redirect our thinking about the construction of gender in at least one of the early societies of the Mediterranean, namely the Greek Neolithic. A first step toward 'engendering' the Greek Neolithic, this chapter reconsiders aspects of both human figurines and mortuary data.

The Greek Neolithic

The Greek Neolithic spans approximately three millennia, ca. 6500–3200 BC (calibrated). Although our understanding of this complex and changing period remains fragmentary, it is generally agreed that the introduction of the Neolithic into Greece is associated with the emergence of small, sedentary villages where subsistence was based on cereal agriculture (mostly wheats, barleys and a limited range of legumes), some collecting (shellfish, nuts, wild fruit) and animal husbandry (primarily sheep, goat, cattle and pigs).

Neolithic Greece is usually defined as an egalitarian society, though status of some kind probably existed and was likely to have been based on age, gender, sex and the (archaeologically unretrievable) force of one's personality.[6] Individual households formed the basic economic unit within each community, and extensive networks of exchange or trade facilitated the circulation of commodities and finished products, both utilitarian and prestige.[7]

The system of exchange in Neolithic Greece most likely required itinerant individuals, who transported not only goods but information and ideas. These individuals would have functioned as roving artisans, peddlers of valued raw materials and finished products, and messengers circulating among villages. Women, possibly exchanged as brides, herders or transhumant pastoralists (if such existed), may have fulfilled some of these roles.

For the most part, the literature paints these individuals, as well as other members of Greek Neolithic society, as faceless. Telling, perhaps, is that they are not entirely without gender, even if the references are casual or implicit. Many scholars working in the field (both male and female) would probably conjure up images of men as tool-makers, itinerant craftsmen, herders, procurers of raw materials, and women as gatherers, primary caretakers, household potters and perhaps weavers. These ascriptions are primarily based on modern bias and ethnographic analogues that have not been tested against the ancient evidence. In addition, since modern Western notions tend to devalue the role of household caretaker, the unspoken presumption is that women's status was subordinate to that of men in Neolithic Greece.

In attempting to recover data that provide more accurate information about gender and gender relations in early Greek society, we can profitably look at two sources of evidence: human figurines and human burials. While these two forms of symbolic expression are likely to have projected very different sets of meanings for members of Greek society, it is noteworthy that, in both spheres, women are more visible in the archaeological record. Moreover, among the figurines there is a notable percentage of sexless or sexually ambiguous examples. How we might interpret these patterns is a matter for consideration.

Human images in the Greek Neolithic

The Greek Neolithic has produced more than 1200 published figurines and countless unpublished examples in private collections.[8] Only a small percentage can be sexed reliably as male or female. Many of the pieces are uninformative fragments, others display no clear sexual attributes, still others appear to be sexless (at least to the modern eye) or intentionally 'unisex', and at least one appears to be an androgyne, exhibiting both male and female sexual characteristics.[9]

Though clearly part of the repertoire, males appear in significantly fewer numbers. Sites and regions with relatively large samples produce comparable sex patterns. Sitagroi, a site in northern Greece with middle and late Neolithic material, yielded 220 possible figurines, approximately 80 of which can be classified as definitely/probably female or male, sexless, or sexually ambiguous. Of that subset, 50 per cent are sexless or sexually ambiguous, 48 per cent are definitely or probably female, and approximately 1 per cent is possibly male. Achilleion, a small village in central Greece of early and middle Neolithic date, yielded close to 200 possible figurines, of which 74 are 'sexable': 72 per cent of the subset are definitely or probably female, 25 per cent sexless or sexually ambiguous and 3 per cent male. For all of southern Greece, which produced only 65 'sexable' figurines for the entire Neolithic, 83 per cent are definitely or probably female, 15 per cent are sexless or sexually ambiguous, and approximately 1 per cent is male.[10]

Males appear most often as tetrapodal images (Figure 1.1a).[11] Representations of male phalluses have been recovered from a few Neolithic sites in Greece, though claims of phallic-headed figures are debatable.[12] A few possible examples of ithyphallic men complete the repertoire.

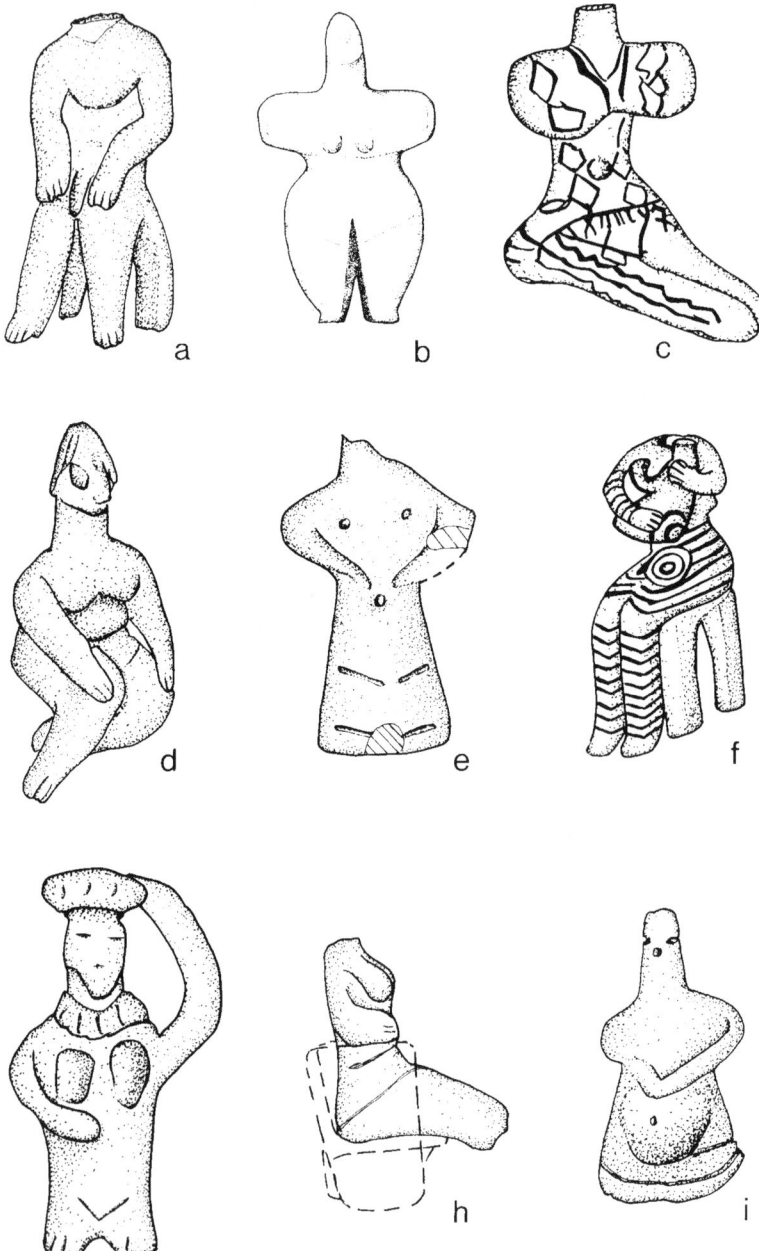

Figure 1.1   Male and female figurines

a   Male tetrapodal figurine (clay), Middle Neolithic, Pyrasos; height 0.07 m
Source: After Gimbutas (1989), Figure 282.

b   Female standing figurine (stone), Middle or Late Neolithic, Aegina; height 0.106 m
Source: After Welter (1954).

c   Female seated figurine (clay), Late Neolithic, Franchthi Cave; height 0.095 m

d   Female seated figurine (clay), Middle Neolithic, region of Pharsala; height 0.07 m
Source: After Theocharis (1973), Plate 38.

e   Probable female seated figurine (clay), Middle Neolithic, Achilleion; height 0.042 m
Source: After Gimbutas *et al.* (1989), Figure 7.11.1.

f   Kourotrophic figurine (clay), Late Neolithic, Thessaly; height 0.16 m
Source: After Theocharis (1973), Plate 56.

g   Female figurine carrying a bundle on her head (clay), Early Neolithic, Prodromos; height ca. 0.060 m?

h   Female seated figurine probably designed to sit in a chair (clay), Middle Neolithic (?), Achilleion; height 0.054 m
Source: After Gimbutas *et al.*

i   Possible pregnant figurine (clay), Neolithic, Magoula Karamoular; height 0.058 m
Source: After Theocharis 1973 Plate 201.

The majority of male figures are modelled from clay, which was readily available at most sites. Though some of the male images are well made, few suggest great investment of production time.[13]

Females figurines are treated quite differently. Women appear in a variety of postures with a range of painted or incised decoration and are occasionally designed from materials other than the ubiquitous clay. Although no one has yet undertaken a detailed and rigorous study of gesture and posture, it is clear that a few main types are popular: standing with arms curled to or under the breasts (Figure 1.1b); seated with legs either extended or folded with arms curled towards the breasts (Figure 1.1c); seated with legs either extended or folded and arms resting on the thighs or stomach (Figure 1.1d); and standing with hands placed on the stomach or upper thighs (Figure 1.1e). There are also some kourotrophic females (Figure 1.1f), women carrying bundles (Figure 1.1g), a few women on chairs (Figure 1.1h), and possibly pregnant images (Figure 1.1i).[14]

Of particular note on many of the female figures are their decorative elements – painted or incised marks which possibly reflect ritual attire or adornment. Curiously, designs on some of these ancient figurines are similar to dress, tattoo, body paint and scarification known today among ethnographic societies. These bodily adornments commonly accompany a wide variety of ritual ceremonies, indicate tribal affiliations, signal pre- and post-betrothal status, or pre- and post-menses states, and the like. Whether the ancient decorative elements popular on Greek Neolithic figurines functioned as comparable symbols is not known. Nor can we be sure that the patterns on these images actually mimicked contemporary bodily adornment.[15] Whatever the meanings, the Neolithic figurine-makers, who may have been adult males or females or occasionally children, expended a good deal of effort decorating some of these female images. Moreover, the choice of designs by makers at different villages is sometimes close enough to suggest face-to-face contact among makers at separate settlements, travelling craftsmen/women, or possible inter-village exchange of figurines.[16]

The remainder of the Greek corpus contains a high percentage of sexless or sexually ambiguous pieces and at least one example of a dual-sexed image (see Naomi Hamilton, Chapter 2 in this volume for comparable patterns among prehistoric figurines of south-eastern Europe). The sexless images are fairly schematic, with only minimal indications of features; the possible dual-sexed pieces are also relatively simple.

Both the sexless and androgynous images raise intriguing questions regarding the notion of gender and the portrayal of sex in the Greek Neolithic. Were the sexless images viewed as truly 'neuter', transcending sexual classification altogether? Or, were they seen as somehow subsuming both male and female sexes? In the latter case, the image would not have been seen as actually sexless but rather as capable of moving in and out of various sexual categories (e.g. male, female or dual). The explicit lack of sexual attributes would have presented the users with a choice whereby the designation of sex might be determined by the image's particular use at a given time or by temporary clothing or ornamentation. A comparable signalling of sex by distinct cultural, not biological, markers is known from the ethnographic record. The sex of ancestor and spirit figurines from modern Indonesia, for example, is indicated by special kinds of hair knots, earrings placed in one ear or the other, or by gesture and posture.[17] If, on the other hand, these images were considered truly neuter and devoid of any sex or gender, they might have been employed as signifiers for concepts that were without sexual or gender connotations. The 'nkisi' figurines of west equatorial Africa seem to represent just such neuter images. They appear to be intentionally designed as asexual protective spirits which are employed in a variety of rituals, including initiation rites and medical curing ceremonies.[18]

The dual-sexed images, which admittedly are quite rare in Greece,[19] may have embodied a different concept of sex or gender. In these androgynous pieces, care is taken to represent the primary sexual characteristics of both males and females, foregrounding rather than suppressing biological traits.

Unlike the sexless images, which may subsume both sexes by avoiding the notation of sexual traits, these images portray both sexes by explicitly depicting breasts and genitals.[20]

Taken in aggregate, the corpus of Neolithic figurines urges us to contemplate gender ascriptions that include more than the traditional male/female, either/or dichotomies. If we jettison the conventional binary opposition we are left with the possibility that the early preliterate communities of Neolithic Greece employed multiple or even fluid gender categories, at least in their visual repertoire. Such categories would include male, female, neuter, dual-sexed, and possibly a dynamic classification that moved in and out of sexual/gender identities. Certainly, the existence of several genders, gender-crossing and shifting categories is known from a variety of cultures, both in the historic past and the present.[21]

As many feminists have observed, the presumption of a universal binary gender system exerts a hegemonic force in research that has often limited investigation of gender configurations within cultures. Not all cultures form beliefs about the sexes based on 'logical oppositions or complementarities; the sexes appear more as gradations on a scale'.[22] These kinds of observations have a bearing on our attempts to understand sex/gender representations in the visual record of preliterate societies. While we confront profound frustrations in trying to decipher, for example, precisely what the early human portrayals of Neolithic Greece reveal about gender relations and attitudes, we need to be wary of imposing Western norms of sexual/gender identity on the archaeological evidence.

The most extensively discussed aspect of these images in terms of function has been their identification as goddesses, although that work has concentrated almost exclusively on female images. Scholars such as Marija Gimbutas, whose provocative and controversial works have found their way into popular feminist writings, propose that the abundance of female figurines in prehistoric contexts of the Mediterranean (and south-eastern Europe) reflects an early pan-Mediterranean belief in a Great Mother Goddess. Moreover the worship of this Great Goddess, purportedly, implies a matriarchal social structure, and a time when women either ruled supreme or at least in partnership with men.[23]

As critiqued more extensively elsewhere, and briefly summarized here, there are serious flaws with this proposal.[24] First, as discussed above, not all of the figurines are female and any cogent interpretation of these images should take into account the number of sexless or sexually ambiguous pieces. Second, the relationship in any society between its religious symbolism and everyday social behaviours is complex. Religious symbolism is rarely epiphenomonemal. Even if one could prove that some of the figurines from early Greece reflect the worship of a Great Mother Goddess, it is misleading to assume a direct correspondence between what appears to be the elevated status of women in the religious sphere with an elevated status in the social and political spheres. Third, current arguments in support of an early Mother Goddess worship tend to cast women and matriarchies as nurturing, sensitive and pacific as opposed to patriarchies which are viewed as aggressive, brutal and violent. Such unidimensional portrayals are most likely incorrect. Finally, the myth of an early Mother Goddess and a primordial matriarchy forces feminists into a conundrum by assuming that their elevated status and power were principally based on their reproductive capacities. Such conclusions overlook the complex nature of gender structures in the past and seriously limit the definitions of female power. Viewed from that essentialist perspective, the myth of the Great Goddess projects mysogynistic overtones.

To some extent then, the acceptance of the Mother Goddess proposal poses feminists with a dilemma. On the one hand, the idea of an all-powerful female goddess is seductive, underscoring women's less than satisfactory contemporary status and providing ammunition to all who would wish to recapture the alleged 'Golden Age' of gender relations. On further analysis, however, the Mother Goddess notion relegates women to a static and conventional role where power is ultimately embedded in biological capabilities.

Burials in Neolithic Greece

While the figurines offer a tantalizing source of evidence to help us gain insight into gender and gender ideologies of Neolithic Greece, we can go only so far with this corpus. It is imperative, therefore, to consider other aspects of the material record that may corroborate or contradict inferences drawn from the figurines or, perhaps, offer alternate possibilities. One area of study that holds promise is that of mortuary data.

The most recent comprehensive study of burial practices in Neolithic Greece was published in 1981.[25] At that time, only some 30 sites from the hundreds known yielded evidence of human burials. Although the data are still preliminary and must await new analysis, it is clear that cremation, and secondary and primary burial were all practised. During most of the Neolithic the dead, who were routinely given few or no burial goods, were inhumed in unmarked graves within settlements or, at the end of the period, sometimes in formal cemeteries located outside habitation areas. The few published accounts of these burials indicate that women are not only more visible than men in the mortuary record but that they received more burial goods than their male counterparts. The examples, though restricted, are instructive.

At the site of Kephala, a small and fairly impoverished community in the Aegean occupied briefly at the end of the Neolithic, a formal cemetery was located immediately adjacent to the settlement; 25 of the skeletons were identified as female and 21 as males, the remaining being unsexed. Of the sexed skeletons, six females received some kind of grave good, as opposed to only one male.[26] Women were given 'scoops', a curious object whose function remains a mystery, marble (which was a rare commodity at this site) or clay bowls, and possibly obsidian blades, whose uses were probably multiple. The only male associated with a grave gift had a flint scraper placed by his right arm.

At Franchthi Cave on the Greek mainland, a smaller mortuary sample reveals comparable patterns. Of the 10 formally buried adults, nine are female; the only male was apparently buried together with an adult female. In the rare cases that scattered bone could be sexed, women again appear to outnumber men. As at Kephala, women occasionally receive grave goods: three of the adult females are associated with various objects, including pottery, a spindle whorl, a rubbing stone, and various bone and stone tools. An infant, possibly female,[27] was laid to rest with a fine marble bowl and half a clay vessel. Neither the one adult male, nor any of the possibly male children, receive grave goods of any kind.[28] Similar patterns are suggested at other Greek Neolithic sites, including Tharrounia and Lerna.[29]

Only on the rarest occasions can we speculate about the possible occupation of the deceased, based on associated grave goods and skeletal stress. For example, Fr 59 at Franchthi Cave was a primary intramural burial of an adult female. This woman received an extraordinary number of artifacts: 11 items in all, consisting of a complete clay pot, six bone points and four obsidian tools. According to one physical anthropologist who examined the skeleton, the considerable wear of the incisors may indicate thread-biting – an activity associated with weaving and spinning.[30] The tools given to the deceased could have served both purposes. While these conclusions are highly speculative, it is striking that, relatively speaking, this woman was lavished with useful items at her death.

Several basic questions about the social roles of men and women arise out of the mortuary evidence. The problem of small samples notwithstanding, why are there more women than men buried in and near Greek Neolithic sites? Where, indeed, are the adult males at sites like Franchthi Cave? Why favour women over men for grave goods?

Currently, it is difficult to offer good answers to these questions. There are, however, some provocative parallels at other Neolithic sites that may ultimately cast light on the Greek data. The greater visibility of women in burials is not a phenomenon confined to Neolithic Greece. Other Neolithic sites throughout the Mediterranean display similar patterns, though the impression may be somewhat erroneous, given that burials are often under-published and the sexing of skeletons is controversial. One site with a fairly sizeable sample of interments is Abu Hureyra in northern Syria. The ratio of women to men is nearly 5 to 3 ($n = 87$) with the dead buried under house floors or in pits within the confines of household courtyards.[31] Women appear to predominate within the houses. Analysis of skeletal stress suggests that women engaged in grinding, spinning and the production of baskets and mats.[32] The *in situ* locations of saddle querns indicate that grinding was carried out within the houses, and it is arguable that the other activities were also tied to household production.

Theya Molleson (1994) has suggested that if these kinds of activities were seen as defining the social roles of women at Abu Hureyra, then the physical boundaries of the house might have been equated with a predominately female domain. By burying women within the house, both the ideological role and the geographical boundaries associated with women during their lifetimes were maintained after death.[33]

Given the limited Greek data and the very incomplete state of publication of Greek burials, Molleson's model is not currently applicable to the Greek Neolithic. As more Greek data are compiled, her suggestions may yet prove useful. Her model does, nonetheless, draw us back into the parochial view that 'women's work' was principally domestic. The problem lies not with the fact that female roles in the past may, indeed, have included a large component of domestic activities but with the fact that modern perceptions equate domestic work with, as it were, devalued currency. It is far more salutary to revise our thinking about the possible worth of domestic roles in the past and to consider how they may have contributed to the larger socio–cultural functioning of early village societies.

Although these endeavours to 'engender' the Greek Neolithic yield mostly conjecture, the evidence suggests that this preliterate society constructed a fairly broad-based view of gender, at least in its permanent visual record. Human figurines seem to portray intermediate categories of sex or gender beyond the strict male/female classification and preference is given to female and sexless images. While the mortuary data do not corroborate the possible existence of 'other' genders, they do suggest, in accordance with the figurine data, that women were accorded a certain level of attention not given to men, at least in a way that is archaeologically recognizable. Whether the motivations for greater visibility of women in both spheres were similar or even linked is difficult to know, given current evidence. Nor do we know whether the preference given to women in burials indicates that deceased women had responsibilities to (or power over) the living that men did not.

Definitions of gender as well as relationships between males and females in preliterate societies were probably no less complex than those in our own culture. Alliances, resistances and power struggles shifted as the status quo was challenged, renegotiated and redefined in subtle ways. Indeed, sexual asymmetries surely varied in nature, some being permeable and overlapping, others formal and institutionalized, and still others informal and casual. The challenge for Aegean prehistorians is to tease out these constructs from the material record, despite formidable obstacles.

Notes

* I would like to thank Tracey Cullen, Steve Bank, and most significantly my father, Anselm Talalay, for many insights and helpful comments. My appreciation also to all of the participants at the Conference who provided such lively discussion, especially Naomi Hamilton whose provocative presentation on figurines of the eastern Mediterranean (Chapter 2 in this volume) had a direct bearing on this chapter. Part of this chapter is based on an earlier article in *Gender and History*, 6 (1994).

1. Shapiro (1992), pp. 1–23.
2. See, for example, Conkey and Spector (1984), pp. 1–7; Nelson and Kehoe (1990); Conkey and Williams (1991), pp. 102–39; Gero and Conkey (1991); Walde and Willows (1991); Gilchrist (1991), pp. 495–501; Wylie (1992); Claassen (1992); Dommasnes (1992); Brown (1993), pp. 238–71; Nixon (1993), pp. 1–23; Marcus (1993), pp. 157–78; Gilchrist (1994).
3. See, for example, James (1959); Gimbutas (1974, 1982, 1989a).
4. See Talalay (1994), pp. 165–83.
5. Ucko (1968); Hayden (1986), pp. 17–30; Talalay (1993).
6. For discussion of possible social ranking in the Greek Neolithic, see Halstead (1993), pp. 603–9.
7. Perles (1992), pp. 115–64; Perles and Perles (1993), pp. 355–416.
8. For the purposes of this preliminary overview, the Neolithic is treated as an undifferentiated chronological period although I fully recognize that different types of figurines were popular during certain phases. Shifting ideas of gender may also have characterized the various phases of the Neolithic. Such refinement must await future study. For reports on Neolithic figurines from Greece, see Tsountas (1908); Wace and Thompson (1912); Ucko (1968); Hourmouziadis (1973); Theocaris (1973): Gimbutas (1986), pp. 225–301; Phelps (1987), pp. 233–53; Gimbutas (1989b), pp. 171–250; Talalay (1993).
9. Sexing of prehistoric figurines is not a simple task; even the best studies suffer from subjectivity. For this study, sexing of figures is based on the following criteria: definite females are identified by the appearance of female genitalia and/or breasts which do not appear to represent male nipples; probable females by breasts and the occurrence of secondary traits that occur repeatedly on definite females (e.g. certain design patterns or physical attributes such as wide, ample hips); definite males are identified by male genitalia; possible males by secondary traits that occur repeatedly on definite males (often this may be reflected by posture); dual-sexed images are identified by the appearance of male genitalia and breasts that do not appear to depict male nipples; and sexless or sexually ambiguous pieces by the absence of any recognizable sexual attributes or any secondary traits that repeatedly occur on sexable images.
10. Gimbutas (1986, 1989b).
11. The use of tetrapodal configurations for males requires further study. The only interpretive discussion of which I am aware refers to these seated figures as 'enthroned' males who, it is suggested, are related to a Year God (see Gimbutas, 1989a), pp. 181–2).
12. See Gimbutas (1989b), pp. 198–200.
13. Unfortunately, the archaeological contexts of the male images are either unknown or unenlightening.
14. The question of the function and use of these images is a matter of debate. Although I am of the opinion that they were multifunctional, serving a host of

purposes (e.g. contracts, items of sympathetic magic, dolls or toys, ancestor images, see Talalay 1993, pp. 45–51, 72–9), others have argued that the female figurines, at least, represent goddesses. Attempts to understand the possible links between these images and gender constructs in Neolithic Greece are partially stymied by our inability to clearly and convincingly 'prove' the possible functions of these items.

15. The ethnographic record occasionally shows design elements on figurines from a given group that directly mimic the patterns employed by that group to adorn the human body. The best example I know is from the Tabwa of Africa, see Roberts and Mauer (1985) p. 130. A particularly intriguing set of design elements from Neolithic Greece derives from Sitagroi. In the corps of approximately 200 figurines is a subset of female images that show three incised vertical lines between the breasts and five vertical lines along the back (Gimbutas, 1986, see drawings on pp. 228, 232, 241–3, 248, 268).

16. See Talalay (1993).

17. Greub (1988), p. 238.

18. Greub (1988), pp. 38ff.

19. See, for example, Gimbutas (1989a), Figure 283.

20. The possibility also exists that the dual-sexed images were intended to represent a third gender, e.g. hermaphrodites.

21. For discussions on varying 'non-traditional' gender constructions, see Shore (1981), pp. 192–215; Whitehead (1981), pp. 80–115; Bolin (1992), pp. 13–39.

22. Ortner and Whitehead (1981), pp. 6–7.

23. Gimbutas (1986, 1989a, 1989b).

24. Talalay (1994).

25. Jacobsen and Cullen (1981), pp. 79–101.

26. Coleman (1977). Unfortunately, the Kephala data and mortuary evidence from other Greek Neolithic sites yield very small samples. The patterns cannot, therefore, be considered 'statistically significant'.

28. T. Cullen, personal communication; Cullen and Cook (forthcoming).

29. T. Cullen, personal communication.

30. Angel (n.d.), p. 41; see also Smith and Cook (1991).

31. Molleson (1994), pp. 70–6.

32. Study of the Abu Hureyra bones and teeth suggest that pulling canes through teeth while weaving baskets resulted in grooves on the front teeth. The particular type of wear was confined to female skeletons. Evidence for extended grinding of grain by females who probably positioned themselves on their knees and repeatedly pushed and pulled on the rubbing stone of a saddle quern was suggested by damaged and hyperflexed big toes, bony growths of the vertebrae, and other abnormalities along the shaft of the femur and the knee.

33. Molleson (1994) p. 75; see also Hodder (1990).

Bibliography

Angel, J.L. (n.d.) 'The Human Skeletal Material from Franchthi Cave', unpublished ms.

Bolin, A. (1992) 'Coming of Age among Transexuals', in T. Whitehead and B. Reid (eds), *Gender Constructs and Social Issues* (Chicago).

Brown, S. (1993) 'Feminist Research in Archaeology: What does it mean? Why is it taking so long?', in N. Rabinowicz and A. Richilin (eds), *Feminist Theory and the Classics* (New York).

Claassen, C. (ed.) (1992) *Exploring Gender through Archaeology* (Madison).

Coleman, J. (1977) *Kephala: A Late Neolithic settlement and cemetery: Keos*, vol. 1 (Princeton).

Conkey, M. and J. Spector (1984) 'Archaeology and the Study of Gender', in M. Schiffer (ed.), *Advances in Archaeological Method and Theory*, vol. 7 (New York).

Conkey, M. and S. Williams (1991) 'Original Narratives: The political economy of gender in archaeology', in M. di Leonardo (ed.), *Gender at the Crossroads of Knowledge: Feminist anthropology in the postmodern era* (Berkeley).

Cullen, T. and D.C. Cook (forthcoming) *Mortuary, Ritual and Human Biology at Franchthi Cave, Greece*.

Demoules, J.P. and C. Perles (1993) 'The Greek Neolithic: A new review', *Journal of World Prehistory*, 7.

Dommasnes, L. (1992) 'Two Decades of Women in Prehistory and in Archaeology in Norway: A review', *Norwegian Archaeological Review*, 25.

Gero, J. and M. Conkey (eds) (1991) *Engendering Archaeology: Women and prehistory* (Oxford).

(1991) 'Women's Archaeology? Political feminism, gender theory and historical revision', *Antiquity*, 65.

Gilchrist, R. (1994) *Gender and Material Culture* (London and New York).

Gimbutas, M. (1974) *The Gods and Goddesses of Old Europe* (Berkeley).

Gimbutas, M. (1982) *The Gods and Goddesses of Old Europe*, rev. edn (Berkeley).

Gimbutas, M. (1986) 'Mythical Imagery of Sitagroi Society', in C. Renfrew, M. Gimbutas and E. Elster (eds), *Excavations at Sitagroi* (Los Angeles).

Gimbutas, M. (1989a) *The Language of the Goddess* (San Francisco).

Gimbutas, M. (1989b) 'Figurines and Cult Equipment: Their role in the reconstruction of Neolithic religion', in M. Gimbutas, S. Winn and D. Shimabuku (eds), *Archilleion: A Neolithic settlement in Thessaly, Greece, 6400–5600 BC* (Los Angeles).

Gimbutas, M., S. Winn and D. Shimabuku (eds) (1989) *Archilleion: A Neolithic settlement in Thessaly, Greece, 6400–5600 BC* (Los Angeles).

Greub, S. (ed.) (1988) *Expressions of Belief: Masterpieces of African, Oceanic and Indonesian art from the Museum voor Volkenkunde, Rotterdam* (New York).

Halstead, P. (1993) '*Spondylus* Shell Ornaments from Late Neolithic Dimini, Greece: Specialised manufacture or unequal accumulation?', *Antiquity*, 67.

Hayden, B. (1986) 'Old Europe: Sacred matriarchy or complementary opposition?', in A. Bonnano (ed.), *Archaeology and fertility cult in the Ancient Mediterranean* (Amsterdam).

Hodder, I. (1990) *The Domestication of Europe* (Oxford).

Hourmouziadis, G.C. (1973) *I Anthropomorphi Idoloplastiki tis Neolithikis Thessalias* (Anthropomorphic Sculpture of Neolithic Thessaly) (Volos).

Jacobsen, T. and T. Cullen (1981) 'A Consideration of Mortuary Practices in Neolithic Greece: Burials from Franchthi Cave', in S. Humphreys and H. King (eds), *Mortality and Immortality: The anthropology and archaeology of death* (London).

James, E.O. (1959) *The Cult of the Mother-Goddess* (New York).

Marcus, M. (1993) 'Incorporating the Body: Adornment, gender, and social identity in ancient Iran', *Cambridge Archaeological Journal*, 3.

Molleson, T. (1994) 'The Eloquent Bones of Abu Hureyra', *Scientific American*, 271.

Nelson, S. and A. Kehoe (eds), (1990) *Powers of Observation: Alternative views in archaeology* (Washington, DC).

Nixon, L. (1993) 'Gender Bias in Archaeology', in L. Archer and S. Fishler (eds), *Women in Ancient Societies: 'An Illusion of the Night'* (London).

Ortner, S. and H. Whitehead (eds) (1981) *Sexual Meanings* (Cambridge).

Perles, C. (1992) 'Systems of Exchange and Organisation of Production in Neolithic Greece', *Journal of Mediterranean Archaeology*, 5.

Perles, J.P. and C. Perles (1993) 'The Greek Neolithic: A new review', *Journal of World Prehistory*, 7.

Phelps, W. (1987) 'Prehistoric Figurines from Corinth', *Hesperia*, 56.

Roberts, A. and E. Mauer (eds) (1985) *Tabwa, The Rising of a New Moon: A century of Tabwa art* (Ann Arbor).

Shapiro, A.L. (1992) 'History and Feminist Theory; Or talking back to the beadle' in A.L. Shapiro (ed.), *History and Feminist Theory* (Middletown, Conn,), pp. 1–23.

Shore, B. (1981) 'Sexuality and Gender in Samoa: Conceptions and missed conceptions', in S. Ortner and H. Whitehead (eds), *Sexual Meanings* (Cambridge).

Smith, S.K. and D.C. Cook (1991) 'Mesolithic to Modern Dental Wear at Franchthi Cave, Greece', paper presented at the Annual Meeting of the Society for American Anthropology (New Orleans).

Talalay, L.E. (1993) *Deities, Dolls and Devices: Neolithic figurines from Franchthi Cave, Greece* (Bloomington).

Talalay, L.E. (1994) 'A Feminist Boomerang: The great goddess of Greek prehistory', *Gender and History*, 6.

Theocharis, D. (1973) *Neolithic Greece* (Athens).

Tsountas, C. (1908) *Ai Proistorikai Akropoleis Diminiou kai Sesklou* (Athens).

Ucko, P. (1968) *Anthropomorphic Figurines* (London).

Wace, A. and M. Thompson (1912) *Prehistoric Thessaly* (Cambridge).

Walde, D. and Willows, N.D. (eds) (1991) *The Archaeology of Gender* (Calgary).

Welter, G. (1954) 'Aeginerica xxv–xxxvi', *Archaeologischer Anzeiger*, 69.

Whitehead, H. (1981) 'The Bow and the Burden Strap: A new look at institutionalised homosexuality in native North America', in S. Ortner and H. Whitehead (eds), *Sexual Meanings* (Cambridge).

Wylie, A. (1992) 'Feminist Theories of Social Power: Some implications for a processual archaeology', *The Norwegian Archaeological Review*, 25, pp. 51–68.

2
Ungendering Archaeology: Concepts of Sex and Gender in Figurine Studies in Prehistory*

Naomi Hamilton

This chapter is concerned with the interpretation of prehistoric anthropomorphic figurines from eastern Europe and the Near East, and a methodology which classifies figures primarily by sex and then translates sex into stereotyped Western gender roles which may have no relevance to prehistory. The study of figurines is one of the few ways in which attempts have been made to address the roles of women in the past, but the discussion which has taken place demonstrates the need for a theory of gender and gender relations to support these attempts. Here I will examine some problems with traditional studies and their underlying ideologies, and will suggest other approaches which may be more enlightening.

Considerable numbers of largely female figurines were first uncovered at prehistoric sites in the Near East and Europe at the turn of the century. Many more have been found since then, and their interpretation is still dominated by early theories. In general, scholars are split between those who see these figures as evidence of goddess worship, and those who oppose this interpretation in various ways. I suggest that this argument is inspired not so much by compelling evidence either way as by ideology concerning sex and gender roles both past and present. There can be little doubt that if the figures had been predominantly male they would initially have been viewed as gods or leaders, and that when later questioned by modern scholars, the alternatives put forward would have been rather different from those frequently offered for female ones.

I am not concerned here with whether or not these figures represent goddesses but with the response to this view, and its relevance to theories of gender. There have been two main approaches to the 'problem' of figurines being mainly female: either to offer alternative interpretations for female figures; or to challenge the view that they really are female. A number of these studies seem to be motivated by anxiety about gender roles and a confusion of sex with gender, rather than with problems intrinsic to the evidence.

Using the first approach, a range of interpretations of female figures has been put forward, but they often seem heavily influenced by Western attitudes to gender – hence ancient pornography, portraits of marriageable daughters, fertility charms, substitute wives, sexual servants for the dead, children's dolls and so on have all been suggested. Some of these ideas have been propounded quite recently, a number with no attempt at contextual analysis. For example, Bronze Age Cypriot figurines such as those in Figure 2.1a and 2.1b have attracted considerable attention: thus Vassos Karageorghis (1981) commented that

> terracotta female figures holding infants or groups of male and female figures have been found in tombs, and perhaps served as female 'companions' to the male.[1]

Orphanides (1983) suggested the figures

> may represent the female servant(s) of the dead.[2] It seems reasonable that, in the Near Eastern society of those times, their companionship or service to their husbands or masters ... was primarily sexual.

Desmond Morris (1985) suggested that the plank idols were fertility charms, but then felt they are so unsexual that perhaps they were 'substitute figures – effigies of widows placed in their husband's graves to accompany them in death, thereby avoiding the unhappy entombment of the real widows'.[3] No one has questioned why, for instance, only the male dead should need companions, and in fact my own preliminary examination of the material from the Early/Middle Bronze Age cemetery at Vounous suggests that most if not all figurines were found with female skeletons, while Paraskevi Baxevani's analysis of the Lapithos material also suggests that plank idols occur with females.[4] These theories, then, are purely wishful thinking.

The second approach has been to question the female attribution of many figures. Merrillees (1980) points out that although plank idols are generally assumed to be female, not all of them have breasts and therefore their sex must be in doubt.[5] However, he goes on to remark that the small breasts represented could also be men's, making all plank idols male. Where does this take us in terms of the interpretations just mentioned, and the apparent occurrence of plank idols with females? If we follow Morris, these should be substitute *widowers* to avoid their unhappy entombment with their wives – or according to Orphanides they are there to satisfy the

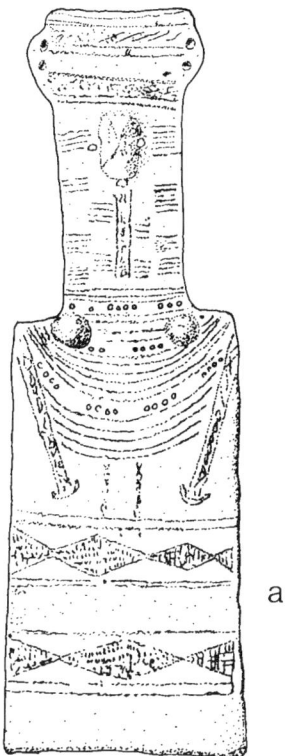
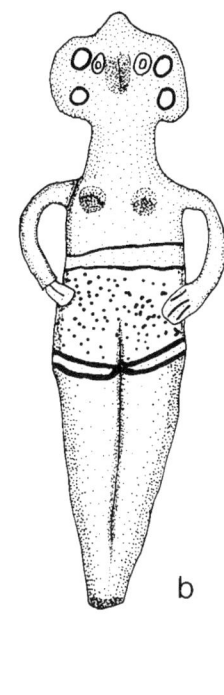

Figure 2.1   Cypriot 'plank idol' and figurine
a   Cypriot Early/Middle Bronze Age 'plank' idol; height ca. 275 mm
Source: After Nick Dooley.
b   Cypriot Late Bronze Age figurine: height 157 mm

sexual appetites of dead females in the next world. However, I am not convinced that all plank idols are male. The absence of breasts is itself problematic as a sole indicator of maleness; to suggest that the presence of small breasts can also signify maleness requires a strong supporting argument to be taken seriously. There are no known instances of true plank idols with male genitals, and this may well be because the figures are clothed. Therefore it might seem more sensible to suggest that breastless ones are male or sexless, and breasted ones are female. However, in the end it is simply a matter of opinion endlessly disputed. Of course, if we believe they are all female, logic would suggest that if Morris and Orphanides are correct, a substantial proportion of the female population was lesbian – and that this was socially recognized at least in burial rites. Something tells me I would have difficulty in persuading the establishment of the plausibility of this view, yet it is the result of mixing their long-held beliefs with an analysis of the data.

In a widely quoted study, Ucko (1968) discussed a considerable number of figures from Egypt and Crete, with some from Greece and the Near East for comparative purposes. He offered a range of ethnographic examples of what female figurines could be used for rather than being goddesses, idols or dominant women and also looked for the missing men, while recognising sexless figures.[6] However, although ostensibly applying objective measures to analyze the figures, his methods of both sexing and counting are open to question. Just one example can illustrate the problems – the sexing of the Cretan material, for which he recognized only breasts and penes as positive sex indicators, regarding apparent sexual triangles as leg muscles and waist or hip lines (Figure 2.2a, 2.2b). Table 2.1 shows numbers of figures of undisputed sex, then when the uncertain ones have been distributed. Table 2.2 demonstrates the result if Ucko had accepted that sexual triangles are shown. The proportions of male, female, and no-sex vary widely according to counting methods. Nevertheless, the number of male figurines remained very low, and perhaps as a consequence of this, Ucko's conclusion pays little attention to explaining the laboriously discovered male figures, concentrating instead on dismantling the often poorly supported goddess theories and examining alternatives for the female figures. However, his dismissal of their use in sympathetic magic to encourage the birth of children, on the grounds that this 'would imply, if the figurine

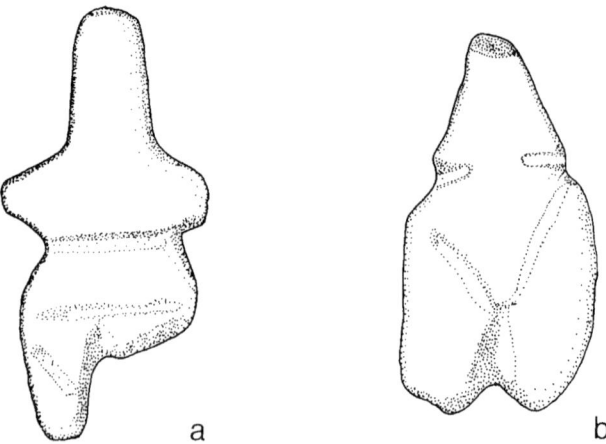

a   b

Figure 2.2   a and b Cretan figurines with 'leg muscles and waist lines'; height a 55 mm; b 51 mm

Source: After Ucko, Cretan Figures 93, 94.

Table 2.1 Ucko's Cretan figurines – not recognizing sexual triangles

	Female	Male	No-sex	Can't say
Definite	27	5	28	13
Possible	11.5	4.5	14	–
Total	38.5	9.5	42	13

Source: Ucko (1968).

Table 2.2 Ucko's Cretan figurines – recognizing sexual triangles

	Female	Male	No-sex	Can't say
Definite	35.0	5.0	21	13
Possible	11.5	4.5	14	–
Total	46.5	9.5	35	13

Source: Ucko (1968).

complement is representative, that girls were much more frequently desired than boys,'[7] and his support for their use as servant figures since 'the sexes of the figurines ... could ... be easily explained by this interpretation'[8] does give the impression that he is ideologically motivated in his attitude to female roles, and it is little surprise to read his conclusion that many of the figures were children's' dolls – a function which he appears to understand as having no social significance.

Broman's analysis of early neolithic Mesopotamian figurines is also interesting. Concerning the numerous female figures, she suggested their frequent occurrence in rubbish dumps and occupation debris was accounted for by their use as wish-vehicles, used for a specific moment and discarded afterwards. In her analysis of the Tepe Sarab assemblage (1990), no clearly male figures could be found, but she discussed a group of 18 sexless torsos with the 'extended arm' position, a tiny proportion of the 650 anthropomorphic figures at the site:

The only human figurines that could be considered male are of this type. Not only are the fragments small, but they are also rather crudely modelled ... For the male form ... the most important aspect is that of the all-embracing posture of the arms. Could this mean social power in the form of leadership?[9]

This interpretive leap from a few crude figures to male leadership seems to owe more to socially constructed expectation than to the evidence.

The point of the foregoing is not to be unpleasant at the expense of hard-working scholars, but to illustrate the need to expose and then put aside for good the attitudes to gender roles which are hidden in archaeological interpretation, and the problems of regarding sex and gender as synonymous. In the social sciences the separation between biological or physiological sex, and social roles which constitute gender, is old news,[10] but archaeologists have been slow to make use of it. What *has* happened is that the term 'gender' has recently been borrowed into archaeological work on figurines and burials as a substitute for the word 'sex', presumably because gender *sounds* much more scientific and precise, while in practice it is widely misused. The gender of figurines does not depend upon physical attributes – which show only sex – but upon social ones, and if we are interested in how early societies operated, it is gender rather than sex which we should investigate, and the relationships between sex and gender. The problem, of course, is finding out what gender consisted of in the society in question, and how to recognize it via prehistoric figures which generally only indicate – or fail to indicate – sex.

I would suggest that the first thing to do is to become familiar with the ethnographic comparisons concerning the range of gender roles known in recent societies, and with how these might be indicated. According to anthropological research, all known human groups appear to have some form of gender division which relates in some way to the two main sexes. However, sex and gender are not inevitably linked in the way they have been in the modern Western world. Put simply, a male does not have to be a man. Examples of sex–gender dissonance, fluidity, or simply difference from Western conceptions can be found in many societies. For instance, studies on Papua New Guinea have shown the enormous range of attitudes to sex and gender held by different groups living on one large island,[11] and other examples can be found around the world: the indigenous North American *berdache* who adopt a gender belonging generally to the other sex;[12] young male wives for Azande warriors who can later be re-transformed into men;[13] Omani male prostitutes who, it has been claimed, become women;[14] the Indian *hijras* – males dedicated to a goddess, who dress as women and have the power to curse.[15] Yet in modern Western society gender-crossers are so unacceptable that they increasingly resort to surgery – thus becoming sex-crossers;[16] on the other hand, the Wana of south-east Asia believe that the two sexes are biologically basically the same, that it is cultural aspects – gender– which cause difference;[17] and the Western pre-Enlightenment view was also that male and female bodies were more similar than different, with gender being the basic division.[18]

This brief review of examples, by no means exhaustive but chosen to demonstrate the widespread nature of the data, shows that the primacy given by modern Western culture to the biological differences between males and females in determining their role in society is not universal or absolute. It would be wise, therefore, to allow that prehistoric cultures may have had at least as wide a range of options available as those known from historical periods. Indeed, there is such variety that it is valid to question whether gender has always been a feature of human society. I suggest that, rather than arguing over the sex of figurines which have no sex indicated, these figures could give valuable information about the development and constitution of gender in prehistoric society. There are several ways in which this could be approached, and here I want to consider figurines with ambiguous indication of sex – either being dual-sexed, or sexless.

The development of a sex-linked gender system presupposes not just the recognition of sexual differences but their elevation to a major structuring principle. If sex is not indicated on figurines, it is reasonable to suppose that it was not considered relevant – perhaps because the users of the figures knew what sex was indicated, because they were meant to be sexless, or children, or because sex was not perceived as important – yet we prefer to assume that sex was indicated through coded symbols. Dual sexed figures, though a small minority, may be a key to discovering the development and nature of gender relations. Such figures are often interpreted as 'really' belonging to one or other of the two acceptable sexes, but recognizing their ambiguity may be more fruitful. It is worth noting that in some societies with more flexible attitudes to sex and gender, official 'gender-crossers' may have special activities allocated to them, such as being a shaman, match-maker, corpse-handler, head of household; or special abilities attributed to them such as cursing or healing; while in others they simply take their place in their chosen gender role.

A number of ambiguous figures invite enquiry. For instance, a Sesklo culture group from neolithic Greece – a female (Figure 2.3a) was thought by the excavator to represent a female centaur,[19] but was later interpreted as a seated figure, a goddess or perhaps a woman on a birth stool;[20] several similar male figures (Figure 2.3b)[21] are often viewed as enthroned men, but another has well-defined breasts and penis (Figure 2.4).[22] Is it a male on a birth stool? – one who believes, like the Wana, that males can give birth and breast feed? If we take the traditional view that men were in charge and sat on thrones, is this an enthroned female, borrowing a penis from the characteristics of normal throne-sitters? Perhaps instead we have a 'gender-crosser' to whom special abilities are attributed and who is therefore the group leader or head of household? Maybe it would be simpler after all to return to deities and postulate a gynandrous divinity? We may never know who was really represented, but we should note the problems raised.

Another ambiguous neolithic group comes from the Tisza culture in Hungary – three female figures/anthropomorphic pots are known, with sexual triangles and small breasts (one is broken but breasts are assumed) and the well known 'Sickle God' is claimed to be definitely male though it has no sex indicated.[23] What, then, do we make of one with small breasts

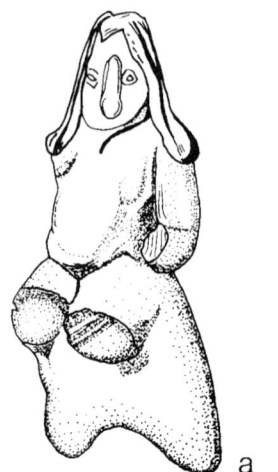

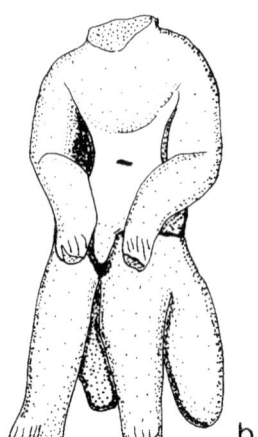

Figure 2.3   Greek Neolithic Sesklo figure
a   Female; no scale
Source: After Tsountas.
b   Male; height ca. 70 mm.

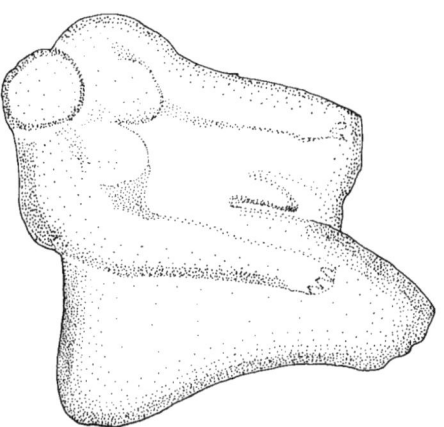

Figure 2.4   Greek Neolithic dual-sexed Sesklo figure; height ca. 70 mm

and penis?[24] It brings into question not just the sexing of the Sickle God, but also the validity of seeking two discrete sexes.

A group of dancers from Kamilari in Crete is described as having unclear sex,[25] but they have breasts and penes and seem to be dual-sexed. Dancing is known to have many uses in religious and/or ritual behaviour, and it is plausible to suggest that this scene represents something of this nature: perhaps the acquisition, or celebration through ritual dance, of the attributes of both sexes, which could derive either from beliefs that there is little difference between them – which may imply also that gender was a low-key concept – or from cultures such as the Hua in Papua New Guinea where male dominance is coupled with a secret belief among men in the superiority of women and its attendant efforts to acquire female power for themselves.[26] A different interpretation returns to gender-crossers as shamans – indeed, shamans in societies without institutionalized gender-crossers are often believed to be dual-sexed, this being a sign of superhuman qualities.[27] Of course, Merrillees' point about male breasts should not be dismissed out of hand – males are sometimes shown with breasts, especially in Egypt and the Cyclades. However, in assessing whether male breasts or dual sex are intended, comparison with female figures is helpful. For instance, a male figurine from the neolithic site of Cafer Hoyuk in Turkey has appliqué penis and small breasts, but female figurines have large pendulous appliqué breasts.[28] Therefore one can be fairly confident that a male rather than a dual-sexed person is represented, although a degree of androgyny cannot definitely be ruled out without a larger number of male figures for comparison.

Let us look briefly at Cyprus. The majority of neolithic figures are sexless, but several are thought to show mixed sex. Figure 2.5 from Sotira-Arkolies,

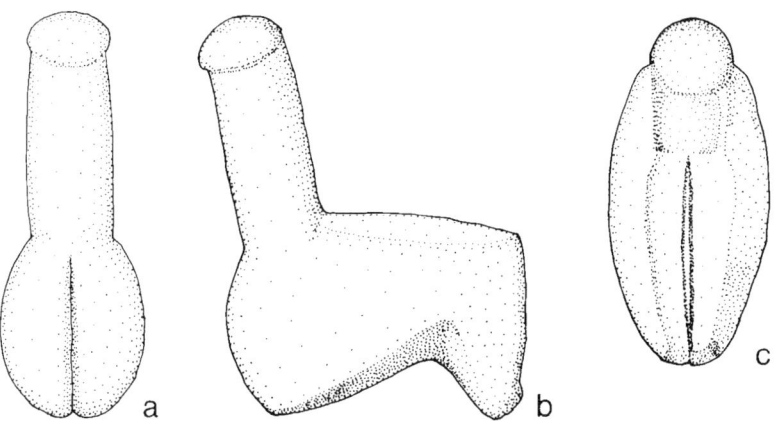

Figure 2.5   Cypriot phallic and vulvic Neolithic figure from Sotira-Arkolies; height 161mm
a   Back view
b   Side view
c   View from above

is apparently both phallic and vulvic according to how it is viewed.[29] An interesting comparison is found in a figure from Tepe Yahya in Iran – ostensibly female, it is phallic when seen from above.[30] These figures do not show the sexual division we find so 'natural'. The plank idols have been dealt with above, but it is interesting that they occur in multiple versions (Figure 2.6a);[31] Karageorghis states that it is not clear which one of the pair is female since the potter has put a breast on each side[32] – a comment which illustrates how deeply the male/female pairing is embedded in interpretation. A number of specific figurines have disputed sex – for instance, still in the Bronze Age Figure 2.6b[33] has been seen as a breasted

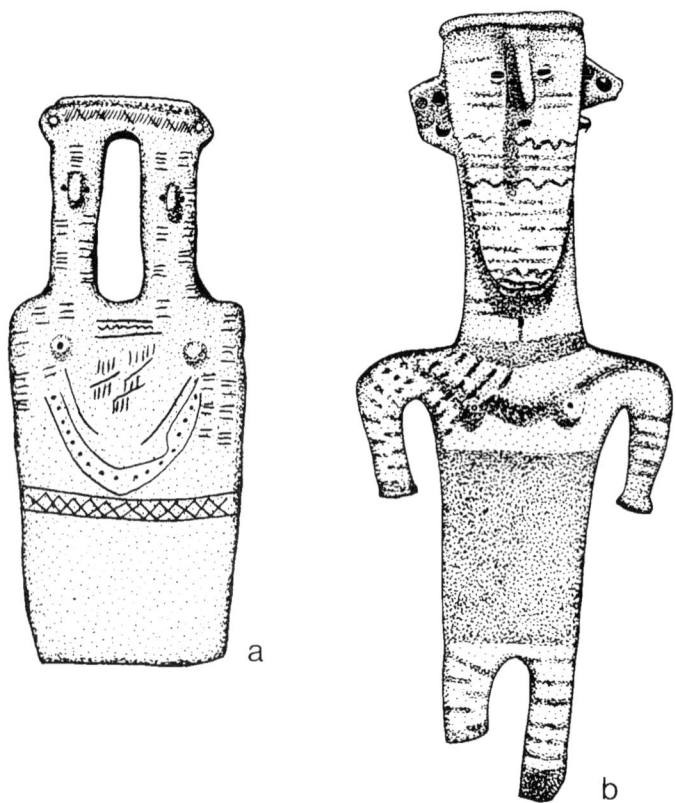

a

b

Figure 2.6   Cypriot 'plank' idol and figure
a   Cypriot Early/Middle Bronze Age double 'plank' idol; height 238 mm
b   Cypriot Middle Bronze Age figure of uncertain sex; height ca. 340 mm

Source: Courtesy of Desmond Morris.

man, a bearded woman or a long-faced woman; while Figure 2.7a is described by Karageorghis as male, adding that the breasts may not be a significant characteristic;[34] and Figure 2.7b was published as a hermaphrodite,[35] a description questioned by Karageorghis.[36] A Mycenaean-style figure was published as a bearded male with breasts,[37] but no genitals are visible – why is it not a bearded female? – or perhaps it is something more than either of these simplistic terms suggests. At the 1991 Göteborg Congress, Karageorghis showed a slide of Iron Age toy soldiers, one of which had breasts.[38] He commented that breasts have no significance when they occur with beards. I cannot agree. It is highly unlikely that breasts were added to a soldier by accident, and therefore they must be significant. What they signify is probably far more interesting than the fact that most toy soldiers do not have breasts, but is more difficult to determine.

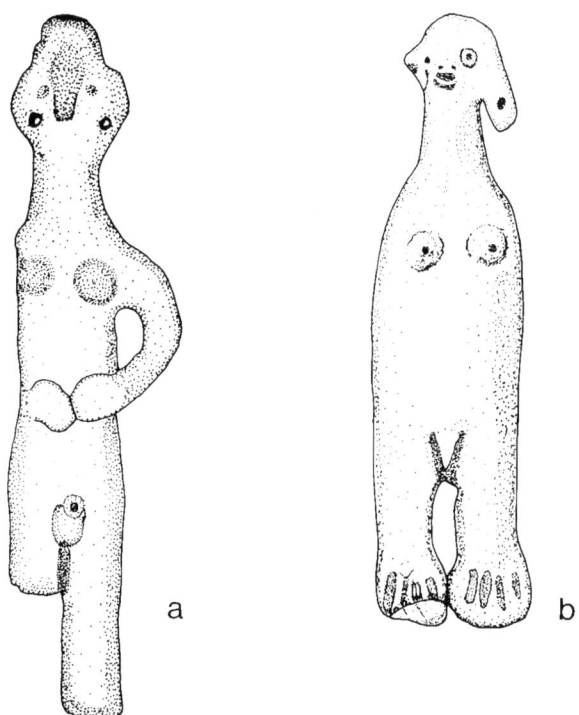

Figure 2.7   Cypriot figures
a   Cypriot Middle Bronze Age dual-sexed figure; height 171 mm
b   Cypriot Early/Middle Bronze Age 'hermaphrodite' figure; no scale

To conclude, archaeologists have traditionally assumed that certain aspects of human life can be taken as universal 'givens', primeval and changing only superficially. A division of human groups into two mutually exclusive categories of male and female, accompanied by a sexual division of labour resembling that of historical Western societies, has been one of these unquestioned universals. Figurine studies have fallen into line with this ethos, with the emphasis on sexing figurines, and interpretations following conservative attitudes to sex and gender roles, thus bolstering traditional assumptions. However, a glance at anthropology has shown that many cultures do not have the simplistic gender divisions that archaeologists have assumed to be standard, and a brief look at the artefactual evidence has shown that many figurines defy straightforward sexing, being either sexless or dual-sexed. How then do we interpret figurines such as these? I believe it is essential to take them at face value, as anomalies either within our concepts, or within their accompanying material culture. Sexless figures may well reflect an absence of sex as a structuring feature of society. Exceptional figures may represent genuinely dual-sexed individuals, or they may have been gender-crossers – which presupposes clear gender boundaries to cross. The fact that indication of sex is erratic and clear males very rare in the prehistoric figurines complement suggests either that for some reason figurines were not associated with males, or that maleness was not an important concept at the time. All these problems are relevant to the state of gender ideology in archaeology, and it seems clear that interpretation of figurines must take into account other information about the culture, rather than forcing figurines into preconceived sex and gender pigeonholes, and then using the results to interpret social structures. Archaeologists must therefore be aware not only of their own cultural biases, but of how sex and gender operate in other societies, and how they may be expressed in material culture. After all, if societies known to be strongly gendered produced mainly sexed figurines, logic suggests that if sex is rarely or ambiguously indicated, that society had different gender concepts and structures from our own.

Notes

*   I would like to thank Helen Loney and Andy Hoaen for long and helpful discussions of drafts of this paper; Dr Trevor Watkins for reading and commenting on the text; Desmond Morris for providing me with Figures 2.6a and 2.6b; Müge Sevketoglu for drawing all the other figures and helping in countless ways; Glasgow Museums, Art Gallery and Museum Kelvingrove for supplying a photograph of the figurine shown in Figure 2.7a; Professor Ucko for permission to reproduce Figure 2.2, and Dr Stuart Swiny for permission to reproduce Figure 2.5

1. Karageorghis (1981).
2. Orphanides (1983), p. 446.
3. Morris (1985), p. 162.
4. Baxevani, personal communication.

5. Merrillees, in Morris (1985), p. 162.
6. Ucko (1968).
7. Ucko (1968), pp. 436–7.
8. Ucko (1968), p. 432.
9. Broman (1990), pp. 12–13.
10. Ortner and Whitehead (1981); Caplan, 'Introduction', in Caplan (1987).
11. Mead (1935); Meigs (1976), pp. 393–407; Poole (1981), pp. 116–65; Brown and Buchbinder (1976); and many more.
12. For example, Whitehead (1981).
13. Evans-Pritchard, summarized in Caplan (1987), pp. 21–2.
14. Wikan (1977, 1978).
15. Nanda (1990).
16. Raymond (1979).
17. Atkinson (1990).
18. Laquer (1990), Chapter 1: Martin (1987), Chapter 1.
19. Tsountas (1908), Plate 33.4a.
20. Vassits (1908), p. 327; Wace and Thompson (1912), p. 68.
21. Gimbutas (1989), Figure 282; Wace and Thompson (1912).
22. Gimbutas (1989), Figure 283.
23. Kalicz (1970), Plates 32–37, p. 41.
24. Kalicz *et al.* (1987), Figures 14–16, pp. 53ff.
25. Goddison (1989), Figure 184.
26. Meigs (1976).
27. Eliade (1964), p. 257.
28. Renda (1993), pp. 45, 17–19.
29. Swiny and Swiny (1983), pp. 56–9.
30. Lamberg-Karlovsky and Meadow (1970), pp. 12–17.
31. Morris (1985), Figure 221.
32. Karageorghis (1991), p. 91.
33. Morris (1985), Figure 250.
34. Karageorghis (1991), p. 180.
35. Ohnefalsch-Richter (1893), n. **, p. 143, Plate XXXVI.1.
36. Karageorghis (1991), p. 180.
37. Nikolaou (19), pp. 47–57.
38. Karageorghis (1992), Figure 2, p. 182.

Bibliography

Atkinson, J. (1990) 'How Gender makes a Difference in Wana Society', in J. Atkinson and S. Errington (eds), *Power and Difference: Gender in Island Southeast Asia* (Stanford).

Broman, V. (1990) *Figurines and Other Clay Objects from Sarab and Cayön*ü

Brown, P. and G. Buchbinder (eds) (1976) *Man and Woman in the New Guinea Highlands* (Washington, DC).

Caplan, P. (ed.) (1987) *The Cultural Construction of Sexuality* (London).

Eliade, M. (1964) *Shamanism: Archaic techniques of Ecstasy* (London).

Evans-Pritchard, E. (n.d.) 'Sexual Inversion among the Azande', *American Anthropologist*, 72.

Gimbutas, M. (1989) *The Language of the Goddess* (London).

Goodison, L. (1989) *Death, Women and the Sun* (London).

Kalicz, N. (1970) *Clay Gods. The Neolithic period and Copper Age in Hungary* (Budapest).

Kalicz, N. *et al.* (eds) (1989) *The Late Neolithic of the Tisza Region* (Budapest).

Karageorghis, V. (1981) *Ancient Cyprus* (Baton Rouge and London).

Karageorghis, V. (1991) *The Coroplastic Art of Ancient Cyprus 1* (Nicosia).

Karageorghis, V. (1992) 'Soldiers and Toys in the Coroplastic Art of Cyprus', in P. Astrom (ed.), *Acta Cypria 2. Proceedings of the 1991 Göteborg Congress on Cypriot Archaeology* (Göteborg).

Lamberg-Karlovsky, C. and R.H. Meadow (1970) 'A Unique Female Figurine. The Neolithic at Tepe Yahya', *Archaeology*, 23.

Laqueur, T. (1990) *Making Sex: Body and gender from the Greeks to Freud* (Cambridge, Mass.).

Martin, E. (1987) *The Woman in the Body. A cultural analysis of reproduction* (Milton Keynes).

Mead, M. (1935) *Sex and Temperament in Three Primitive Societies* (London).

Meigs, A.S. (1976) 'Male Pregnancy and the Reduction of Sexual Opposition in a New Guinea Highlands Society', *Ethnology*, 14.

Merrillees, R.S. (1980) 'Representation of the Human Form in Prehistoric Cyprus', *Opuscula Atheniensia*, XIII: (12) p. 174.

Morris, D. (1985) *The Art of Ancient Cyprus* (London).

Nanda, S. (1990) *Neither Man nor Woman: The Hijras of India* (Belmont, California).

Nikolaou, K. (1972) 'Mycenaean Terracotta Figurines in the Cyprus Museum', *Opuscula Atheniensia*, V, pp. 47–57.

Ohnefalsch-Richter, M. (1893) *Kypros, the Bible and Homer* (London).

Orphanides, A.G. (1983) *Bronze Age Anthropomorphic Figurines in the Cesnola Collection at the Metropolitan Museum of Art* (Göteborg).

Ortner, S. and H. Whitehead, (eds) (1981) *Sexual Meanings. The cultural construction of gender and sexuality* (Cambridge).

Poole, F.J.P. (1981) 'Transforming "Natural" Woman: Female ritual leaders and gender ideology among Bimin-Kuskusmin', in S. Ortner and H. Whitehead (eds), *Sexual Meanings. The cultural construction of gender and sexuality* (Cambridge).

Raymond, J. (1979) *The Transsexual Empire* (Boston).

Renda, G. (ed.) (1993) *Woman in Anatolia. 9000 Years of Anatolian women* (Istanbul).

Swiny, H. and S. Swiny (1983) 'An Anthropomorphic Figurine from the Sotira area' in *Report of the Department of Antiquities* (Nicosia).

Tsountas, C. (1908) *Ai Proistorikai Akropoleis Dimhniou kai Sesklou* (Athens).

Ucko, P.J. (1968) *Anthropomorphic Figurines of Predynastic Egypt and Neolithic Crete with Comparative Material from the Prehistoric Near East and Mainland* Greece (London).

Vassits [Vasic], M.M. (1908) 'South-east Elements in Pre-Historic Servia', in *Annual Report of the British School at Athens*, XIV.

Wace, A.J.B. and M.S. Thompson (1912) *Prehistoric Thessaly* (Cambridge).

Whitehead, H. (1981) 'The Bow and the Burden Strap: A new look at institutionalised homosexuality in native North America', in S. Ortner and H. Whitehead (eds), *Sexual Meanings. The cultural construction of gender and sexuality* (Cambridge).

Wikan, U. (1977) 'Man becomes Woman: Transsexualism in Oman as a key to gender roles', *Man*, 12.

Wikan, U. (1978) 'The Omani Xanith: A third gender role?', *Man*, 13.

3

Gender Constructs in the Material Culture of Seventh-century Anasazi Farmers in North-eastern Arizona*

Kelley Hays-Gilpin

In comparing designs on pottery, baskets, textiles, figurines and rock art from a group of shallow caves in northeastern Arizona, I noted there were at least two distinct decorative styles in use at the same time. Archaeologists often treat decorative styles as diagnostic of particular time periods and cultural traditions. I will argue here that these two art styles have something to do with gender.

My results do not provide law-like generalizations or cognitive universals about gender. Rather, the goal of this study is to learn something about the role of gender as a way of classifying people, work and ideas at a particular time in the Anasazi cultural tradition of the southwestern United States. My primary method is examining material culture as a structured set of differences. This method does not treat objects as passive reflections of cognitive, social or utilitarian norms, but as actively modified and reinterpreted in ongoing processes of culture change.[1] Along the way, I will provide alternative interpretations and highlight ambiguities, contradictions and instances where I make assumptions that cannot be verified or that require further support.

Broken Flute Cave

The Prayer Rock District is located on the east side of the Lukachukai mountains in extreme northeastern Arizona.[2] People who lived here were the ancestors of contemporary Pueblo Indians, such as the Hopi, Zuni and Acoma people. In the 1930s, Earl Morris excavated about a dozen caves in this area. He called the largest one Broken Flute Cave (Figure 3.1), for two

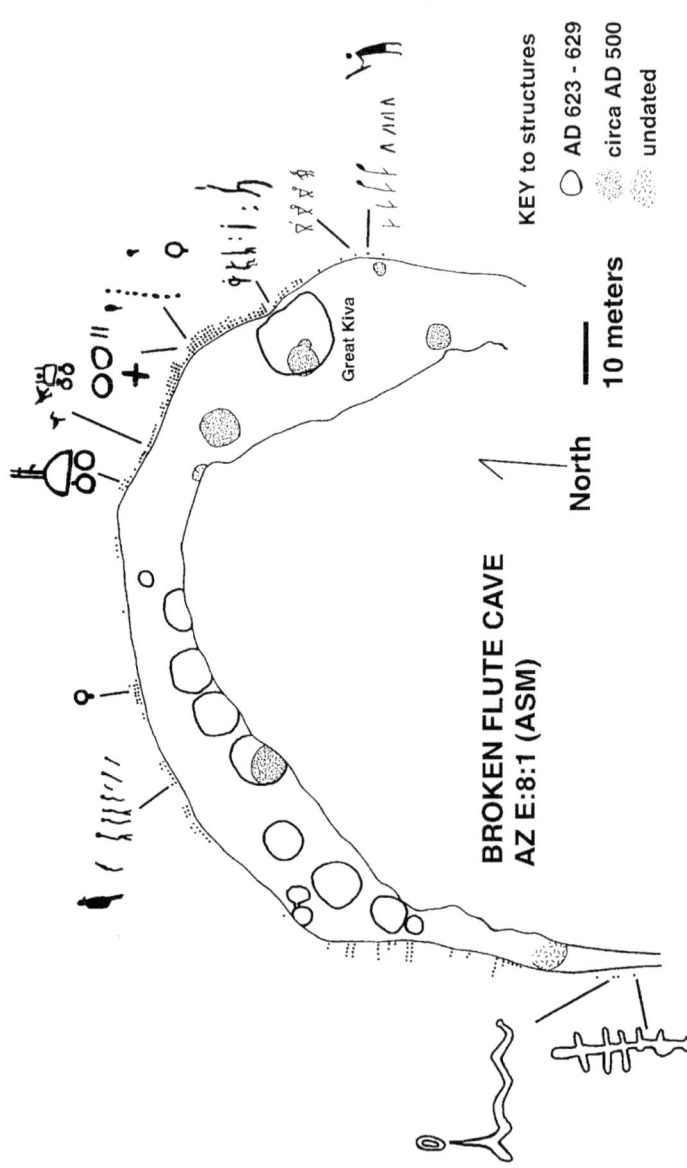

Figure 3.1   Broken Flute Cave, northeastern Arizona, showing location and density of rock art (one element or element cluster), and selected rock art motifs

Source: Author.

broken flutes held laid in the grave of an elderly man there. I located and studied the artefacts and excavation notes, and recorded all the cave's rock art. The site had two well dated occupations belonging to the Basketmaker III period, ca AD 400–700. The Basketmakers grew corn, beans and squash, as their descendants do today, but at that time they lived in pithouses rather than the familiar masonry and adobe apartment-like pueblos. Most of the time, these pithouses were clustered on flat alluvial terraces near good farmland. Rarely, Basketmakers built in shallow caves, like Broken Flute, where dry conditions preserved a wide range of perishable artifacts and architectural material. Clusters of tree-ring dates provide excellent chronological control.

Several small pithouses in Broken Flute Cave were occupied around AD 500. These early structures are aceramic or contain early, undecorated pottery. A few small, and many larger, pithouses have construction dates between AD 623 to about 635.[3] A maximum of 12 may date to this interval; they have hearths, storage features, milling equipment and all the other features of habitation structures in contemporaneous open-air sites. Many storage cists and one probable ritual structure called a 'great kiva' are associated with this seventh-century occupation. Pithouses in several other nearby rockshelters dated a few decades later in the same century and produced similar artefacts and pithouses, but had no great kivas. Two contrasting art styles are present in the seventh-century artefacts and rock art. The painted pots found in the pithouses have designs that clearly derive from the same style as basket and textile decoration, and contrast with rock art. Designs on the pottery, baskets and textiles are made up of small, repeated, geometric units, usually organized by rotational symmetry (Figures 3.2–3.3). The occasional birds and animals depicted on these objects are always rectilinear, and made up of small geometric units (Figure 3.2c–e). This style does not simply result from constraints imposed by weaving, twinning and stitching, because the pottery and some of the textiles are painted. This style is associated with portable household items and women's clothing and activities – particularly aprons (Figure 3.3) which have menstrual stained fringe and are found only on female burials (no female burials were found in Broken Flute Cave, but many contemporaneous ones come from the Canyon de Chelly area about 60 km away). Note also that carrying baskets and tump lines, tray baskets and pottery are all associated with gathering, preparing, storing and serving food and drink. These objects were found in the residential portion of the site.

The second style is found only in rock art.[4] It emphasizes human, animal and bird figures. Simple geometric elements such as zigzags, circles and squiggly lines are also frequent. These units are usually isolated, but are sometimes repeated by translation. In most cases, each unit is asymmetrical or bilateral. Rotational symmetry is absent, curvilinear lines are common, and the stepped elements found in the first style do not appear. This

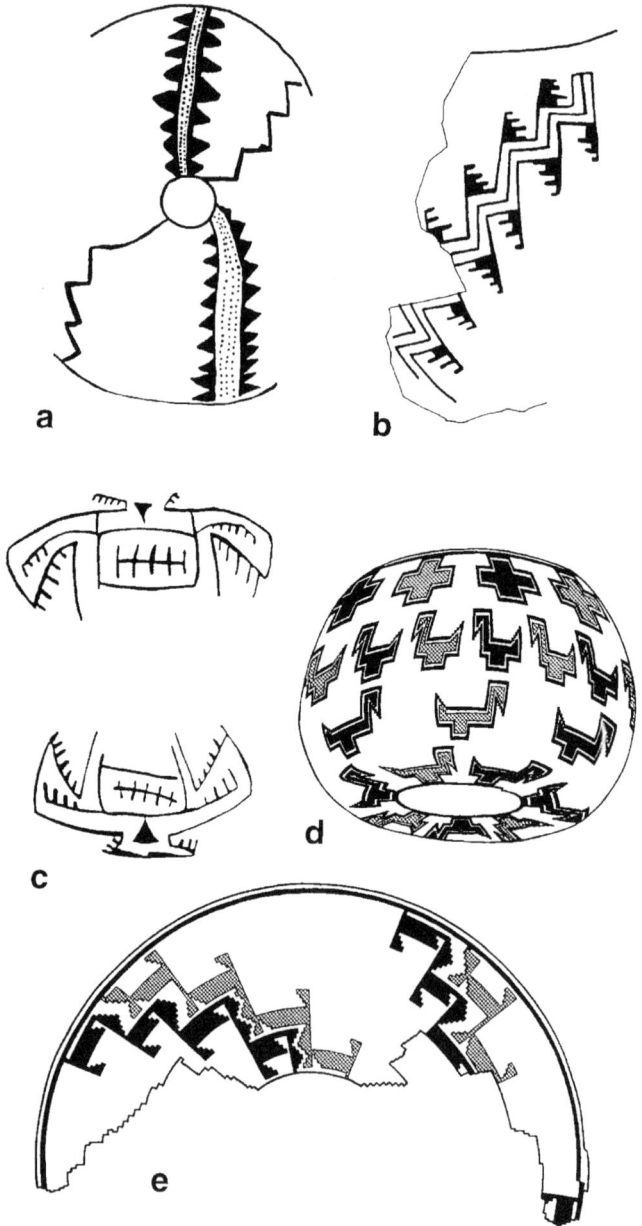

Figure 3.2   Designs on painted pottery bowl (a, c) and jar (b) interiors; coiled baskets with black and red designs (d, e)

Source: Courtesy of the Carnegie Institute of Washington.

Figure 3.3   Decorated textiles
a   Painted tump band
b   Women's string aprons with woven decoration, black, white and yellow

Source: Author.

second style is associated with immobile natural features of the landscape. Many of the human figures are clearly phallic, and none has female features. Most of the rock art in Broken Flute Cave appears in the east half of the cave, which contains no seventh-century houses, but holds human burials (two adult males and several infants) and a probable ritual structure of the kind known as a 'Basketmaker III great kiva'.[5] It is possible that the high density of rock art in the east half of the cave resulted from the addition of seventh-century work to some put there during use of the earlier structures in that area. The great kiva may have been built in this location because of the rock art that was already there. Or most of the rock art may have been put where it is during activities that took place in this structure in the seventh century. Several design elements (Figure 3.1) appear near the great kiva that are rare or do not appear in the west half of the site, and they do not appear in the other shelters – processions of humans, mostly phallic, possible masks and lobed circles, a figure I will discuss further, all indicating some kind of ritual activities.

We have, then, two art styles with different architectural and functional associations. The partitioning of styles coincides, though perhaps not perfectly, with several spatial and conceptual dichotomies: household/community architecture and by extension, household/community levels of social organization, female/male, and possibly secular/sacred activities. Even if no *conceptual* separation was made corresponding to Western ideas of sacred and secular, *behaviours* in the two halves of the site clearly differed, based on the distribution of thermal, storage and mortuary features.

Gender most parsimoniously explains this stylistic partitioning of Basketmaker visual arts and their spatial distributions. Gender – not merely sex, but gender as a symbolic way of contrasting people, space, work and abstract concepts – could have subsumed the other dichotomies mentioned. For the purposes of this study, I am making the assumption that the Basketmakers had a binary system of gender classification like that of their descendants. This does not deny that some individuals could have crossed gender categories or had ambiguous roles, as they do today.

Sex, gender and gender ideology

Recent studies by primatologists and cultural anthropologists show that the man-the-hunter/woman-the-gatherer model is oversimplified and far less biologically driven than previously thought. Division of labour by sex is varied and flexible, especially when variability in individual life cycles is considered.[6] The construction of gender categories is even more flexible, and proceeds in part from cultural ideas about sex, in part from the division of labour and in part from other culturally and historically specific factors. Yet there are strong patterns in the ethnographic record that are often applied to archaeological cases when there is little or no direct evidence. The consistent associations seen between sex and particular kinds of work are not biologically but socially determined; analogy must therefore be applied cautiously and other lines of evidence supporting a gendered division of labour pursued.

My interpretation of the Broken Flute Cave data could be used simply to extend the stylistic associations of objects to the norms about division of labour derived from comparative ethnography. In a majority of cases, ethnographers have noted women gathering and processing food, making pottery, baskets and off-loom textiles and they associate group ritual activities, large-game hunting and warfare with men. Although it is wise to ask to what degree these associations reflect biases of the ethnographers and archaeologists who cite them, it appears that the division of labour by gender in native North America fits this model rather well. This is not to say that labour is divided by sex – the well described case of the North American *berdache* demonstrates that, on most of this continent, choice of work traditionally determined gender identity, not biological sex (see also volume 2).

The evidence for gendered division of labour in Broken Flute Cave, at least for the classification of female work, does not rest wholly on ethnographic analogy, on the fact that these items are usually made and used by women in living horticultural societies (or by male *berdaches*, for which physical evidence is lacking in most archaeological cases including this one). Blood on the string aprons is a sound link with menstruation and hence with female sex. So is the fact these aprons are only found on the female Basketmaker burials (aprons on burials are not necessarily bloodstained – it appears that women wore aprons all the time and discarded them after their periods; of discarded aprons, the majority are bloodied but not decorated, and a small number are both bloodied and decorated). The uniformity in structure and content of the design style makes the link to other textiles, to baskets, and the pottery.

Ethnographically, both generally and in the Pueblos, men usually control most ritual activities even though women may often take part or have their own rituals. Men usually hunt large game and almost always take charge of warfare. There is a weak link between men and ritual in the rock art in Broken Flute Cave, between men and hunting in rock art in other Basketmaker sites (but not here), and between men and armed conflict in that the two adult males buried in Broken Flute Cave had suffered serious head wounds. In this case the evidence for women's work is relatively strong, although that for men's work is weak.

What interests me now is why a high degree of decorative intensity and skill was going into women's artefacts (perhaps I should say 'female-gendered' artefacts) at this time and place. This partitioning of design styles among the different media in Basketmaker times did not persist through time. By the AD 1200s in nearby Puebloan sites, basket designs are very simple and pottery is much more elaborate. Rock art contains many designs that are found in both pottery and elaborate loom-woven textiles.[7]

An 'eco-feminist' interpretation might be that Basketmaker portable art was a celebration of womanhood in the old days before men succeeded in completely taking over the religion, trade routes, political power and even textile production. I would argue instead that intensification of artefact and architectural decoration often goes along with social tensions and even conflicts.[8] Basketmaker people may have experienced a loss of flexibility in the organization of labour as they settled down in larger communities and made a greater commitment to farming. In such a situation, there should also be an increase in social specialization. Beyond child-bearing and nursing, sexual division of labour is the classification of work by criteria that have nothing to do with reproductive anatomy. As subsistence systems become more specialized, so do social roles. This happens in the realm of food production and processing, religious practice, and in the way use-rights of all kinds are allocated.

Arguing from ethnographic analogy only so far, Basketmaker women probably did most of the farm labour beyond the initial clearing of fields. This is the weak link in the scenario I am about to present because other kinds of evidence are unavailable. In societies where women do most of the farming, residence is often matrilocal, and matrilineal descent and inheritance of land use-rights often follows. Women usually have a great deal of sexual and economic autonomy.[9] According autonomy and importance to women does not reverse the usual stereotypes and place men in passive positions; as already noted, men probably hunted, conducted rituals and defended the settlement, perhaps even engaging in warfare (most of the pithouses were burned with tools and food supplies still in them).

If the period from the fifth to the seventh century was the time when the matrilocal residence pattern seen in the historic western pueblos (such as Hopi and Zuni) was forming, we can well imagine that there were some tensions and conflicts in Broken Flute Cave. This was a relatively large community for its place and time – other sites in the same canyon dating to the 480s–early 500s, and later in the 680s, had two to five households. Still, with 6–12 households, Broken Flute Cave was not big enough to be an endogamous community. If residence was matrilocal, then at least some males changed communities to marry, and the male power base in ritual and warfare would have been dispersed while female production remained concentrated. Uniformity of decorative styles across a fairly large area does suggest that women were not isolated, however. Women themselves may have travelled and traded (ideas, objects, or both), or men may have traded on behalf of women.

Much remains ambiguous about the division of labour by sex, gender roles, the role of decoration and the role of gender as a key structuring principle in this dynamic and changing Basketmaker world. I will explore two aspects of the Broken Flute Cave assemblage that do not fit the model of a simplistic male/female stylistic partitioning: the lobed circle motif in rock art and ceramic figurines.

Gender imagery in rock art

A Utah rock art specialist has suggested that lobed circles in Basketmaker rock art are uterine symbols.[10] Others have suggested they were badges of office worn by senior males in their roles as priests.[11] Both may be correct – the circle with the lobe projecting up, especially when depicted on masks and the chests of male figures, probably represents the turquoise mosaic pendants found in nearby Canyon del Muerto on two male Basketmaker burials, and in structure fill in Broken Flute Cave.[12] These were probably worn by males as an emblem of a restricted social role – that is, one that was not held by all males. With lobes projecting down, especially when depicted on the abdomens of female figures, these circles quite plausibly represent wombs. When they appear unattached, usually in pairs, they could refer simultaneously to both concepts and perhaps conflate other meanings as well.

The lobed circle may represent the expropriation of a symbol of female reproductive capabilities into the realm of male-dominated ritual activities. Although this is a female symbol in a fundamental, representational way, it was apparently used in the context of men's activities. It appears on male burials, appears near the phallic procession scenes in Broken Flute Cave and at other sites and does not appear in objects used and worn by women.

Men may have devised communal rituals partly as a means to integrate men from different natal communities into the community of their spouses. If matrilocality was becoming the dominant post-marital residence pattern, men moved between residence groups. One role of men became to reproduce the social order on an extracommunity scale through rituals. They also may have asserted their importance against the increasingly for-malized economic contributions of women – when women grow rather than gather plants, and when the group stays in one area for many seasons, control over arable land imparts a new kind of power. In asserting their perceived roles as managers of the supernatural or ritual domain, in con-trast to the agricultural and child-bearing domain of women, men expro-priated symbols of female reproductive powers, the lobed circles as both uterus and badge of office.

In addition, Basketmakers probably partook of the common and probably Mesoamerican-derived symbolic conflation of maize and female spiritual beings, the Corn Maidens and Corn Mothers,[13] and a cosmology that compares human emergence from the underworld to this world to passage through the birth canal. The historic pueblo kiva, which often has the shape of a lobed circle or rectangle with a southern projection, is viewed as a metaphorical womb, with the sipapu, a simple tubular hole in the floor, as symbolic birth canal.[14] In the Pueblo world, women are said to possess fertility and the ability to give birth to new life naturally and physically, but men must obtain by other means the ability to help maize grow and help game animals proliferate. They do this through obtaining ritual knowledge and practices that include manipulating symbols of female reproductive powers.

Figurines

A second kind of image that clearly relates to ideas about female gender but is stylistically ambiguous is ceramic figurines (Figure 3.4). Human figurines represent people of the female sex because they have breasts and a cleft crotch that is sometimes covered with a fibre apron. Carrying basket figurines are the same shape as full-sized conical coiled carrying baskets found with tump bands in Basketmaker III sites.[15] Figurines are clearly representational and curvilinear rather than geometric and rectilinear. The aprons and breasts seen on the figurines are not found in Basketmaker III period rock art in this area – even non-phallic rock art figures do not have these characteristics. The simple punctate designs on the female figures seem to represent beads, and the designs on the basket figures are somewhat similar to the repeated geometric units found in what I have called the 'female' decorative style but are much simplified. A pornographic interpretation – which has been suggested for many European Upper Paleolithic figurines – is unlikely given the association of Basketmaker female figurines with carrying basket figurines.

In Broken Flute Cave, the figurines came from pithouse fill in the west side of the site. Earl Morris (1951) suggested they are evidence for a cult of female and plant fertility, and that the fill of certain burned pithouses was somehow used as a locus for fertility rituals.[16] This is plausible (although the concept of fertility would need close scrutiny), but another explanation is at least plausible. The figurines could have been made by or for little girls as part of their socialization as women, mothers, gatherers and farmers. Children probably played in the ruins of the disused houses and lost, discarded, or hid away their toys as these depressions filled with refuse from the active households nearby. The figurines represent one way women taught girls about women's work. The elaboration of the other portable artefacts described here is another way women asserted what they saw as their roles and property. Textiles and baskets, in particular, show considerable labour investment in decorating the objects used in women's work in a particular style. This highly visible labour investment suggests that women's work and property were contestable at that time.

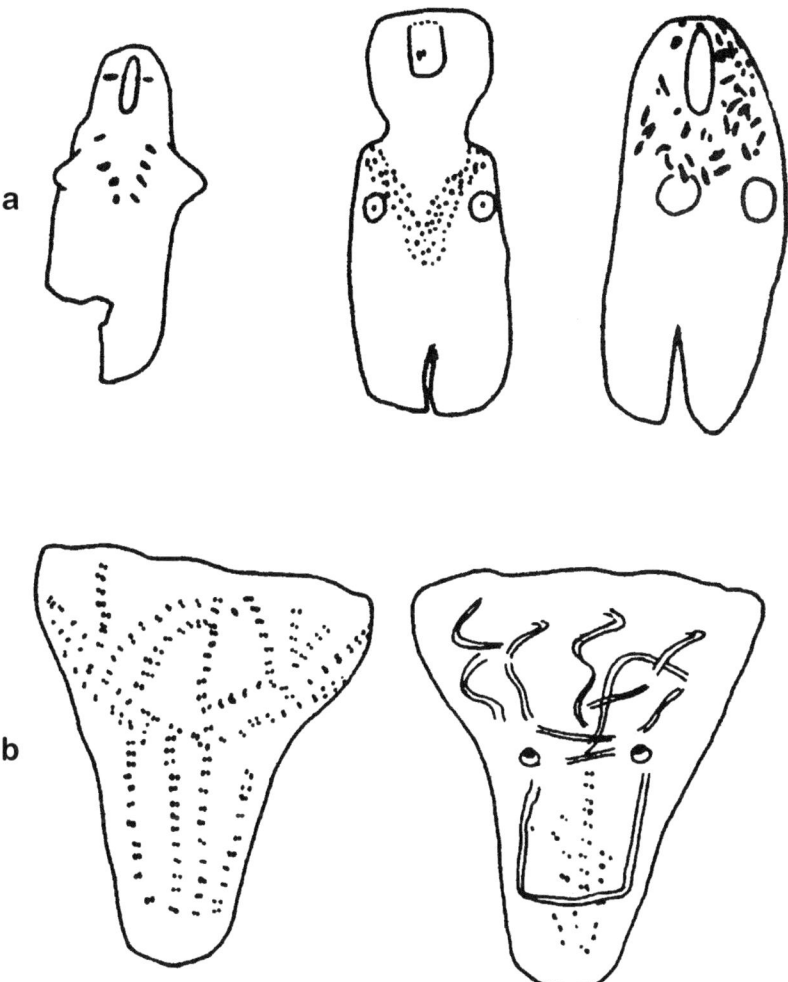

Figure 3.4   Fired clay figurines
a   Women
b   Carrying basket, front and back

In spite of the Pueblo ideology that male and female roles are complementary (as opposed to male dominating female), it is not difficult to find evidence of gender tensions and even conflicts in contemporary Pueblo society. It is more than probable that such tensions existed in the past, with roles constantly being re-negotiated.

Some directions for future research

In future research, a more detailed study of the Prayer Rock District architecture could be fruitfully combined with an ethnographic study of the habitations of matrilocal families versus other kinds. This is being done for the European Neolithic, where floor areas and configurations are emerging as important.[17] The fifth and early sixth-century structures in Broken Flute Cave and contemporaneous sites are much smaller and simpler than most of the seventh-century ones. The fifth-century occupants of Broken Flute Cave may have lived in nuclear family groups but the seventh-century people were building houses for extended matrilocal families. I would also like to see if we can find evidence for similar processes in other sites, even ones that lack the excellent preservation of Broken Flute Cave.

My interpretation of what was going on in Broken Flute Cave is incomplete and likely to remain so. It cannot directly be applied to other times and places, and it does not 'predict the past'. It does provide an interpretation that accounts for a great deal of the data, weighs against some other possible interpretations and suggests a framework for further inquiry. It demonstrates what can happen when we assume that many of the meanings artefacts had for their makers are not only accessible to archaeologists but essential to interpreting past lifeways.

Humans tend to dichotomize the material, social, philosophical and political worlds – men's work/women's work, elite/commoner, objective/subjective, science/art, science/humanism, social science/natural science, processual archaeology/post-processual archaeology, prehistoric/historic. This must not be seen as an innate drive that is always necessary and inevitable. Making dichotomies must be seen in every case as a goal-directed strategy even when not done consciously. Binary classification is a tool to help make sense of the world and to impose a particular sense on others. Although other kinds of classification are used, binaries are extremely common and are most easily recognized in material culture. Understanding of the past and the present can be moved forward by identifying and challenging such dichotomies, whether we are classifying our own methods and theories in the present or trying to discover past categories in art styles, architecture or organization of labour. Gender categories are a particularly good place to start. What people or activities are in both categories or neither? What mediates the two? What changes over time? What is hidden, subverted, or redirected by categorizing experience in this way?

Notes

* Special thanks to Dan Boone of Northern Arizona University's Research Imaging Laboratory for his generous assistance with the illustrations, to the Arizona State Museum, American Museum of Natural History, United States National Museum of Natural History for collections access, and to the University of Arizona Graduate College for funding.
1. Hodder (1982), p. 10, (1992).
2. Morris (1931); Morris (1980); Hays (1991, 1992).
3. Ahlstrom (1985); Bannister, Dean and Gell (1966); Morris (1980).
4. Hays (1991).
5. Adler and Wilshusen (1990), pp. 133–46; Marshall *et al.* (1979).
6. Lancaster (1989), pp. 96–115; Martin and Voorhies (1975).
7. Larralde (1977).
8. Hays (1993), pp. 81–92; Soffer (1985); Wobst (1977), pp. 317–34.
9. Martin and Voorhies (1975).
10. Manning (1992), pp. 1–37.
11. Cole (1989), pp. 59–87, (1990); Hurst and Pachak (1989); Patterson and Patterson (1992), pp. 187–211.
12. Hurst and Pachak (1989); Manning (1992); Morris (1980).
13. See Black (1984), pp. 279–88, for Hopi examples.
14. Young (1987), pp. 436–45.
15. Morris and Burgh (1941).
16. Morris (1951), pp. 33–40.
17. Ehrenberg (1989).

Bibliography

Adler, M.A. and R.H. Wilshusen (1990) 'Large-scale Integrative Facilities in Tribal Societies: Cross-cultural and Southwestern US examples', *World Archaeology*, 2, pp. 133–46.

Ahlstrom, R.V.N. (1985) 'The Interpretation of Archaeological Tree-Ring Dates', PhD dissertation, University of Arizona (Ann Arbor).

Bannister, B., J.S. Dean and E.A.M. Gell (1966) *Tree-Ring Dates from Arizona E: Chinle-De Chelly-Red Rock Area.*, Laboratory of Tree-Ring Research, University of Arizona (Tucson).

Black, M. (1984) 'Maidens and Mothers: An analysis of Hopi corn metaphors', *Ethnology*, 23, pp. 279–88.

Cole, S. (1989) 'Iconography and Symbolism in Basketmaker Rock Art', in *Rock Art of the Western Canyons*, Colorado Archaeological Society Memoir 3 (Denver), pp. 59–87.

Cole, S. (1990) *Legacy on Stone* (Boulder).

Ehrenberg, M. (1989) *Women in Prehistory* (Norman, Oklahoma).

Hays, K.A. (1991) 'Rock Art of the Prayer Rock District, Apache County, Arizona: A descriptive report', report to the Navajo Nation Historical Preservation Department and Arizona State Museum; also on file Museum of Northern Arizona, UCLA Rock Art Archives and Library of Congress.

Hays, K.A. (1992) 'Anasazi Ceramics as Text and Tool: Toward a theory of ceramic design "Messaging",' PhD dissertation, University of Arizona (Ann Arbor).

Hays, K.A. (1993) 'When is a Symbol Archaeologically Meaningful?' in N. Yoffee and A. Sherratt (eds), *Archaeological Theory: Who Sets the Agenda?* (Cambridge), pp. 81–92.

Hodder, I. (1982) 'Theoretical Archaeology: A reactionary view', in I. Hodder (ed.), *Symbolic and Structural Archaeology* (Cambridge) pp. 1–16.

Hodder, I. (1992) *Theory and Practice in Archaeology* (New York).

Hurst, W. and J. Pachak (1989) *Spirit Windows: Native American Rock Art of Southeastern Utah*, Spirit Windows Project (Blanding).

Lancaster, J. B. (1989) 'Women in Biosocial Perspective' in S. Morgen (ed.), *Gender and Anthropology: Critical reviews for research and teaching*, American Anthropological Association (Washington DC), pp. 96–115.

Larralde, S. (1977) 'Pottery and Textile Design Relationships in Prehistoric Arizona, 1100–1350 AD', unpublished Master's Thesis, University of Denver.

Manning, S.J. (1992) 'The Lobed Circle Image in the Basketmaker Petroglyphs of Southeastern Utah', *Utah Archaeology*, pp. 1–37.

Marshall, M.P., J.R. Stein, R. W. Loose and J.E. Novotny (1979) *Anasazi Communities of the San Juan Basin*, Public Service Company of New Mexico and Historic Conservation and Recreation Service (Albuquerque).

Martin, M.K. and B. Voorhies (1975) *Female of the Species* (New York).

Morris, E.H. (1931) 'Field Notes and Catalog of Artefacts Collected by the 1931 Carnegie Expedition', Arizona State Museum Archives A-133.

Morris, E.H. (1951) 'Basketmaker III Human Figurines from Northeastern Arizona', *American Antiquity*, 17, pp. 33–40.

Morris, E.H. and R. F. Burgh (1941) *Anasazi Basketry, Basket Maker II Through Pueblo III: Study based on specimens from the San Juan River Country* (Washington, DC).

Morris, E.A. (1980) 'Basketmaker Caves in the Prayer Rock District, Northeastern Arizona, Anthropological Papers of the University of Arizona, 35 (Tucson).

Patterson, A. and M. Patterson (1992) 'The Rock Art of Bluff, Utah and the Pendant Circle Complex', *Utah Rock Art*, 12, pp. 187–211.

Soffer, O. (1985) *The Upper Paleolithic of the Central Russian Plain* (New York).

Wobst, H.M. (1977) 'Stylistic Behavior and Information Exchange', in C.E. Cleland (ed.), For the Director: Research Essays in Honor of James Bennett Griffin, *University of Michigan, Museum of Anthropology, Anthropological Papers*, 61 (Ann Arbor), pp. 317–34.

Young, M.J. (1987) 'Women, Reproduction, and Religion in Western Puebloan Society', *Journal of American Folklore*, 100, pp. 436–45.

4

Shaman Images in San Rock Art: A Question of Gender*

Judith Stevenson

Conkey and Spector (1984) discussed androcentric biases and how certain assumptions about human behaviour underlie archaeological research.[1] They stressed that these assumptions must be examined and evaluated in the light of recent feminist research. Conkey and Williams continued in the 1990s to challenge the privileging of the commonly accepted techno–environmental model used in archaeology because of the tacit association of this type of data with male categories. Knowledge about archaeological reconstructions or interpretations involving gender in the past is, of course, closely related to the socio–political history of archaeology, with strong male bias firmly entrenched. Feminist enquiry has revealed problems about how archeologists have 'gendered' the past by applying stereotypical notions about men and women to specific kinds of artefacts and activities. This notion of a gender-specific ideology has roots, not in the generic prehistory of men and women, but in western European social institutions which may have emerged during the Industrial Revolution of the nineteenth century: mainly the nuclear family and a gender-based division of labour.[2]

This ideology has influenced archaeological interpretations of other cultures and has led to gender-biased interpretations. For example, a female found buried with a grinding stone is assumed to have used this artefact in life. If a male was buried with the same grinding stone, it was either because he had manufactured it, or because it had a religious–symbolic meaning. As Spector and Whelan (1988) forcefully pointed out, however, most archaeologists, when making statements about the activities and social roles of men and women and their relative positions to each other in the past, rarely define their sources for their assumptions about gendered behaviour and never seem to confirm or validate them.[3]

It is not surprising, then, to find similar gender assumptions and androcentric bias in the interpretation of the San paintings and engravings of

Southern Africa. This art form has been dated to as far back as 26 000 years[4] and was still being produced until the end of the nineteenth century. Its enigmatic images, however, puzzled researchers for years until Lewis-Williams (1981) utilized ethnographic sources to unlock the meanings of the art.[5] One of the most valuable sources of ethnographic information is the Bleek and Lloyd collection, compiled in the 1870s. This comprehensive corpus of southern San ethnography has served to record the now extinct /Xam culture, the creators of much of the art (see Figure 4.1 for a distribution of San groups in southern Africa). The Bleek–Lloyd work was recorded in phonetic script from the /Xam people in their own language, and contains almost 12 000 pages of verbatim accounts of folklore, mythology, and descriptions of daily life.

The Bleek–Lloyd ethnography, however, is not easy to interpret and apply to the art. Like the art, the San belief system and way of life is expressed through idiom and metaphor.[6] In order to understand it, it must be interpreted for Western minds. We must learn to 'unravel the highly complex and nuanced symbols, metaphors, and implications of San

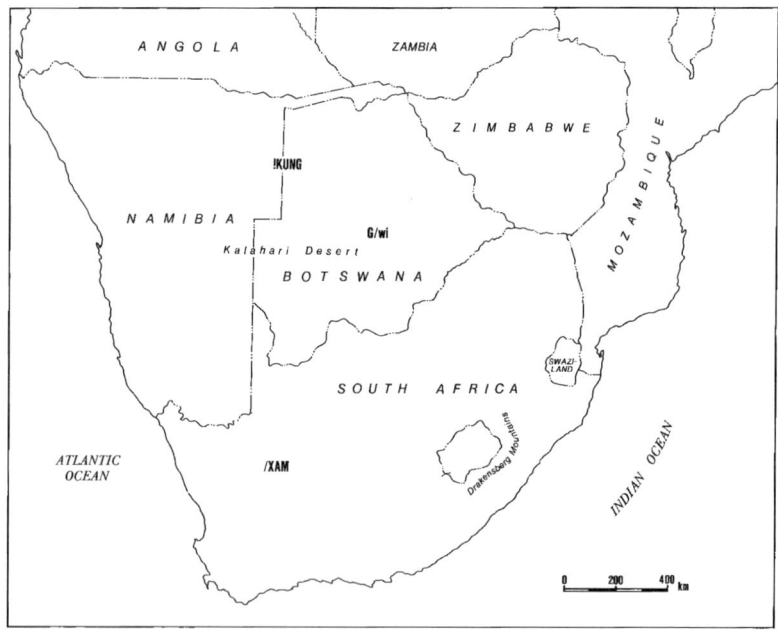

Figure 4.1   Distribution map of San groups

shamanism'.[7] This chapter, then, reflects some of my own emergent thoughts and observations about San rock art analysis within the scope of ethnoarchaeological research, my view being that the majority of San rock art research is permeated with androcentrism. I agree with Conkey and Spector that, in general 'the contributions, activities, perceptions, and perspectives of females are trivialized, stereotyped, or simply ignored'.[8] Sexual asymmetry in interpretations is prevalent, with males presented as dominant and females subordinate. This asymmetry has created an incorrect reading of the art. I do, however, caution that this type of analysis is only a preliminary step which is critical to further investigation of the San culture and, by extension, their art. I stress, furthermore, that this chapter is not intended to be critical or accusatory, but is offered with the intention of identifying male bias in current rock art research. Moreover, I hope to begin to transcend the androcentrism which limits our knowledge about San images by restricting the questions that we ask, and by biasing the data which we record.[9]

Gender is a generating and causal principle which is capable of producing certain motifs in the art which may not have been recognized through past investigations, mostly because we, as Westerners, have not understood or recognized the role of gender in San cosmology and worldview, and how it applies to their art. Most of the notable rock art researchers, Lewis-Williams, Dowson, Yates *et al.*, Parkington *et al.* and Vinnicombe, but with the notable exception of Solomon, have generally focused on a male experience, and have not addressed the correlation between male and female experience in San society and gender images in the art.[10] They have all agreed with the observation that 'the paintings... reflect a distinctly masculine bias'.[11] I argue, however, that it is our Western vision of the art which carries this masculine bias, and that we must learn to interpret San visual metaphors more broadly, and include women's experience.

Human image making grows out of complex associations and motivations. Figure 4.2 illustrates a complex panel of therianthropic figures, snakes, antelope, and other symbolic depictions. Lewis-Williams has pointed out, rightly, that it is difficult to understand the complexities of symbolic relationships.[12] It is also important, however, to recognize that all humans, both male and female, have participated in the construction of those symbolic relationships. This is true in San society, as it is in any other society. I argue that we must tighten the link between gender as a way of life, and all of the principles, expressions and constructions that it may encompass, and the construction of San art. Despite the lack of what Westerners would describe as collateral evidence for women's participation in the art, we must begin to admit that there may indeed be evidence which we have not recognized. Female participation is expressed in the art, but is expressed in symbolic, metaphorical ways which are complex as often contradictory.

48

Figure 4.2 Complex panel, Kwazulu/Natal, South Africa

Source: Rock Art Research Unit, University of Witwatersrand.

Archaeologists in southern Africa have called for a rejection of Eurocentric interpretations,[13] and have worked steadily towards vigorous and constant revision of theoretical stances.[14] Despite this, women have generally been neglected in rock art research. While researchers have been urged to move towards more polysemic interpretations of the art, gender-related studies have not been given adequate attention. While researchers have also called for detailed application of ethnographic evidence, women's roles have been marginalized. Researchers have cited references and passages selectively which support their assumptions regarding the role of women and men in San society, while ignoring other potentially important information. Archaeologists have perpetuated stereotypic notions exemplified by the socially constrained roles of Man-the-Hunter and Woman-the-Gatherer (Figure 4.3). The result has been an interpretation of San art which is skewed. Practical applications and interpretations have, therefore, been flawed. While it is important to recognize that many of the examples of androcentrism in rock art research have been the result of androcentric bias found in the ethnographies used, it must also be noted that archaeologists have accepted these sources as objective and valid. They have failed to recognize that androcentric bias in archaeology is, in reality, a reflection of the 'tyranny' of the ethnographic record and how it has structured archaeological models.[15]

Figure 4.3   Kwazulu/Natal figures
a   'Man-the-Hunter'
b   'Woman-the-Gatherer'
Source: Rock Art Research Unit, University of Witwatersrand.

Parkington, Manhire and Yates focus on the intent of Bushman paintings in the Western Cape Province.[16] Despite their claims, in 1990, that it is important to 'study the role of *both* men and women in human evolution' (p. 8, emphasis mine) they consider only male ritual and male experience within San society. Figure 4.4 illustrates the site under discussion. The authors find continued 'significant' associations of karosses with bows, arrows and quivers, and a 'virtual absence' of female karossed figures, and conclude that this bias towards males is an intentional one by the San artist.

I argue that one can hardly confirm that any karossed figure is either male or female because the kaross covers any identifying primary sexual characteristics in both males and females. Why assume they are male? The authors cite ethnographic references from the Kalahari describing male initiation rituals at which women are excluded, and describe this scene as an initiation event, based on that evidence. They state that all of the 50 human figures in this painting are 'apparently male'. They argue that the kaross-clad figures represent initiated male hunters with an association with the eland. I argue, however, that the karossed figures could just as easily be identified as women.

Figure 4.4   Karossed figures from the Western Cape, South Africa

Source: Reproduced by kind permission of Professor John Parkington.

The authors use selective ethnographic argument from the Kalahari to support their male initiation hypothesis, but ethnography from the Kalahari could suggest other readings. Richard Lee (1979), for example, has stated unequivocally that !Kung men never wear karosses.[17] They are exclusively women's garments. Based on ethnography drawn from the Kalahari, then, these figures could be women. Furthermore, I argue that it is impossible to say for sure that the 'sticks' carried by the karossed figures are either bows, arrows, or dancing sticks, as argued by the authors. They *could* just as easily be digging sticks, or walking sticks, or dancing sticks which are all used by both men and women.[18] The authors go on to state that 'the … elands paintings symbolize the councils of men', and argue that the eland is associated with male hunters.[19] This is an exclusionary argument which ignores strong ethnographic evidence that the eland is equally associated with women. For example, Biesele (1993), Lewis-Williams (1981), Vinnicombe (1972) and the Bleek–Lloyd material all give ample evidence for a clear relationship between eland and San women during ritual.[20]

Figure 4.4   Karossed figures from the Western Cape, South Africa

Source: Reproduced by kind permission of Professor John Parkington.

Rock art researchers are greatly indebted to Lewis-Williams' pioneering work in San rock art and its complex meanings during the past thirty-plus years. His research has clearly established that the art has a largely shamanic component.[21] Furthermore, this position is now widely accepted within the archaeological community.[22] Ethnographic studies have supported that fact that the San belief system is highly dependent on shamanism and that shamanic rituals play a critical role in San society.[23] Despite Lewis-Williams' capacity for constant revision of his theoretical positions (i.e. ethnographic analogy and symbolism,[24] structural marxism[25] and neuropsychology[26]), however, he has not included women in his research. While he calls, continuously, for a polysemic reading of the art, and for detailed application of ethnographic evidence, he gives little attention to women's role. While Lewis-Williams has taken great pains to caution against the use of 'simplistic ethnographic analogues',[27] he himself has not been cautious regarding the subject of gender.

While Lewis-Williams has repeated in his publications the well documented fact that 30 per cent of the women became shamans,[28] he generally describes the male experience in trancing and shamanism, and does not give women sufficient attention. Women trancers are rarely discussed or described. Yet women, as well as men, have this experience of trancing, and thus one of healing, rain-making, and game manipulation. The evidence for this has not been ignored perhaps, but certainly it has been marginalized. Women are powerful contributors to San social structure. We know that shamanism played a critical role in mediating San society, and we must see women as full participants in, and controllers of, those social forces. Proper attention has not been given to the full richness of female participation in both the construction and implementation of shamanism. Women participated as shamans along with men and held power to protect the people and to act as intermediaries between reality and non-reality and to maintain contact with the supernatural. Through their participation in trancing and shamanism, they were significantly involved in economic affairs and San construction of society.[29] I argue that this is reflected in the art through metaphor.

It is generally accepted that there are three categories of shamanism. These have been widely discussed, however, in the context of male experience. It must be emphasized that there is a considerable body of ethnographic evidence, both published and unpublished, which describes female shamanic experience, and which has not been well referenced by rock art researchers.[30]

The first under discussion is the 'curer'. Figure 4.5 shows a tracing of a site with women shamans bleeding from the nose. Curing shamans are described as healing through either a curing dance,[31] or a special ritual where the healer is said to draw the sickness out of the ill person and then 'sneeze' it out through their nose.[32] This healing process often induced

Figure 4.5   Female shamans bleeding from the nose, the Eastern Cape, South Africa

Source: Rock Art Research Unit, University of Witwatersrand.

nasal haemorrhage, with the blood being rubbed on the patient in order that the smell would keep evil away. There are clear descriptions of female curers found in the Bleek–Lloyd ethnography. In fact, there is an entire subsection of four pages devoted to 'The Sorceress !Kwara-an' in 'Beliefs and Customs of the /Xam Bushmen, Part VII: Sorcerers'.[33] In this section !Kwara-an is described in the same process of taking sickness from a patient, experiencing nasal haemorrhage, and rubbing the blood on her patient. Also, my preliminary review of one of Bleek's unpublished notebooks revealed a description of 'one old woman and young girls' who came together for a healing ritual which included blood.[34]

The second category of shaman is the shaman of the game. Figure 4.6 shows a redrawing of a female shaman with a rhebok head. The sorcerers of the game control the movements of antelope and bring game to the hunters. While Bleek–Lloyd is widely referenced regarding game shamans, we need to give attention to female participation in this role. There is a clear description of a woman beating the ground with a bored stone in order to ensure her husband's hunting success, and a further reference to a woman beating a stone on the ground to call game.[35] An additional passage quotes a female shaman, 'I must allow the springbok to travel, thou doesn't seem to think [that] I seem truly to possess springbok that I am a springbok enchantress'.[36] These passages are cited in relatively few numbers as compared to references to male shamans.[37]

The third category is the rain shaman who captured the dangerous rain animals so that they can be led over drought-ridden lands to make rain. Figure 4.7 illustrates a site in Lesotho redrawn in the 1870s by J.M. Orpen which depicts a rain animal with human figures. In 1874 Orpen published an article which included comments by a southern San informant who interpreted these images. This informant, Dia!kwain, when shown the copy of this painting, made particularly provocative comments on it. He stated,

we see here a water thing, or water cow, which, in the lower part, is discovered by a Bushman, behind whom a *Bushwoman* stands ... the two men are preceded by two *Bushwomen*, of whom one wears a cap on her head.[38]

While Lewis-Williams has discussed this site carefully and has cited Dia!kwain's comments regarding the paintings, he has referred to all of the human figures as 'men'.[39] One must keep in mind that Lewis-Williams wrote this article in 1980 and did not, at the time, consider the implications of Dia!kwain's comments. The point is, however, that there have been, and continue to be, androcentric interpretations of the paintings. Further examination of Dia!kwain's comments leads to an enquiry into San notions of gender positions and depictions which have not been explored. What were the connections in Dia!kwain's mind when he ascribed the

Figure 4.6   Female shaman with rhebok head, the Eastern Cape, South Africa

Source: Rock Art Research Unit, University of Witwatersrand.

Figure 4.7   Rain shamans, Lesotho
Source: After Orpen (1874).

female gender to half of the human images in this painting? To the Western eye, there are no obvious gendering characteristics which would make one identify any of the figures as female. In fact, three of the figures carry spears, which Westerners would identify as male. What kind of gender ideologies were operating in the San culture, both by the viewer, Dia!kwain, and the unknown artist? What lines of enquiry may we follow to investigate San ideologies of gender representations as expressed by Dia!kwain? How might these ideologies correspond to what San women 'did'? How might new gendered readings of the images lead us to new ideas about how the San structured the world and, further, how they negotiated that world? Finally, how do these questions impact archaeological enquiry into 'engendered' research? Questions such as these can be resolved only through further inquiry which frees us from assumptive biases.

There are many figures in the art which have not been discussed within the context of gender ascriptions. Therianthropic figures, which combine human and animal characteristics, are generally considered to be shamans in trance. Figure 4.8 gives an example of therianthropic figures: note the antelope heads and the hoofed feet on the anthropomorphic figures. In the literature these are frequently referred to as male.[40] It has generally been argued that the paintings show a paucity of female figures and female shamanic activity.[41] This, of course, leads to the obvious question of 'why so few?' if 30 per cent of the women are shamans? I argue, however, that the images do not always show us female shamans in ways that we, as out-

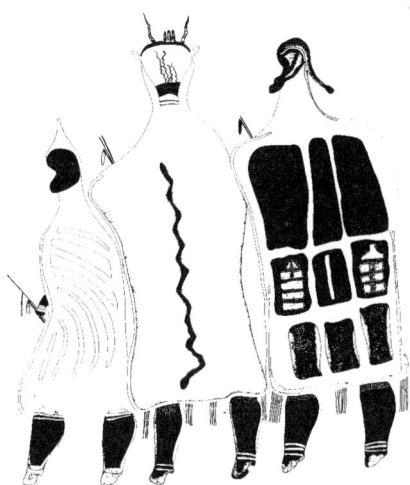

Figure 4.8   Therianthropic figures, Kwazulu/Natal, South Africa

Source: Rock Art Research Unit, University of Witwatersrand.

siders to the San culture, have understood. Close examination of some of the figures may reveal clues which will make it clear that there are depictions of female shamans, but that we have not recognized them. Figures 4.9–4.11, are three examples which move towards 'engendering' the art.[42]

The elephant therianthrope shown in Figure 4.9 is identifiable as a female. This can be seen by its angled forehead, which differs from a bull's more rounded one, its small tusks, its small trunk, and its lack of large prominent ears. This is a *female* therianthrope, and thus possibly a *female* shaman which has not been previously recognized.

The antelope head on the therianthrope in Figure 4.10 has been identified as a female rhebok, from the lack of horns and by the shape and size of the ears. Again, I argue that this is possibly a *female* shaman.

Most of us can tell a male lion from a female lion (Figure 4.11). Paintings of lions have been interpreted as depicting shamans in trance who travel by night on shamanic missions. They have not, however, been discussed in the context of being a representation of a female shaman, and what that may imply. This is a female lion, and thus possibly a *female* shaman.

The point in all of this is not that I have the determining and correct answers to questions regarding male biased assumptions in the images. But, rather, it is critical for rock art researchers to become aware of androcentric research biases, and to begin to challenge them. The question is *not only* 'is it male or female?', as this misdirects our analysis and interpretations

Figure 4.9   Elephant therianthrope, Orange Free State, South Africa

Source: Rock Art Research Unit, University of Witwatersrand.

'towards a search for a clear, consistent, and patterned evidence of activities differentiated by sex'.[43] This misses the point. As I stated at the beginning of this chapter, this process of gender ascription is preliminary to deeper analysis. A simplistic 'either-or-ing' of the images does a disservice to the complexity of 'engendering' San art. Sex linkages with the images in the

Figure 4.10   Female therianthrope, Kwazulu/Natal, South Africa
Source: Rock Art Research Unit, University of Witwatersrand.

Figure 4.11   Female lion, the Western Cape, South Africa
Source: Rock Art Research Unit, University of Witwatersrand.

paintings may, indeed, be contradictory, subjective, decentred, dynamic representations which we do not understand.[44] It is our duty not to treat them simplistically, because shamanic gender contexts may not be a matter of explicit, standardized, or normative categories in San worldview.[45]

I caution against a reductionist analysis of gender ascription and argue for a plurality of standpoints which can withstand multiple probings into the complexities of gender relations and their connections to shamanism. This theoretical stance is imperative because there do appear to be contradictory and confusing sexual representations in the images.

Sometimes male and female characteristics are combined in the same figure. Figure 4.12 illustrates a gynandromorphic eland engraving from the Magaliesberg area which shows sexual characteristics of both male and female eland.[46] A female eland is characterized by a smallish dewlap hanging down from the neck, while the male displays a bulky, fatty dewlap which is very large in comparison. The belly lines on the eland engraving show both the female stomach, in contrast to the male belly complete with a penis.

In addition to sexual composites, however, there are other aggregated conflations found in the images. Human, animal, female, male, and shamanic characteristics are all combined in different ways, with different attributes standing out in different contexts. For example, an hallucinatory figure (Figure 4.13a) from the Drakensberg shows a posture which characterizes female images. The swollen body with spread legs, the vulva patch and genital emission have been connected to femaleness through an association with the potency of amniotic fluid, along with linkages between menstrual blood and rain.[47] The bows, arrows, and quiver, on the other hand, are closely related to male ritual and shamanic activity.[48] Figure

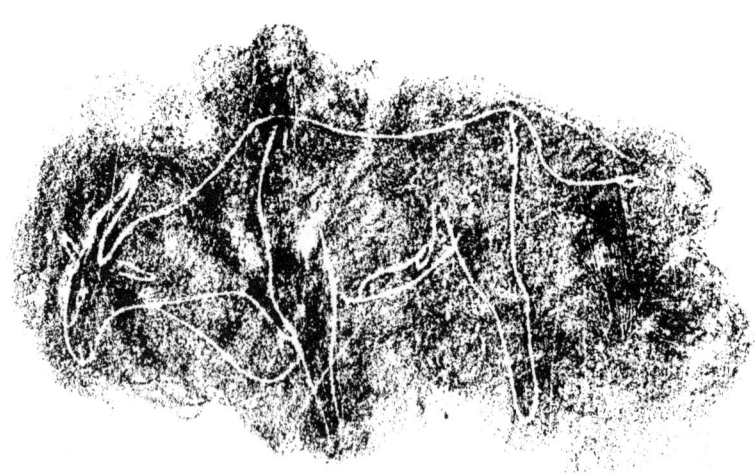

Figure 4.12   Gynandromorphic eland, PVW, South Africa

Source: Rock Art Research Unit, University of Witwatersrand.

a   b

Figure 4.13   a, b Gynandromorphic therianthropes, Kwazulu/Natal South Africa

Source: Rock Art Research Unit, University of Witwatersrand.

4.13b also illustrates a therianthrope from the Drakensberg which incorporates a female rhebok head on a human body with an erect penis.

As these three examples indicate, San gynandromorphic figures encompass complex, but sometimes incongruous motifs which do not lend themselves to a naive reductionist interpretation. The art reflects more than straightforward depictions of gender roles in society. For the San, metaphor permeates their entire expressive life. In fact, one could say that metaphor is a way of life.[49] The metaphors of the art likewise are permeated with complex symbols which serve to link the individual San with his or her society. But metaphor in San society broadly overlaps and mixes up themes and motifs, creating a richly complex layering of meanings about social processes. These themes are all-inclusive. The metaphors are all representations of potency, or power.[50] As Biesele stated in 1993,

> womanly power and manly power and the power of shamans, of *n/omkxaosi*, are really one power, a power in turn coterminous with the identical powers of creation and healing.[51]

The metaphors are all equivalent, and so can be mixed together, jumbled up, intersected, and conflated without the San viewers of the art finding any contradictions. It is our Western insistence on division of gender, our own gender ideology of separate spheres, which makes these images seem confusing and contradictory. Instead of tenaciously clinging to stereotypical linkages of male and female to specific roles within the art, it is perhaps more important to see that all of these image – male, female, gynandromorphic, shaman, human and animal – show different metaphorical aspects, with different nuances of supernatural power. This power permeates the entire society, and is a way of life. Both men and women take equal responsibility in maintaining social cohesion and inspiring renewal of nature. It is important to see San women in this context. They are not an autonomous category of inevitable separation, but rather they operate within a rich multiplicity of roles and social relations and social responsibilities. They are equal to men in creating specific connections to representations of ideology in the art.

Notes

* I am grateful to Professor David Lewis-Williams, Director of the Rock Art Research Unit at the University of the Witwatersrand, for comments and discussion. I thank Professor John Parkington for his kind permission in using the redrawing of the rock art site from the Western Cape Province. All other redrawings are used courtesy of the Rock Art Research Unit. I also thank Kaye Reed of State University of New York at Stoney Brook for her animal identifications, along with the Jagger Library of the University of Cape Town who provided access to the Bleek and Lloyd manuscripts. Special thanks goes to Anne Holliday for her assistance in the rock art redrawings.
 1. Conkey and Spector (1984).
 2. Conkey with Williams (1991); see also Wolff (1990).
 3. Spector and Whelan (1988).
 4. Wendt (1976), pp. 5–11.
 5. Lewis-Williams (1981).
 6. Lewis-Williams (1990), p. 41.
 7. Lewis-Williams (1990), p. 45.
 8. Conkey and Spector (1984), p. 13.
 9. Conkey and Spector (1984); Harding (ed.) (1987); Wylie (1991), pp. 31–56.
10. Lewis-Williams (1982), pp. 429–49, (1990), (1992), pp. 56–60; Lewis-Williams and Dowson (1989); Yates, Parkington and Manhire (1990); Parkington, Vinnicombe (1972), pp. 124–33, (1976); Solomon (1989), (1992), pp. 291–329.
11. Lewis-Williams (1990).
12. Biesele (1983), pp. 54–60, (1993), pp. 188–93; Lewis-Williams (1990).
13. Lewis-Williams (1983), pp. 3–13, (1984a), pp. 225-52, (1989), pp. 47–52, (1993), pp. 45–50; Mazel (1987); Solomon (1992).
14. Dowson and Lewis-Williams (1994a); Mazel (1987); Solomon (1992).
15. After Conkey and Spector (1984).
16. Parkington, Manhire and Yates (n.d.).
17. Lee (1979), p. 124.
18. Bleek (1923), p. 51; Bleek and Lloyd (1911), p. 361; Guenther (1986), p. 114; Lee (1979), p. 123.
19. Parkington, Manhire and Yates (n.d.).

20. Biesele (1993); Bleek and Lloyd (1911); Lewis-Williams (1981); Solomon (1992); Vinnicombe (1976).
21. Lewis-Williams (1981), (1982), (1983), (1984a), (1989), pp. 47–52, (1992).
22. Deacon (1994); Hall (1994), pp. 61–82; Huffman (1983), pp. 49–53; Maggs and Sealy (1983), pp. 44–8; Yates, Golson and Hall (1985), pp. 70–80; Yates and Manhire (1991), pp. 3–11.
23. Biesele (1993); Bleek (1936), pp. 131–61; Bleek and Lloyd (1911); Katz (1982); Lee (1979); Marshall (1976); Shostak (1981); Thomas (1959).
24. Lewis-Williams (1981).
25. Lewis-Williams (1982).
26. With Dowson (1988), pp. 116–28.
27. Lewis-Williams (1991).
28. Lewis-Williams (1990); Lewis-Williams and Dowson (1989).
29. After Lewis-Williams (1982); Lewis-Williams (1984b), pp. 58–66.
30. Bleek (1936), pp. 131–62; Bleek and Lloyd (1911), Bleek and Lloyd (1866–77).
31. Katz (1982).
32. Bleek (1935), pp. 2–5.
33. Bleek (1935).
34. B.I. 58. The Bleek and Lloyd manuscripts are catalogued in the following manner. Wilhelm Bleek's notebooks are notated differently from Lucy Lloyd's. In Bleek's system the first letter is 'B' for his name, followed by a roman numeral which designates the number of the notebook, followed by the page number. Lloyd developed her own system which designated separate notebooks for each informant. The first letter is 'L', followed by a roman numeral which designates the informant, followed by the number of the notebook, followed by a page number.
35. Bleek (1935), pp. 40–3; Bleek (1936), p. 135.
36. LV. 10. 4740.
37. See Lewis-Williams (1980); Lewis-Williams and Dowson (1989).
38. Orpen (1874), pp. 1–13, emphasis mine.
39. Lewis-Williams (1980).
40. Lewis-Williams (1990); Lewis-Williams and Dowson (1989); Yates, Golson and Hall (1985).
41. Lewis-Williams, personal communication.
42. Kaye-Reed, personal communication.
43. After Handsman (1991), p. 339.
44. Haraway (1983).
45. After Handsman (1991), p. 339.
46. Dowson (1988).
47. Solomon (1992), pp. 313–17.
48. Lewis-Williams (1981), (1982); Lewis-Williams and Dowson (1989); Solomon (1992), pp. 301–3.
49. After Biesele (1993), pp. 23–7.
50. Biesele (1978), pp. 921–47.
51. Biesele (1993), p. 202.

Bibliography

Biesele, M. (1978) 'Sapience and Scarce Resources: Communication systems in evolutionary perspective', *Social Science Information*, 17, pp. 921–47.

Biesele, M. (1983) 'Interpretation in Rock Art and Folklore: Communication systems in evolutionary perspective', *South African Archeological Bulletin Goodwin Series*, 4 (June), pp. 54–60.

Biesele, M. (1991) *Women Like Meat* (Bloomington and Indianapolis).

Bleek, D. (1923) *The Mantis and his Friends* (Cape Town).

Bleek, D. (1933a) 'Beliefs and Customs of the /Xam Bushmen. Part V: The rain', *Bantu Studies*, 7, pp. 297–312.

Bleek, D. (1933b) 'Beliefs and Customs of the /Xam Bushmen. Part VI: Rainmaking', *Bantu Studies*, 7, pp. 375–92.

Bleek, D. (1935) 'Beliefs and Customs of the /Xam Bushmen. Part VII: Sorcerers', *Bantu Studies*, 9, pp. 1–47.

Bleek, D. (1936) 'Beliefs and Customs of the /Xam Bushmen. More about sorcerors and charms', *Bantu Studies*, 10, pp. 131–62.

Bleek, W.H.I. and Lloyd, L.C. (1866–77), unpublished manuscripts, Jagger Library, University of Cape Town.

Bleek, W.H.I. and Lloyd, L.C. (1911) *Specimens of Bushmen Folklore* (London).

Campbell, C. (n.d.) 'Art in Crisis: Contact period rock art in the south-eastern mountains of Southern Africa', unpublished MA thesis, University of the Witwatersrand, Johannesburg.

Conkey, M. and Spector, J. (1984) 'Archaeology and the Study of Gender', in M. Schiffer (ed.), *Advances in Archaeological Method and Theory*, vol. 7.

Conkey, M. with Williams, S. (1991) 'Original Narratives: The political economy of gender in archaeology', in M. di Leonardo, (ed.), *Gender at the Crossroads of Knowledge: Feminist anthropology in the postmodern era* (Berkeley).

Deacon, J. (1986) '"My place is the Bitterpits": The home territory of Bleek and Lloyd's /Xam San Informants', *African Studies Journal*.

Deacon, J. (1988) 'The Power of a Place in Understanding San Rock Engravings', *World Archaeology*, 20, pp. 129–40.

Dowson, T. (1988) 'Revelations of Religious Reality: The individual in San rock art', *World Archaeology*, 20, pp. 116–28.

Dowson, T. and Lewis-Williams, J.D. (1994a) *Contested Images: Diversity in Southern African rock art research* (Johannesburg).

Dowson, T. and Lewis-Williams, J.D. (1994b) 'Aspects of Rock Art Research: A critical perspective', in T. Dowson, J.D. and Lewis-Williams (eds), *Contested Images: Diversity in Southern African rock art research* (Johannesburg), pp. 201–22.

Guenther, M. (1986) *The Nharo Bushmen of Botswana: Tradition and change* (Hamburg).

Hall, S. (1994) 'Images of Interaction: Rock art and sequence in the Eastern Cape', in Dowson, T. and Lewis-Williams, D. (eds), *Contested Images: Diversity in Southern African rock art research* (Johannesburg), pp. 61–82.

Handsman, R., (1991) 'Whose Art was Found at Lepenski Vir? Gender relations and power in archaeology', in J. Gero and M. Conkey (eds), *Engendering Archaeology* (Oxford), pp. 329–65.

Haraway, D. (1983) 'Why has the Sex/Gender System become Visible Only Now?', in S. Harding and M. Hintekka, (eds), *Discovering Reality: Feminist perspectives on epistemology, metaphysics, methodology, and philosophy of science* (Boston).

Harding, S. (1987a) 'Introduction: Is there a feminist method?' in S. Harding (ed.), *Feminism and Methodology: Social science issues* (Bloomington and Indianapolis), pp. 1–14.

Harding, S. (1987b) 'Conclusion: Epistemological questions', in S. Harding, (ed.), *Feminism and Methodology: Social science issues* (Bloomington and Indianapolis), pp. 181–90.

Harding, S. (ed.) (1987) *Feminism and Methodology: Social science issues* (Bloomington and Indianapolis).

Huffman, T. (1983) 'The Trance Hypothesis and the Rock Art of Zimbabwe', *South African Archaeological Society, Goodwin Series*, 4, pp. 49–53.

Katz, R. (1982) *Boiling Energy: Community healing among the Kalahari !Kung* (Cambridge and London).

Lee, R. (1979) *The !Kung San: Men, women, and work in a foraging society* (Cambridge).

Lewis-Williams, J. D. (1980) 'Ethnography and Iconography: Aspects of southern San thought and art', *Man*, 15, pp. 467–82.

Lewis-Williams, J. D. (1981) *Believing and Seeing: Symbolic meanings in Southern San rock paintings* (London).

Lewis-Williams, J. D. (1982) 'The Economic and Social Context of Southern San Rock Art', *Current Anthropology*, 23, pp. 429–49.

Lewis-Williams, J. D. (1983) 'Introductory Essay: Science and rock art', *South African Archaeological Society Goodwin Series*, 4, pp. 3–13.

Lewis-Williams, J. D. (1984a) 'Ideological Continuities in Prehistoric Southern Africa: The evidence of rock art', in C. Schrire, (ed.), *Past and Present in Hunter-gatherer studies* (New York), pp. 225–52.

Lewis-Williams, J. D. (1984b) 'The Empiricist Impasse in Southern African Rock Art Studies', *South African Archaeological Bulletin*, 39, pp. 58–66.

Lewis-Williams, J. D. (n.d.) 'Reality and Non-reality in San Rock Art', Twenty-fifth Raymond Dart Lecture, Institute for the Study of Man in Africa (Johannesburg).

Lewis-Williams, J. D. (1989) 'Southern Africa's Place in the Archaeology of Human Understanding', *South African Journal of Science*, 85, pp. 47–52.

Lewis-Williams, J. D. (1990) *Discovering Southern African Rock Art* (Cape Town).

Lewis-Williams, J. D. (1991) 'Wrestling with Analogy: A problem in Upper Palaeolithic art research', *Proceedings of the Prehistoric Society*, p. 57.

Lewis-Williams, J. D. (1992), 'Ethnographic Evidence Relating to 'Trancing' and 'Shamans' among Northern Bushmen', *South African Archaeological Bulletin*, 47, pp. 56–60.

Lewis-Williams, J. D. (1993), 'South African Archaeology in the 1990s', *South African Archaeological Bulletin*, 48, pp. 45–50.

Lewis-Williams, J. D. and T. A. Dowson (1989) *Images of Power: Understanding Bushman rock art* (Johannesburg).

Lewis-Williams, J. D. and J. H. N. Loubser (1986) 'Deceptive Appearances: A critique of southern African rock art studies', in F. Wendorf and A. E. Close (eds), *Advances in World Archaeology Vol 5* (New York), pp. 253–89.

Maggs, T. and Sealy, J. (1983) 'Elephants in Boxes', *South African Archaeology Society, Goodwin Series*, 4, pp. 44–8.

Marshall, L. (1976) *The !Kung of the Nyae Nyae* (Cambridge).

Mazel, A. (1987) 'The Archaeological Past from the Changing Present: Towards a critical assessment of South African Later Stone Age studies from the early 1960s to the early 1980s', in J. Parkington and M. Hall (eds), *Papers in the Prehistory of the Western Cape*, BAR International Series, 332 (Oxford).

Mazel, A. (1993) 'Gender and the Hunter-Gatherer Archaeological Record: A view from the Thekula Basin', *South African Archaeological Bulletin*, 47, pp. 122–6.

Orpen, J.M. (1874) 'A Glimpse into the Mythology of the Maluti Bushmen', *Cape Monthly Magazine*, 9 (49), pp. 1–13.

Parkington, J.A. Manhire, and R. Yates 'Reading San Images', in J. Deacon, and T. Dowson (eds), *Voices from the Past: /Xam Bushmen and the Bleek and Lloyd Collection* (Johannesburg).

Shostak, M. (1981) *Nisa: The Life and Words of a !Kung Woman* (New York).

Solomon, A. (1989) 'Division of the Earth: Gender, symbolism, and the archaeology of the southern San', unpublished MA thesis, University of Cape Town.

Solomon, A., (1992) 'Gender, Representation, and Power in San Ethnography and Rock Art', *Journal of Anthropology and Archaeology*, 11, pp. 291–329.

Spector, J. and M. Whelan (1988) 'Incorporating Gender into Archaeology Courses', in S. Morgan (ed.), *Gender and Anthropology* (Washington, DC).

Thomas, E.M. (1959) *The Harmless People* (Cape Town).

Vinnecombe, P. (1972) 'Motivation in African Rock Art', *Antiquity*, 46, pp. 124–33.

Vinnecombe, P. (1976) *People of the Eland: Rock paintings of the Drakensberg Bushmen as a reflection of their life and thought* (Pietermaritzburg).

Yates, R. and A. Manhire (1991) 'Shamanism and Rock Paintings: Aspects of the use of rock art in the south-west Cape, South Africa', *South African Archaeological Bulletin*, 46, pp. 3–11.

Yates, R.,J. Parkington and A. Manhire (n.d.) *Pictures from the Past: A History of the interpretation of rock paintings and engravings of Southern Africa* (Pietermaritzburg).

Yates, R.,J. Golson and M. Hall, (1985) 'Trance Performance: The rock art of Boontjieskloof and Sevilla', *South African Archaeological Bulletin*, 40, pp. 70–80.

Wendt, W. E. (1976) 'Art Mobilier' from the Apollo 11 Cave, South West Africa: Africa's oldest dated works of art', *South African Archaeological Bulletin*, 31, pp. 5–11.

Wolff, J. (1990) *Feminine Sentences: Essays of women and culture* (Berkeley and Los Angeles).

Wylie, A. (1991) 'Gender Theory and the Archaeological Record: Why is there no archaeology of gender?', in J. Gero and M. Conkey (eds), *Engendering Archaeology* (Oxford), pp. 31–56.

Part II

Representing Gender in the Early Mediterranean World

5
Engendering Ambiguity in Minoan Crete: It's a Drag to be a King

Louise A. Hitchcock

At the 1993 meeting of the Theoretical Archaeology Group, a discussant accused me of essentialism for reifying the dualistic categories of Male/Female in my study of Minoan bronze figurines. I very much would have liked to have presented a trendy Lacanian post-structuralist account of a multiplicity of hitherto neglected genders. However, as Shanks, Tilley, and Hodder tell us: in a post-processual and a post-structural archaeology, an anything-goes relativism is resisted by the evidence which constrains our interpretations.[1] 'Post-processual' archaeology began as a critique of the scientific paradigms and the anthropological orientation favoured by 'New' or processual archaeology, and the empiricist practices of traditional archaeology. It has sought to re-insert a historical content into archaeology, open up debate about the practice of archaeology, and accept theoretical diversity that has often paralleled post-structuralist critique.[2]

Although the evidence is textually mediated,[3] and the facts exist only within the context of a narrative,[4] there was no way of getting around the clear male/female distinctions in the figurines. The presence of ambiguity was conspicuously absent. I suppose that I might have interpreted them as cross-dressers; however, Shanks and Tilley might have accused me of creating an idealized past.[5] Still, in turning my search for ambiguity to the medium of fresco painting in my quest for Derrida's *différance* and sublation or the breaking down of simplistic dichotomies,[6] the Minoans didn't abandon me – they never do.

As I noted above, gender roles in Minoan art of Late Bronze Age Crete (ca.1700–1450 BC) are almost always clearly defined (Figure 5.1). Dress conventions generally include a kilt with cod-piece for males, and a flounced skirt with open bodice for females. Men wore their hair in long 'snaky' locks

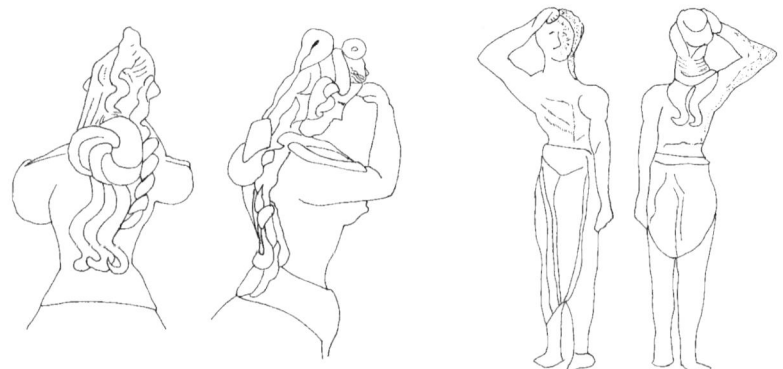

Figure 5.1   'Typical' Minoan figures (all drawings are by the author)
a   Female
b   Male

Source: After Evans.

down the back and shoulders. Women's hair styles were similar, but often included a great curl on the top of the head which fell down the back. Gender was further distinguished by skin pigmentation: reddish brown for males, white for females. This convention was borrowed from Egyptian art.

Notable exceptions to these 'rules' can be found in the bull-leaping fresco and in the so-called 'Priest-King' relief fresco, both from Knossos. In both frescoes the individuals are depicted with the white skin pigmentation of females, and the long snaky locks, kilt and cod-piece of males. Despite these anomalies, Minoan archaeologists have tried to force these representations into preconceived essentialist male/female cultural categories.[7]

The bull-leaper has been interpreted as a female dressed as a male or as a male whose white skin colouring is a convention for representing temporal sequences. The 'Priest-King' has been alternately interpreted as male and female, but most efforts have focused on making a 'proper' reconstruction of the fresco, which is fragmentary. I would like to suggest that it is possible to break out of this simplistic binarism by exploring the possibility of other gender constructions and their implications for our understanding of Minoan social structure and how Aegean archaeology constructs itself as a discipline in relation to its object of study.

I want to begin by first reviewing the evidence for each fresco, how it is interpreted and how those interpretations are constructed and constrained within a discourse where the categories of male/female are treated as transparent and natural. Then I will briefly discuss how these interpretations reflect and reify gender roles in the present. I will conclude by suggesting other plausible interpretations based on evidence from contemporary Bronze Age societies in Egypt and Mesopotamia. In doing this, my goal is to emphasize the 'otherness' of the past, and 'open out the field of meanings'[8] for Minoan material culture with regard to gender issues.

The Priest-King (Figure 5.2)

What remains of the original fresco is fragmentary and includes a crown of lilies normally associated with Minoan sphinxes; the upper torso which preserves a lock of hair, lily necklace, and clenched right hand brought back diagonally across the chest, a small part of the left arm which the excavator, Sir Arthur Evans, believed to be engaged in a downward motion; most of the kilt and cod-piece, the left leg excluding the foot; and a fragment of the right thigh, all rendered in low relief against a background of designs painted 'on the flat'.[9]

In a preliminary report, Evans assigned the fragments to three different figures: the lily-crown to a Minoan king, the torso to a boxer, and the leg to a third male figure. However, he later restored it as a single figure leading a sacred animal which is to be inferred from the cord held by the reconstructed left hand.[10] Evans took it for granted that the figure was a male, making the assumption that the fragments had faded from their original 'reddish brown'.[11] He designated it as the 'Priest-King', based on a combination of Greek legends of King Minos and rather vague references to Anatolian legends of the earthly Son of a Great Mother.[12] He assumed that the 'Priest-King' was leading a Griffin based on its frequent depiction on seal stones and its 'specially sacred relation to the Minoan Goddess'.

The fragments are dated to Late Minoan I (ca. 1700–1450 BC) and were found at different levels in a basement room below what Evans reconstructs as the North–South Corridor leading from the 'Corridor of the Processions' to the Central Court of the 'Palace at Knossos'.[13] There the 'Priest-King' takes his place in a processional scheme including some 536 figures reconstructed from even more fragmentary evidence. The reconstructed original can be seen in the Heraklion Museum in Crete, while a replica placed on the site, which is also heavily reconstructed, reifies Evans' totalizing narrative of Minoan history to the thousands of tourists who visit Crete annually.

Needless to say, this account has become increasingly unsatisfactory to Minoan archaeologists over the last 30 years. However, this has not occurred as a result of the impact of the philosophical New Archaeology which has had a negligible impact on Minoan archaeology.[14] Some of these objections to Evans have been recounted by Wolf-Dietrich Niemeier in his reconstruction of the 'Priest-King' (Figure 5.3),[15] and can be summarized as follows: (1) The crown and torso cannot belong to the same figure because lily crowns are worn only by sphinxes and priestesses, but never by men;[16]

Figure 5.2   The 'Priest-King', as restored by Evans

Source: After Marinatos.

(2) The lily crown belonged to a sphinx led by the 'Priest-King';[17] (3) The crown and torso must belong to different figures because the torso's left pectoral muscle indicates a raised position (Figure 5.4) for the left arm while the torso's anatomy is definitely male and probably belongs to a boxer.[18]

Figure 5.3   The 'Priest-King', as restored by Niemeier

Source: After Niemeier.

Figure 5.4   The 'Priest-King', as restored by Coulomb

Source: After Niemeier.

In his definitive study of the Knossos frescoes, Mark Cameron argued that the 'Priest-King' represented a crowned girl athlete leading a bull in a ritual procession prior to participation in bull sports.[19] Stating that human figures in Minoan iconography show a limited range of gestures which recur

Figure 5.5   Minoan figures
a   The 'Mistress of the Mountains'
b   The 'Master Impression'

Source: After Hallager.

almost stereotypically, Niemeier himself suggests that the answer to the 'Priest-King' conundrum lies in finding iconographic parallels where one arm is bent to the body and the other one is raised and outstretched.[20] *Contra* Niemeier, a quantitative analysis of gestures made by Minoan bronze figurines has demonstrated that gestures made by élites were rarely paralleled.[21]

In selecting a parallel, Niemeier oddly dismisses closer parallels from the Theran frescoes or the 'Harvester' vase in favour of the so-called 'Master Impression' (Figure 5.5a), a sealing from the site of Chania in west Crete.[22] Here, a male figure standing atop an architectural façade holds a staff in his outstretched arm, while his other arm is bent behind him with his hand resting in the small of his back. Niemeier associates the crown with either a guardian sphinx or a priestess. Archaeological evidence for the staff is lacking. I would draw your attention to a much closer parallel: the somewhat earlier Akkadian stele of Naram Sin (Figure 5.6) in which the ruler has himself portrayed as a deity by heretically having himself depicted wearing a horned crown.

Marinatos, a historian of religion, notes that the evidence is too fragmentary for a definitive restoration of the 'Priest-King' which she assumes is male based on the rendering of the anatomy while suggesting a thematic link between the lily crown and the lily necklace.[23] I would go further than

Figure 5.6   The Stele of Naram Sin

Marinatos by voicing the objection that none of the reconstructions is acceptable:

(1) they do not tell us anything about the 'Priest-King', only about Minoan iconography
(2) the anatomical debates make a presentist assumption that the goal of the artist was a true depiction rather than an ideal form or a propagandistic representation
(3) they create a fictive closure which reproduces discursive constraints in the discipline of Minoan archaeology which in turn perpetuates contemporary societal norms and prejudices.[24]

The 'Taureador' fresco (Figure 5.7)

I now wish to briefly discuss the 'Taureador' fresco. The fragments were from an upper floor and had fallen into the 'Court of the Stone Spout' in the north half of the east wing of the 'Palace' at Knossos. Evans originally dated them to Late Minoan IB (ca. 1550–1450 BC),[25] although general consensus through the study of stylistic details places them in Late Minoan II/IIIA (ca. 1450–1375 BC)[26] – after the Mycenaean takeover of Knossos and the general destruction of other Minoan centres. The fresco was probably composed of two friezes on two different walls. From the fragments it is possible to restore five panels,[27] although it is possible to restore the entire composition in only one of them. In the words of Evans, the fresco depicts a

> male performer, of the usual ruddy hue, who is turning a back-somersault above the bull, ... two female taureadors [are] distinguished not only by their white skin but by their more ornamental attire.[28]

This is a reference to the variegated hue of the kilts worn by the white figures in contrast to the plain yellow worn by the reddish figure. Evans goes on to tell us that

> the girl acrobat in front seizes the horns of a coursing bull at full gallop, one of which seems to run under her left arm pit. The object of her grip ... seems to be to gain a purchase for a backward somersault over the animal's back, such as is being performed by the boy. The second female performer behind stretches out both her hands as if about to catch the flying figure or at least to steady him when he comes to earth the right way up.

No doubt influenced by a romantic nostalgia for the American West, Evans placed these scenes in what he called the 'Cowboy' class of bull sport representations.

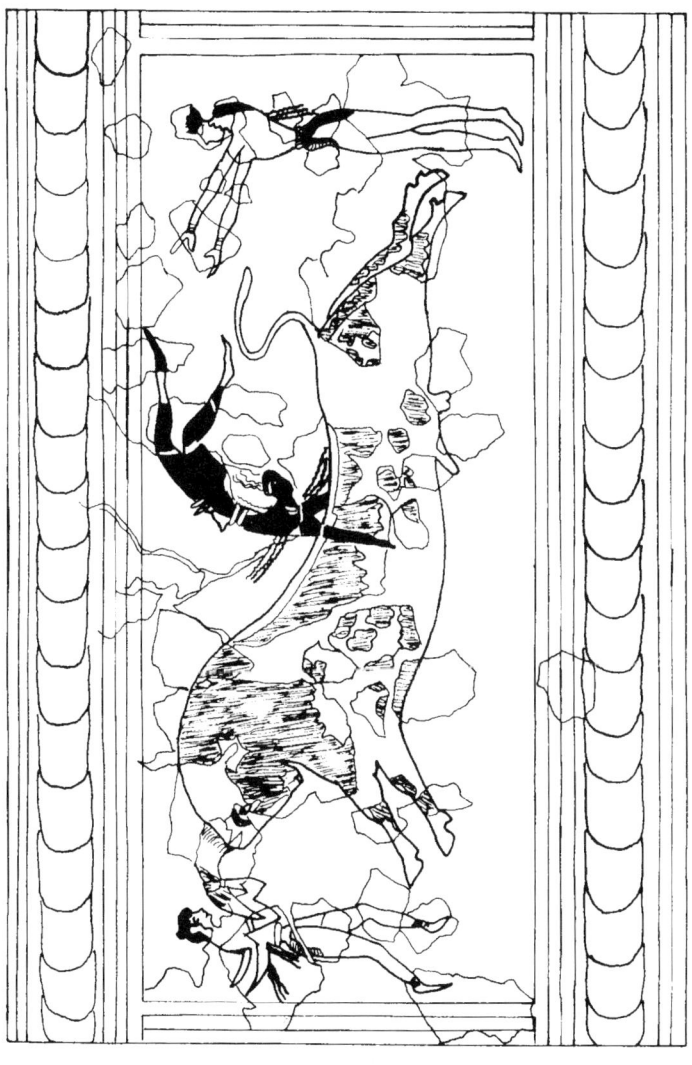

Figure 5.7   The 'Taureador' or Bull-Leaping Fresco

Source: After Marinatos.

Most discussions of Minoan bull sports focus on whether the acrobatics depicted on the fresco are possible,[29] and where they would have taken place:[30] whether in the central courts of the palaces or nearby. Enough representations exist in other media including seals, vessels, sculpture and on a Minoan fresco found in Egypt, to indicate that some sort of contest between humans and bulls took place. In a few instances, the depictions are violent. Until recently, most Aegean archaeologists tended to accept Evans's assumption that the white 'bull-leapers' were female. Cameron saw all of the Knossos frescoes, despite their different styles and chronology, as being thematically linked.[31] He went on to create an ahistorical totalizing narrative which began with a ceremonial assembly to summon the Great Goddess and culminated in a festival in which bull games were celebrated.

Evans' interpretation of female bull-leapers was not challenged until Damiani-Indelicato (1988) suggested that the colour of the bull-leapers was used to indicate temporal sequence.[32] Marinatos also rejects Evans' interpretation based on the depiction of articulated chest muscles, the absence of breasts, the wearing of male clothing, and the observation that the sexes rarely mingle in ritual art.[33] Drawing on Greek myth which makes references to the emergence of young males from a 'feminine guise' through rites of initiation, she believes that the main purpose of bull-leaping was to demonstrate the superiority of human males over the bull through a test of strength. She goes on to suggest that since only dark figures are shown leaping, that colour was an indication of skill level. As a note to this, I would draw attention to Cameron's observation that Minoan artists often neglected to render breasts on large-scale female figures, including the 'Ladies in Blue' and the 'Lady in Red', both from Knossos.[34]

The post-processual critique

Post-processual archaeologists have often been accused of advocating a crippling relativism in which anything can be said about the past and have been criticized for situating the choice between alternative pasts within a political framework.[35] I would respond by putting this criticism back on traditional archaeology. I have illustrated above that the traditional approach uses evidence that is fragmentary and ambiguous to perpetuate and legitimize presentist cultural norms that are male, patriarchal, heterosexual and arbitrarily centred on the fixed categories of male/female by inserting them into the past through an academic framework of textual production that is fixed in the present.[36]

In *Archaeology After Structuralism* (1990), Timothy Yates has suggested that we should let the past signify on its own terms – even if those terms are uncertain, fragmentary, ambiguous, polysemous, or 'Other'.[37] Ambiguity as supplement in Minoan art is put under erasure in the closed narratives recounted above. This suppression mirrors a political subtext of repressing minority genders in contemporary society.[38] In its own small way, then, Minoan archaeology as practised today contributes to the time-less, ahistorical, genealogy of normalcy in which the past becomes mir(ror)ed in the present. Reconstructing an autonomous past, which by the very nature of its autonomy and its difference serves as an agent for change, can be achieved only through a deconstruction of the present.

It is not necessary to write a history of the Minoans based on the sup-pression of difference which faithfully mirrors the present. Minoan Crete existed within a contextual framework of Bronze Age cultures where sexual ambiguity, multiple genders, plurality and difference played a sanctioned role in the dominant social order. For evidence of this, we need not look further than neighbouring Egypt and Mesopotamia where we have addi-tional evidence from textual sources. The gender of Ur-Nanshe (Figure 5.8), a singer whose statue was found in a late third millennium context in the Temple of Ninnizaza at Mari on the Euphrates, has been hotly debated. His – or her – beardless face, long hair and soft features has left Mesopotamian scholars uncertain.[39] Perhaps Ur-Nanshe was an *assinu*, a class of singer of indeterminate gender who performed in the cult of Ishtar: you have the *assinu* sit down and then he sings his *inhu*-songs; that the goddess Ishtar changed the *assinnu* from male to female: the *kurgarrus* and *assinnus* whom

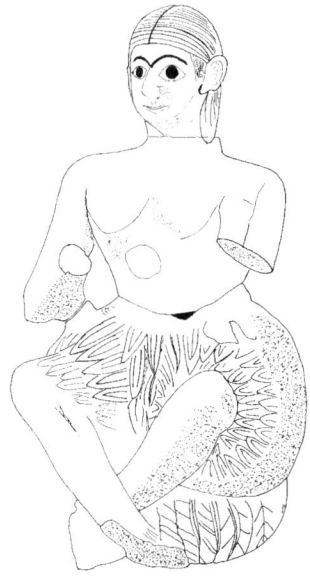

Figure 5.8   The Akkadian singer, Ur-Nanshe

Ishtar had changed from men into women to show the people piety; and that *assinnutu* referred to the position of the *assinnu*: the owner of the sheep will practise *assinnutu*.[40] Oddly, the *Chicago Assyrian Dictionary* deliberately uses the masculine gender in its translation and it is careful to warn us that there is no specific evidence that the *assinnu* was a eunuch or a homosexual; after all, this was 1968.

Even closer to Crete in time and space was the eighteenth-Dynasty reign of the female pharaoh Hatshepsut (ca. 1503–1483 BC). Hatshepsut (Figure 5.9) inserted herself visually and symbolically into the dominant

Figure 5.9   Hatshepsut
a   As Osiris
b   As Pharaoh
c   As a Sphinx

discourse by having herself depicted as a male, a male god, and a sphinx. At Hatshepsut's mortuary temple at Deir el-Babri,[41] 28 statues of Hatshepsut in the mummiform guise of the god Osiris were engaged in the walls and the pillars, and decorated the façades of the temple. Free-standing statues of Hatshepsut as a pharaoh and a sphinx lined the processional way. A fourth depiction shows a white limestone Hatshepsut seated and wearing the male costume of a pharaoh which included short skirt, royal head cloth, and broad collar, but retaining the hint of a female physiognomy. Likewise, textual epithets employed a similar ambiguity.

Framed within this larger Bronze Age context, there is no reason not to suggest similar occurrences for Minoan Crete. It is not unreasonable to suggest that the 'Priest-King' was in fact a 'Priestess-Queen' having herself depicted as a male, a bull-leaper and a sphinx thematically linked by the lily necklace and the lily crown. A male appropriating female symbols of fair skin and a lily-crown to legitimize patriarchal ascension is another possibility and evidence exists for this elsewhere in the male appropriation of female gestures.[42]

A similar suggestion might be put forth for the plaster head of a sphinx from Mycenae (Figure 5.10) whose identification is based solely on its headgear.[43] What are we to make of objects rendered in ivory, such as another bull-leaper (Figure 5.11) from the 'Ivory Deposit' found in a closet of the 'Domestic Quarter' in the east wing of the 'Palace' at Knossos?[44] Surely wood with its darker colour could have been used for males, reserving ivory

Figure 5.10   Plaster head of a 'sphinx' from Mycenae

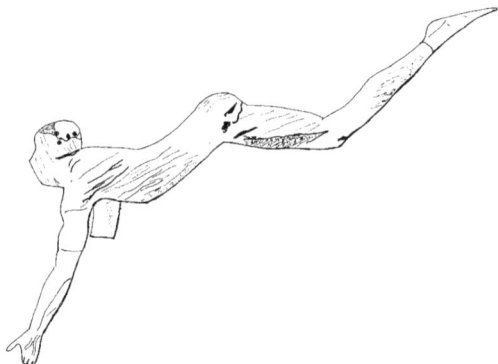

Figure 5.11   Ivory bull-leaper from Knossos

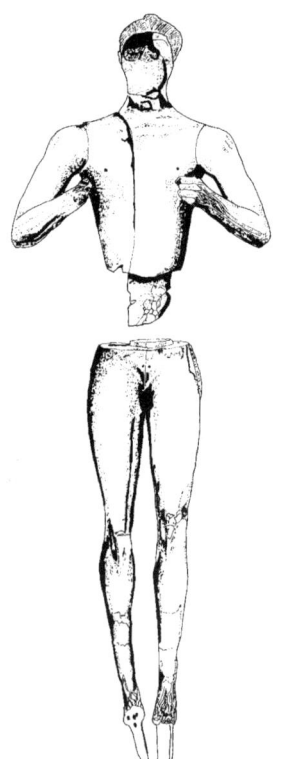

Figure 5.12   Palaikastro 'Zeus'

Source: After MacGillivray and Sackett.

for females? Conversely Homer makes reference to the dying of ivory cheek pieces for horses.[45] Could the chryselephantine statuette from Palaikastro (Figure 5.12), the so-called 'boy Zeus'[46] have actually been a female 'Hera'? Other, more mundane possibilities can be hinted at. Cameron has suggested that skin colours may also reflect social conditions in which women remained indoors, in contrast to men who spent more time outdoors.[47] Might this suggestion be extended to include a rare number of élite males who had achieved a particular class or status? Such a possibility has many parallels in the ethnographic present.

I think that we can conclude several things from this exploration of the Bronze age hermeneutic: that we do not need to write a history of the Minoans that faithfully mirrors the present, that Minoan Crete existed in a social context where plurality, ambiguity and difference contributed to the structuring of the social order and that Minoans chose to privilege certain images as different and distinct from their own cultural norm. It is our social responsibility to the past and the present to promote, defend and explore that difference.

At the beginning of this chapter, I presented a lot of details about the items I wished to discuss. These details served as a rhetorical device[48] to establish my authority as a writer qualified to discuss Minoan and Near Eastern archaeology. I now wish to relinquish some of that authority. A close reading of this text might reveal to you my preferred interpretation of these objects. However, I will choose to leave you with what Christopher Tilley calls a producer text,[49] inviting you, the reader, to write your own conclusions.

Notes

1. Shanks and Tilley (1989), pp. 1–52; Shanks (1990), pp. 294–310; Hodder (1986), (1992).
2. Shanks (1992), nn. 5–9, pp. 211–21; Hodder (1986), (1992).
3. Tilley (1990a), pp. 127–52.
4. Thomas (1991).
5. Shanks and Tilley (1987).
6. Shanks (1992).
7. For example, Gilchrist (1994); Claassen (1975) and Butler (1993).
8. Tilley (1990a).
9. Evans (1928), pp. 774–95.
10. Evans (1900–1901), pp. 15–16; see also Niermeier (1988).
11. Evans (1900–1901), p. 16.
12. Evans (1921a), pp. 1ff.
13. Evans (1928), p. 720.
14. Dyson (1994), pp. 195–206.
15. Niemeier (1987), pp. 65–98, (1988).
16. Bossert (n.d.), pp. 27–8.
17. Palmer (1969), p. 112.
18. Coulumb (1979), pp. 29–50.
19. Cameron (1975), n. 2, p. 122.

20. Niemeier (1987), (1988).
21. For example, Hitchcock (n.d.).
22. Hallager (1985).
23. Marinatos (1993).
24. Tilley (1990a).
25. Evans (1930), pp. 210–11.
26. Immerwahr (1990), pp. 90–2; Cameron (1975).
27. Cameron (1987), pp. 320–8.
28. Evans (1930), pp. 211ff.
29. For example, Pinsent (1983), pp. 259–71; Younger (1976), pp. 125–37; Evans (1921b), pp. 247–59.
30. Graham (1957), pp. 255–62.
31. Cameron (1975).
32. Damiani-Indelicato (1988), pp. 39–47.
33. Marinatos (1989), pp. 219–20, n. 162, p. 260.
34. Cameron (1975), n. 2, p. 122.
35. Shanks and Tilley (1989), p. 195.
36. Yates (1990), pp. 154–202.
37. Yates (1990), p. 159.
38. Nordblah and Yates (1990), pp. 222–37.
39. Postgate (1992), pp. 126–7; Lloyd (1984), p. 11.
40. Civil *et al.* (1968), pp. 341–2.
41. Smith and Simpson (1981), pp. 232ff.; Aldred (1986), pp. 152–3.
42. Hitchcock (1993).
43. Crowley (1989), pp. 40–5.
44. Evans (1930), pp. 428ff.
45. *Iliad* IV, line 141.
46. For example, Macgillivray and Sackett (1989), pp. 26–31, (1991), pp. 121–47.
47. Cameron (1975), p. 52.
48. Olsen (1990), pp. 192–5.
49. Tilley (1990b), pp. 146–7; (1991), pp. 174–83.

Bibliography

Aldred, C. (1986) *Egyptian Art in the Days of the Pharaohs 3100–320 BC* (London).

Bossert, H.T. (n.d.) *Alt Kreta* (Berlin).

Butler, J. (1993) *Bodies that matter: on the discursive limits of sex* (London).

Cameron, M.A.S. (1975) *A General Study of Minoan Frescoes with Particular Reference to Unpublished Wall Paintings from Knossos*, unpublished PhD dissertation (Newcastle-upon-Tyne).

Cameron, M.A.S. (1987) 'The "Palatial" Thematic System in the Knossos Murals', in R. Hägg and N. Marinatos (eds), *The Function of the Minoan Palace* (Stockholm), pp. 320–8.

Civil, M., I. Gelb, B. Landsberger, A.L. Oppenheim and E. Reiner (eds), *Chicago Assyrian Dictionary*, vol. A II (Chicago and Glückstadt), pp. 341–2.

Claassen, C. (1975) 'Questioning Gender: An introduction', in C. Claassen (ed.), *Exploring Gender Through Archaeology: Selected papers from the 1991 Boone Conference* (Madison), pp. 1–10.

Coulomb, J. (1979) 'Le prince aux lis de Knossos reconsidéré', *Bulletin de Correspondance hellenique*, 103 (1979), pp. 29–50.

Crowley, J.L. (1989) 'The Aegean and the East: An investigation into the transference of artistic motifs between the Aegean, Egypt, and the Near East in the Bronze Age', *Studies in Mediterranean Archaeology*, Pocket-book, 51 (Göteborg).

Damiani-Indelicato, S. (1988) 'Were Cretan Girls Playing at Bull Leaping?', *Cretan Studies*, (1994), pp. 39–47.

Dyson, S.L. (1994) 'From New to New Age Archaeology: Archaeological theory and classical archaeology – a 1990s perspective', *American Journal of Archaeology* 97(2), pp. 195–206.

Evans, A.J. (1900–1901) 'The Palace of Knossos, Provisional Report for the Year 1901', *Annual of the British School at Athens*, 7, pp. 1–120.

Evans, A.J. (1921a) *The Palance of Minos at Knossos*, vol. I (London).

Evans, A.J. (1921b) 'On a Minoan Bronze Group of a Galloping Bull and Acrobatic Figure from Crete', *Journal of Hellenic Studies*, 41, pp. 247–59.

Evans, A.J. (1928) *The Palace of Minos at Knossos*, vol. II (London).

Evans, A.J. (1930) *The Palace of Minos at Knossos*, vol. III (London).

Gilchrist, R. (1994) *Gender and Material Culture* (London).

Graham, J.W. (1957) 'The Central Court as the Minoan Bull-Ring', *American Journal of Archaeology*, 61, pp. 255–62.

Hallager, E. (1985) 'The Master Impression', *Studies in Mediterranean Archaeology* (Göteborg).

Hitchcock, L.A. (1993) 'Engendering Domination: A structural and contextual analysis of Minoan Neopalatial Bronze figurines', unpublished paper presented at the American Philological Association Annual Meeting (December 1993) and the Theoretical Archaeology Group, University of Durham (14 December).

Hodder, I. (1986) *Reading the Past* (Cambridge).

Hodder, I. (1992) *Theory and Practice in Archaeology* (London).

Immerwahr, S.A. (1990) *Aegean Painting in the Bronze Age* (Philadelphia).

Lloyd, S. (1984) *The Archaeology of Mesopotamia* (London).

MacGillivray, J.A. and H. Sackett (1989) 'Boyhood of a God', *Archaeology Magazine*, 42(5), pp. 26–31.

MacGillivray, J.A. and H. Sackett (1991) 'Excavations at Palaikastro, 1990', *Annual of the British School of Athens*, 86, pp. 121–47.

Marinatos, N. (1989) 'The Bull as Adversary: Some observations on bull-hunting and bull-leaping', *Ariadne*, 5, pp. 23–32.

Marinatos, N. (1993) *Minoan Religion: Ritual, image and symbol* (Columbia, South Carolina).

Niemeier, W.D. (1987) 'Das Stuckrelief der 'Prinzen mit der Federkrone' aus Knossos und minoische Götterdarstellungen', *Mitteilungen des Deutschen Archäologischen Instituts, Athenische Abteilung*, 102, pp. 65–98.

Niemeier, W.D. (1988) 'The Priest King Fresco from Knossos: A new reconstruction and interpretation', in E.B. French and K.A. Wardle (eds), *Problems in Greek Prehistory* (Bristol), pp. 235–44.

Nordblah, J. and T. Yates (1990) 'This Perfect Body, This Virgin Text: Between sex and gender in archaeology', in I. Bapty and T. Yates (eds), *Archaeology After Structuralism* (London), pp. 222–37.

Olsen, B. (1990) 'Roland Barthes: From sign to text', in C. Tilley (ed.), *Reading Material Culture* (Oxford), pp. 163–205.

Palmer, L.R. (1969) *A New Guide to the Palace of Knossos* (London).

Pinsent, J. (1983) 'Bull-Leaping', in O. Krzyszkowska and L. Nixon (eds), *Minoan Society: Proceedings of the Cambridge Colloquium* (Bristol), pp. 259–71.

Postgate, J.N. (1992) *Early Mesopotamia: Society and economy at the dawn of history* (London).

Shanks, M. (1990) 'Reading the Sign: Responses to archaeology after structuralism', in I. Bapty and T. Yates (eds), *Archaeology After Structuralism* (London), pp. 294–310.

Shanks, M. (1992) *Experiencing the Past: On the character of archaeology* (London).

Shanks, M. and C. Tilley (1987) *Social Theory and Archaeology* (Cambridge).

Shanks, M. and C. Tilley (1989) 'Archaeology into the 1990s', *Norwegian Archaeology Review*, pp. 1–52.

Smith, W.S. and Simpson, W.K. (1981) *The Art and Architecture of Ancient Egypt* (Harmondsworth).

Thomas, J. (1991) *Rethinking the Neolithic* (Cambridge).

Tilley, C. (1990a) 'On Modernity and Archaeological Discourse', in I. Bapty and T. Yates (eds), *Archaeology After Structuralism* (London), pp.127–52.

Tilley, C. (1990b) 'Michel Foucault: Towards an archaeology of archaeology', in C. Tilley (ed.), *Reading Material Culture* (Oxford), pp. 281–347.

Tilley, C. (1991) *Material Culture and Text: The art of ambiguity* (London).

Vercoutter, J. (1956) *L'Egypte et le monde Egéen Préhellénique* (Cairo).

Yates, T. (1990) 'Archaeology Through the Looking Glass', in I. Bapty and T. Yates (eds), *Archaeology After Structuralism* (London), pp. 154–202.

Younger, J.G. (1996) 'Bronze Age Representations of Aegean Bull-leaping', *American Journal of Archaeology*, 80, pp. 125–37.

6
Gender and Burial in Early Colonial Sicily: The Case of Morgantina*

Claire L. Lyons

Introduction

Sicily and South Italy, collectively known as Magna Graecia, were the destinations of one of the first great movements of colonization undertaken by mainland Greeks toward the end of the eighth century BC. Eastern Sicily, in particular, presented both an opportunity and a challenge to Greeks in search of land because of its fertile agricultural plains and abundant natural resources. It was inhabited during the Bronze and Iron Ages by indigenous peoples, whom I shall group under the short-hand term of Sikels. Archaeologically, this region can serve as a laboratory for the examination of exchanges between the colonists who established settlements on the coasts and the original Sikel inhabitants. The ensuing transformation of Sikel culture has usually been considered under the rubric of 'hellenization', a unilateral term that does not adequately take into account the complexity and nuances of inter-cultural contact.

The aim of this chapter is to look at the phenomenon of cultural change during the dynamic period of the seventh and sixth centuries BC, not on the large scale of political or economic development, but in the specific historic context of a single site and even more specifically through the interactions of Greek men with native women. Aspects of their relationships may be fruitfully considered through mortuary evidence. Analysis of the preserved skeletal material identified the sex and age of several individuals which provides a point of departure.[1] Comparative ethnographic data on the situation of Indian women within the colonial communities of the Spanish New World can be useful in helping to reconfigure the examination of gender and material culture in ancient colonial contexts.

It is striking that only rarely and recently has gender been used as an explicit category in the interpretation of the data related to long-term cultural transformations in Sicily. Many of the fundamental monographs on the history of the Western Greek colonies make little or no mention of gender roles as a structuring principle. The question of ethnic interaction tends to be framed in oppositional terms: Greek versus Sikel, civilization versus primitivism, conqueror versus conquered. Yet it is clear that in colonial situations, there is a disruption and redefinition of traditional gender roles on both sides which contributes in large measure to the emergence of hybrid cultural forms.

Recent scholarship has tended to frame the topic of Greek male–Sikel female relations by reference to the question of whether Greek women participated in the colonialist enterprise. The obvious assumption has been that if Greek women were available in some numbers, Greek men would have naturally preferred to marry them.[2] The evidence has been gathered from the texts of Herodotus, Thucydides and other ancient authors. It is fair to state that these literary sources and their intended audience were little interested in whether women took part in the establishment of colonies, and so the fragments of information they offer tend to be contradictory and pertain mainly to persons occupying the upper social strata or quasi-legendary figures. A case has been made that some Greek women may have accompanied their husbands on the voyage to found new cities, such as in the case of the city of Locri in South Italy.[3] The argument has also been put forward that Greek women were required for the transference of the religious cults of the mother cities to the new settlements, and to act as priestesses and celebrants in ceremonies, particularly in the cults of Demeter and Persephone which maintained a powerful presence in Sicily (Graham, 1984, p. 312: 'it is inconceivable that Greeks would ever imagine that the office of priestess could be filled by some native woman').

Although there were certainly occasional exceptions, in the majority of cases it appears that Greek women were not among the bands of colonists of the first generation or two – that is, during the late eighth and early seventh centuries.[5] Many men would thus naturally have sought wives or consorts among the local women. Humphrey[6] emphasizes the role of war, sea-faring, raiding, slave-trading and the establishment of personal alliances by travelling nobles in creating opportunities for young men to acquire status and portable wealth. In this scheme, travel and colonization are connected with an aristocratic male lifestyle of prestige, gift-exchange of status commodities and objects and the acquisition of land and manpower.

If the place of Greek women in western colonial society has been obscured by the scant and contradictory literary testimony, that of indigenous women has also been veiled by the reticence of the sources. In addition to references to intermarriage, for example, between the Greek men and Libyan women of Cyrene, there are accounts of forcible abduction as in the scenario of the Rape of the Sabine and Carian women. The literary record describes inter-ethnic liaisons, whether consensual or forced, with enough frequency to suggest that the concept was not foreign or entirely unacceptable. But the sources are often ambivalent in their treatment of such alliances and it must be remembered that the result of contact in a number of cases would have been servitude or concubinage. Legitimate intermarriage was apparently another option, as witnessed by the marriage of the Phocaean founder of Massalia, Protis, with Gyptis, the daughter of the local king. In fact, intermarriage may have been an intentional strategy adopted by Phocaean colonists.[7] Such negotiated political marriages fit in with the idea of gift-exchange described above, whereby an alliance with a local chieftain's daughter symbolized a transmission of power, legitimated the colonist's claim to the land, facilitated the village's contacts with the outer world and enhanced the status of local élites.

Some of the invisibility of native women can be attributed to research strategies that privilege certain categories of artefact – for example, imported fine ceramics over utilitarian domestic wares – or that place greater emphasis on questions of workshop production and international trade than on the local domestic and funerary contexts in which women's activities are revealed. Good evidence for the presence of indigenous women among the earliest burials at several western colonial sites, such as Pithecusae and Megara Hyblaea, has been gleaned from the typology of their fibulae, the dress pins of iron, bone and amber that are Italic in origin and found exclusively in female burials.[8] As the situation at Morgantina will show, it is important to recognize and highlight those elements of material culture that attest to the dynamic, reciprocal nature of acculturation (or better 'transculturation') and the role that native women played in defining the character of everyday life in these early mixed-population settlements.

Gender relations – the evidence from the burials at Morgantina

The site of Morgantina, occupying a hill-top position known as the Cittadella, was the location of a substantial Iron Age settlement that flourished from the tenth to the eighth centuries BC. In terms of the material culture, particularly the ceramics, this settlement is identified with the Ausonian culture originating in South Italy and attested at Lipari, Lentini and several other Sicilian locales. Its economy was based on subsistence agriculture, hunting, sheep or goat herding, weaving, the manufacture of dairy products and other local crafts such as potting and metallurgy.[9]

It is not until the later seventh century that pottery imported from Greece is found on the Cittadella. The Sikel pottery from the few contact-period contexts that have been excavated is sufficient to demonstrate that the site was continuously occupied from the Iron Age until about the fourth century. In the strata directly beneath a small sacred building decorated with Greek-style architectural terracottas were found fragments of imported wine amphorae inscribed with Greek graffiti and Ionic drinking cups together with great quantities of the lively Sikel geometric pottery that was made locally. An imported Proto-corinthian aryballos or perfume vase was recovered from another late seventh-century context, and the presence of such perfume and wine containers indicates an interest on the part of the natives in obtaining luxury goods. It is tempting to interpret this material as evidence for the establishment of a place of trade or emporion where Greeks and Sikels met, their interactions possibly mediated through the presence of a religious sanctuary.[10] Similarly, the evidence of transport amphorae and table wares closely associated with a sacred building at Monte San Mauro may suggest that such locales were 'privileged places of exchange'.[11]

From about the middle of the sixth century, the Cittadella settlement was very Greek in appearance. A number of buildings decorated with architectural terracottas were constructed as was a fortification wall, and there are clear indications that Greek language and religious iconography were used and understood. Because much Greek pottery was deposited in the necropolis, where Greek burial practices were simultaneously introduced, the excavator of the site linked the hellenization of the Cittadella with the arrival of colonists from one of the Greek cities to the east, perhaps Catania.[12] A study based on the style and iconography of the architectural terracottas hypothesizes that emigré Phocaean settlers made their way to Morgantina,[13] an attractive suggestion that may find some confirmation in the distinctly East Greek pottery styles adapted by local potters.

With the exception of several studies on individual artefact categories and the publication of the Protohistoric settlement, the domestic and civic contexts on the Cittadella have yet to be assessed in detail. For the height of the contact period (late seventh–sixth century), preliminary observations and conclusions rest solely on the evidence of the archaic necropolis; 67 tombs were excavated which can be dated between the later seventh and mid-fifth centuries.[14] The archaeological evidence indicates that the indigenous mortuary ritual continued throughout the lifespan of the cemetery. The majority of adult burials follow the traditional Sikel practice of multiple inhumation in rock-cut chamber tombs, a Bronze Age funerary rite that remained in use even into the fourth century BC. Because burial practices are a conservative element of belief, this suggests that a significant portion of the population maintained its ethnic Sikel identity despite the outwardly Greek appearance of the settlement. Shifts in the character of the mortuary ritual can be observed in the adoption of Greek grave types, mainly for burials of children, and in the nature and function of the tomb furnishings. These changes point to a community defined by an increasingly complex demographic profile with access to a greater range of imported goods and technologies.

Evidence for gender differentiation is preserved in several of the tombs. Tomb 4 is a chamber tomb that contained five adult burials. The chamber is elaborate architecturally, having a pitched ceiling, a sarcophagus at the back and a 'fossa' grave cut into the floor. It also stands out in the great number of grave offerings. The fossa held the remains of a robust adult woman who was over 40 years old at the time of death. In addition to wearing silver rings and bronze fibulae of Greek type (Figure 6.1c, f), she wore two pairs of silver hair spirals of a kind found primarily in indigenous Sicilian contexts (Figure 6.1b) and two or more iron and bone fibulae. Typologically, this form of fibula has been viewed as an element of native costume that persisted in areas of inter-ethnic contact and influenced Greek fibula styles. Her clothing was ornamented with bronze buttons and bosses, following a Sikel rather than Greek fashion both in the form of the ornaments and the quantity (Figure 6.1a). The pottery associated with this

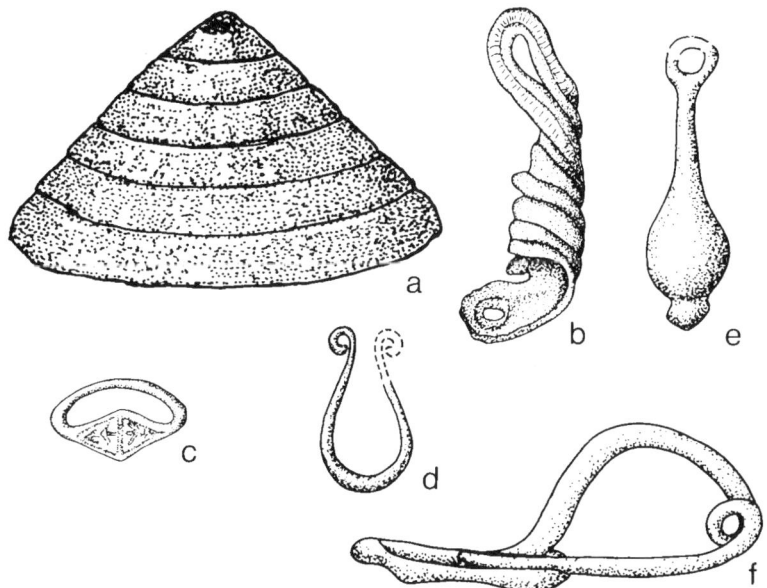

Figure 6.1　Personal ornaments
a　Bronze boss, *inv. 69–500* ; diameter 6 cm
b　Silver hair spiral, *inv. 57–2954*; length 4.4 cm
c　Silver ring, *inv. 57–2 782*; diameter 1.9 cm
d　Bronze pendant, *no inv.*; length 2.2 cm
e　Bronze pendant, *inv. 57–2905*; length 3.8 cm
f　Bronze fibula, *inv. 57–2696*; length 5.6 cm

burial included a small cup and bowl, a container for scented oil called an exaleiptron and a pyxis.

The sex and age of bone fragments preserved in the sarcophagus at the rear of Tomb 4 were not identifiable, but the assortment of jewellery and clothing ornaments was identical to that found in the fossa and it is assumed that this burial, too, was that of an older female. The presence of native jewelry such as silver hair spirals, bronze pendants (Figure 6.1d, e) and several iron and bone fibulae strongly suggests that, in terms of personal ornamentation, this individual identified herself with the indigenous element of the community.

Three other burials in Tomb 4 were mixed together on the floor of the chamber and it was not possible to separate the human remains or the grave furnishings. The typology of the jewellery suggests that at least one of the individuals was female. The pottery assemblage is remarkable for the number of imported vessels used for drinking wine, many of which were decorated with Dionysiac images. As in many other sites on the periphery of the Greek world, the ideology of the symposion was a prominent feature of social practice and is reflected in the large numbers of vase shapes placed in the tombs that were suited for consuming, serving and storing wine. Such symposion pottery tends to be associated with male burials.

Offerings in the form of terracotta masks of the goddess Persephone indicate that some form of Greek religion had been adopted or syncretized with local beliefs. A Greek inscription scratched on a lamp is interpreted as a personal name, 'Thamis', possibly Sikel since it is not attested among Greek names. It demonstrates a degree of Greek literacy among the deceased or their families. The combination of these objects suggests that a group of individuals occupying a position of elevated social status is represented in Tomb 4. Aspects of Greek material culture and social practice pervade this burial context, but the fact that two senior native women occupy privileged burial places (fossa, sarcophagus) within the tomb is significant. The kinds of personal ornaments they wore reflect their gender and ethnic identity and possibly signal their age group affiliation and social status as well.

In Tomb 9, a large chamber containing 17 individual burials, one female and two male inhumations can be securely identified. The woman was small in stature, probably young, and wore only a bronze ring and spiral armlet, unlike the two older women of Tomb 4. Simple bronze jewellery of this sort is common in Sikel burials of the preceding period. Notable among the pots placed near the young woman's remains were a number of imported Corinthian pyxides (Figure 6.2), traditionally considered a female shape used for cosmetics, and several small perfume vessels including prestige imports from East Greece: an aryballos made of faience and two vases in the shape of a sandalled foot and a siren. A significant number of the ceramic shapes, however, were traditional indigenous domestic forms, such as a group of 10 large three-handled bowls. In the case of this burial, the

Figure 6.2 Corinthian pottery from tomb 9
a   Aryballos, *inv. 69–100*; height 10.9 cm
b   Pyxis, *inv. 69–104*; height 12.9 cm
c   Kotyle, *inv. 69–87*; height 8.6 cm

emphasis on cosmetics and scents may imply that this female was of marriageable age and had not yet attained the social status signalled by the profusion of metal ornaments worn by the older females in Tomb 4. Furthermore, the bronze spiral bracelet and the series of indigenous-type bowls reinforce the hypothesis that she may be of Sikel origin.

The two males buried in Tomb 9 were both older men, aged 40–45 years, and their grave goods consisted primarily of symposion pottery – kylikes of various kinds, and shapes for pouring such as oinochoai or for storage such as hydriae. One of these men wore a bronze necklace composed of ringlets with a central biconical bead of a type that has a long local history as far back as the early Iron Age. Parenthetically, the man's necklace and the bronze knife carried by one of the older women in Tomb 4 serve as a caution against simplistic associations of women with jewellery and men with weaponry. The concentration of wine-related vessels in the male burials signals a connection with public display, feasting and hospitality. In a nearby tomb, the prestige value of symposion pottery is evident in the inscription of a masculine Greek name, 'Pyrrhias', on the interior of a wine cup. The character of the grave goods in female burials emphasizes instead status displayed through personal adornment and the link with private, domestic tasks.

Other inhumations of known sex were identified elsewhere in the cemetery but come from confused contexts. Nevertheless, a few biological observations can be made. The burials of two women and one man were preserved in Tomb 16. Tomb 16 is similar to Tomb 4 in that there was a mixture of both Greek and Sikel jewelry and pottery types that can be grouped functionally into two categories: imported pots associated with status goods such as scented oils and especially wine, and domestic shapes produced locally. Of the latter, the majority are large bowls and oinochoai, shapes that are typically found in pairs in pre-Greek Iron Age tombs. The man and one of the women were middle-aged (30–40 years), while the second woman was around 20 years of age. An examination of their well preserved teeth revealed that the older female had the even dentition that has been identified as a characteristic of Greek origin. The younger woman, however, had a pre-molar with a bifurcate root associated by physical anthropologists with South Italian populations and perhaps indicating an Italic origin. If the evidence of dentition can be accepted with some confidence, then several hypotheses concerning the identity of these individuals can be proposed, involving a family or extended family structure in which both ethnic Greek and Sikel women had a place. Such dental evidence or other genetic indicators, for example DNA sampling, may provide biological clues for the issue of intermarriage between individuals of different origins, but they cannot be extended with equal confidence to the question of personal ethnic identity, which is socially constructed and variable.

One final example sheds light on funerary ritual in the later fifth century, when the Cittadella had largely been abandoned following the sack of the site by the Sikel leader Duketios in 459 BC. The indigenous practice of burial in chamber tombs continues and one of these late tombs (tomb 50) contained the remains of a relatively elderly male, about 65, a younger 30-year-old female and a six-year-old child. The bifurcate tooth root of the woman and 'shovelled' central incisors of the child are both characteristics associated with Italic populations. Unfortunately, the objects associated with the burials were mixed, but consisted of a small number of Greek type drinking vessels. For the first time, three pyramidal loom-weights plausibly belonging to the young woman were placed in tomb, a practice that is common in Greek burials but is very rare at Morgantina before the fifth century.

The few other loomweights from the necropolis come from disturbed burial contexts of the fifth century. Two small bronze objects in the form of a rod with a central groove have been tentatively identified as bobbins and were found in Tombs 4 and 17, again in disturbed contexts. They belong to later sixth-century burials (ca. 550–500) on the basis of the associated pottery and because of their small size would have been used to wind finer threads. The various tasks involved in spinning and weaving may have been divided according to age and rank. It is possible that the two bronze bobbins, from wealthier tombs, belonged to individuals of higher status, though this suggestion must remain conjectural. In local seventh–sixth-century funerary contexts generally, the construction of gender was not so closely identified with the production of textiles as it was elsewhere in the Greek world.

The scarcity of artefacts related to textiles, usually connected with female-gendered activity, also extends to the frequently male-gendered category of weaponry. Lance blades and arrow heads were seldom deposited in the tombs and none of the specimens (four of each type) were recovered in a burial of known sex. One spear blade, however, was found lodged in the hip of an individual in Tomb 39 containing many wine-related vase shapes and one may speculate about the likelihood that the wounded person was male. More important, probably, is the general pattern of association between weapons, whether intended for hunting or warfare, and wealthier grave groups furnished with symposion pottery – an allusion to an aristocratic lifestyle emulated by local élites (Tombs 4, 16, 17, 39). Small knife blades, on the other hand, are identified with women, as noted above in the instance of Tomb 4 and perhaps by analogy in burial 3 of Tomb 28. Here an iron knife was placed alongside the deceased, who wore silver hair spirals like the two older indigenous women of Tomb 4.

The assortment of artefacts belonging to burial 3 of Tomb 28 demonstrates that inconsistencies occur which cannot be easily reconciled with the general distribution pattern of object types found in male and female burials. The pattern that emerges from a number of burials described above can be expressed in a series of oppositions:

male	female
symposion vases	household pottery
wine	domestic meals, perfumes
weaponry, hunting	knife, weaving equipment
personal ornaments (rare)	personal and clothing ornaments (frequent)

This pattern is upset in the case of Tomb 28, burial 3. Whereas the metal artefacts (iron knife, hair spirals) can be arguably classed as female, the pottery finds consist almost entirely of symposion shapes. In the absence of osteological data, it is difficult to know whether this is a case of a female who participates in the social ritual of drinking or a male who wears hair ornaments. Does the presence of a libation vase (phiale) in burial 3 and a number of Persephone masks nearby signify that religious practice is in some way a factor? Gender identity is not always neatly attributable to specific artefact types or activities, and there is a degree of blurring and cross-over between the categories of material culture associated with the female and male spheres just as there is, presumably, between female and male social roles.

In the foregoing summary, the presence of imported Greek pottery among the grave offerings of individuals thought to be of native origin furnishes evidence for the consumption of status commodities such as perfumed oils and wine. The household pottery that was found in the tombs and manufactured locally, on the other hand, indicates that foreign goods and the social practices that underlie them were not merely received passively, but were selectively acquired and integrated into existing patterns of use and meaning. In this study, I am making the assumption that women were largely responsible for the production of cooking and storage ceramics and for the preparation and distribution of food. It is notable that nearly half of the 1000 or so pots recovered from the tombs are of local manufacture, a category which includes Sikel-geometric, plain and coarse vessels for food storage and consumption. Over the course of two centuries, some of the characteristically native forms disappear altogether and others take on a Greek appearance.

Several native shapes do persist, descendants of local Iron Age types. For example, large open bowls, many with three vertical loop handles on the run, and countless small trefoil oinochoai ('hellenized' versions of the earlier jug known as a brocchetta) are found in nearly all of the seventh- and sixth-century tombs (Figure 6.3a). Furthermore, the standard Iron Age practice of placing a jug inside a bowl beside the burial continues in the sixth-century tombs. Almost a fifth of all pottery shapes are represented by these oinochoai and bowls, which points to a significant continuity of ritual, representing a typical indigenous meal service and perhaps the perpetuation of the sorts of foods that were eaten.

Local potters imitated selected specialized vase shapes and adopted Greek styles of decoration. Such adaptations tend to recombine elements from both the Greek and the indigenous tradition. For example, one of the more desirable imported vase shapes is the Lakonian black-glazed krater used for mixing and serving wine. A local version approximates the form but embellishes it in the native style with bands and wavy lines (Figure 6.3c). Also in the sixth century, a series of local amphorae, hydriae and askoi begin to be made and decorated in a style that strongly recalls similar ceramics from East Greece and Northern Ionia in the syntax of the bands and 'S-curves' on the shoulders; other elements, however, such as stars or clusters of wavy lines are added in the Sicilian versions (Figure 6.4, 6.5). If this specific style is related to the arrival of Phocaean groups at Morgantina in the mid-sixth century, a hypothesis outlined by Kenfield (1993),[15] then we may see the hybrid decorative schemes as a response on the part of local female potters to accommodate new customs, with the

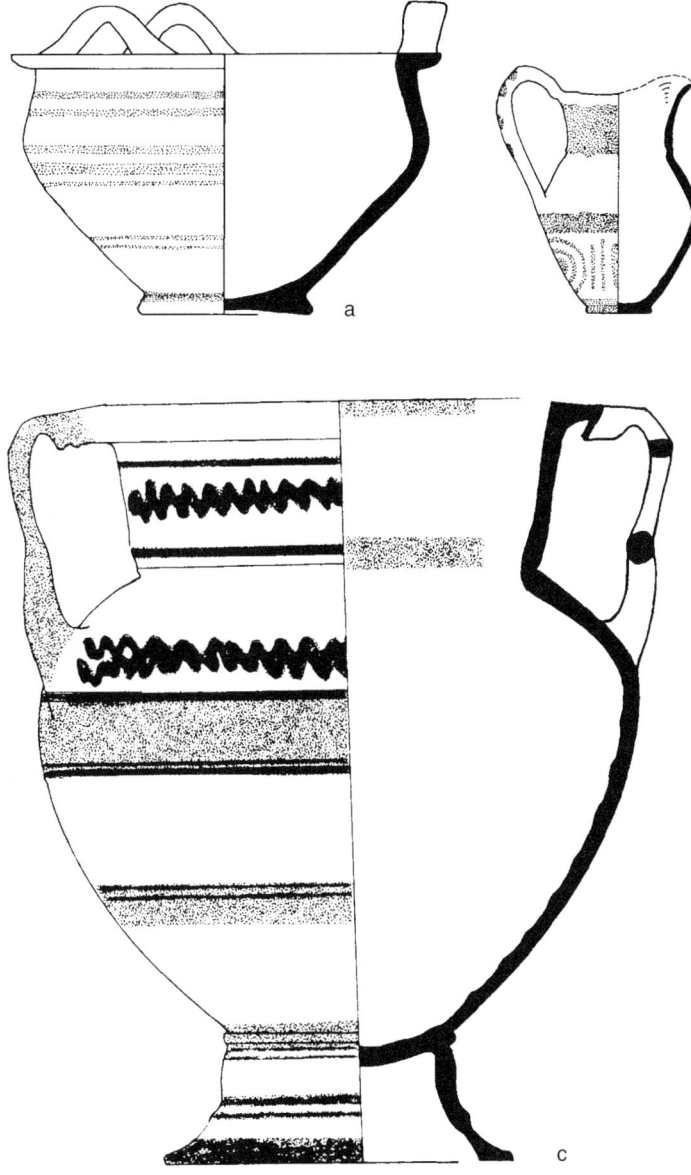

Figure 6.3   Corinthian pottery
a   Local three-handled bowl from Tomb 9, burial 9, *inv. 69–90*; height 10.4 cm
b   Local trefoil oinochoe from Tomb 31, *inv. 70–126*; height 9.9 cm
c   Local stirrup krater from Tomb 17, *inv. 69–558*; height 30.8 cm

a

b

Figure 6.4   Local askoi from Tomb 16
a   *inv. 69–217*; height 16.5 cm
b   *inv. 69–223*; height 21.7 cm

Figure 6.5   Local hydria from Tomb 9, *inv. 69–172*; height 37.0 cm

result that a distinct regional style was disseminated which integrates elements of both cultures.

Gender relations in other colonial sites

Gender-related research at several colonial sites in the Americas has focused
on the consequences of Spanish–Indian intermarriage reflected in material
culture. Although the historical contexts are very different from that of
Greek Sicily, the general patterns that emerge offer interesting parallels and
a useful framework in which to consider the situation in the Mediterranean

world. At the site of St Augustine in Florida, the work of Kathleen Deagan (1985),[16] has yielded provocative evidence that mestizaje (Spanish Native–American intermarriage and descent) had long-term consequences for the development of social structures which can be read in the differential patterning of household artefacts. Objects that are related to the more socially visible male activities, such as fine table wares or architecture, are predominantly European in character, while lower-visibility female tasks such as food preparation are dominated by indigenous types. The social rank of the individuals concerned is an important factor in the degree to which foreign cultural influences were absorbed or resisted. Intermarriage between colonists and the indigenous élites had the greatest impact on the indigenous community which followed the standards established by local leaders. Less political marriages between native women and Spanish men of the lower social strata tended to favour the indigenous culture over that of the colonists. This is shown clearly in the case of household pottery, which did not adopt Spanish types but maintained its native character.

A study of the situation of Indian women in colonial sixteenth-century Peru, based on archival and legal documents, highlights their substantial contributions to regional economies.[17] They provided sources of domestic labour, entered into contracts and dominated local markets. The role of Indian women as mediators between the native and conquest cultures was more significant than that of their male counterparts, by virtue of their access to Spanish households and their resulting acquaintance with Spanish language and customs. Indian men, by contrast, were relegated to the margins of colonial society and exploited for mass labour. The differential impact of colonization on Indian women and men often left men in an inferior position and so undermined social networks within indigenous communities.

Investigation of the strategies adopted by native women in dealing with colonial Spanish society in Ecuador, again supported by notarial records, suggests that innovative approaches with divergent agendas were taken by women acting in different social contexts: noble, common, urban, rural, acculturating, indigenous. The case study of the testament of an urban Indian woman, Maria de Amores, listing a wealth of jewellery and clothing to be transmitted to her heirs, details the contents of her wardrobe which consisted of Indian styles of dress cut from imported luxury textiles. Her dress conformed to no particular rural native style but rather to an upper-class urban Indian fashion which looked back to early colonial traditions in which aristocratic native brides conferred distinction and legitimacy on their Spanish mates. In this instance, a 'hyper-aesthetic version of visible, exterior Indian identity' was coined using materials attractive to Europeans and became emblematic of women in 'cultural mediator' roles.[18] These observations can serve as useful points of comparison in considerations of the permutations of jewellery styles (textiles, alas, are absent) among Sikel and Italic women, as we have seen above in the case of the women in Tomb 4. More thoughtful analysis of female burials from a number of colonized sites in Sicily and elsewhere should ultimately expose the nuances and complexities of cultural change such as are revealed in the better documented New World contexts.

Conclusion

Based on the data from sites like Morgantina and on New World ethnographic parallels, the proposition that the women of mixed-marriage households played a more central role in preserving fundamental aspects of the native lifestyle and in shaping Graeco–Siculan culture merits more serious consideration. In spite of the predominance of Greek material culture at Morgantina, indigenous cultural expression remains lively throughout the first century after the initial contacts (ca. 625 BC) were established. By the mid-fifth century, the character of the grave goods displays less of the diversity and intermingling of colonial and indigenous elements, assuming a more homogenous Greek aspect in the quantity and typology of artefacts. During the sixth century, there is reasonably dependable evidence for group burials based on kinship and consisting of:

(a) women of indigenous origin, occupying positions of status (Tomb 4, burials 4–5)
(b) men of indigenous or mixed origin, occupying positions of status, participating in Greek social ethos of wine amid literate in Greek language (Tomb 9, burial 2; 'Thamis' in Tomb 4)
(c) men likely to be of Greek origin ('Pyrrhias' in Tomb 18).

From the foregoing summary, several preliminary conclusions can be drawn that will need to be tested against the data from the Cittadella habitation and from sites in the region.

- Some native Sikel women achieved positions of social prominence within a community that in outer appearances was profoundly Greek. The evidence for women of Greek origin is lacking with the exception of one case based on dental morphology, a criterion that is contestable and ultimately not helpful in defining ethnic self-identity.
- Elite masculine identity centres around an aristocratic ethos of wine drinking. There is a lack of evidence for lower-status indigenous men in the cemetery, which may lead one to question whether these individuals have been 'put under erasure' – a situation not unfamiliar in modern colonial and post-colonial states. The success of native women in integrating with colonial society may have been a contributing factor to this invisibility.

- The character of the grave furnishings suggests that gender differentiation is manifested in clothing, the type and quantity of personal ornaments, and participation in social rituals such as drinking or domestic tasks related to the preparation of traditional meals. Both sexes enjoyed access to prestige imported goods. The categories of artefacts linked to female and male gender identity are not, however, rigid and there is cross-over. Other factors, including but not limited to class, age, occupation and ethnicity, modified the construction and expression of gender and are integral to social identity.

- The emphasis of traditional scholarship on the material remains of the public, male sphere (for example, trade in status goods, imported pottery) has underemphasized the female, domestic sphere. Closer attention to locally made household pottery, however, reveals a lively, dynamic process of transculturation in which indigenous women are active agents rather than merely the passive receptors of Greek material culture and social practice.

- Finally, the importance of gender roles in structuring the processes of colonization becomes clear when we consider several of the consequences of miscegenation and mixed marriages: the sharing of knowledge between colonists and indigenous peoples, the encouragement of bilingualism and the creation of hybrid forms of artistic, religious and cultural expression.

Notes

I would like to thank the conference organizers, Moira Donald, Linda Hurcombe and Di Cooper for providing the original impetus for my reconsideration of the implications of gender in the Morgantina burials and for creating a stimulating context in which I was the beneficiary of much valuable feedback from colleagues working across disciplines. I am particularly grateful to Theresa Menard and Marianna Nikolaidou for reading and commenting on the final drafts, and to Diane Fane for bibliographic counsel. The inevitable subjectivities of the data and its interpretation remain my own.

1. Becker (1996).
2. Graham (1984), pp. 293–314.
3. Gallo (1983), pp. 723–8.
4. Graham (1984), p. 312.
5. van Compernolle (1983), pp. 1033–49.
6. Humphreys (1978).
7. Gallo (1983), p. 709.
8. Guzzo (1982), pp. 53–61; Coldstream (1993), pp. 89–107.
9. Leighton (1993).
10. Whitehouse and Wilkins (1989), p. 116.
11. Albanese (1996), pp. 89–107.
12. Sjöqvist (1973).
13. Kenfield (1993), pp. 261–9.

14. Lyons (1996).
15. Kenfield (1993), pp. 261–9.
16. Deagan (1985), pp. 281–318.
17. Burkett (1978).
18. Salomon (1988), pp. 337.

Bibliography

Albanese, R.M. (1996) 'Greeks and Indigenous People in Eastern Sicily: Forms of interaction and acculturation', in R. Leighton (ed.), *Early Societies in Sicily: New developments in archaeological research* (London), pp. 167–76.

Becker, M.J. (1996) 'The Human Skeletons from the Archaic Necropolis', in C.L. Lyons, *Morgantina Studies, Vol. V, The Archaic Cemeteries* (Princeton).

Burkett, E.C. (1978) 'Indian Women and White Society: The case of sixteenth-century Peru', in A. Lavrin (ed.), *Latin American Women: Historical perspectives* (Westport), pp. 101–28.

Coldstream, J.N. (1993) 'Mixed Marriages at the Frontiers of the Early Greek World', *Oxford Journal of Archaeology* 12(1), pp. 89–107.

Deagan, K. (1985) 'Spanish Indian Interaction in Sixteenth-century Florida and Hispaniola', in W.W. Fitzhugh (ed.), *Cultures in Contact: The impact of European contacts on Native American cultural institutions, AD 1000–1800* (Washington, DC), pp. 281–318.

Gallo, L. (1983) 'Colonizzazione, demografia e strutture di parentela', in *Modes de contacts et processus de transformation dans les sociétés anciennes (Colloque de Cortone, 24–30 mai 1981)* (Rome), pp. 703–28.

Graham, A.J. (1984) 'Religion. Women and Greek Colonization', in *Religione e citttí nel mondo antico. Centro ricerche e documentazione sull' antichití classica XI (1980–81)* (Rome), pp. 293–314.

Guzzo, P.G. (1982) 'Ipotesi interpretativa su due tipi di fibula con arco ricoperto', in M.L. Gualandi, L. Massei and S. Settis (eds), *Aparchai, Nuove ricerche e studi sulla Magna Grecia e la Sicilia antica in onore di P.E. Arias* (Pisa), pp. 53–61.

Humphreys, S.C. (1978) *Anthropology and the Greeks* (London).

Kenfield, J. (1993) 'The Case for a Phokaian Presence at Morgantina as Evidenced by the Site's Archaic Architectural Terracottas', in J. des Courtils and J.-C. Moretti (eds), *Les grands ateliers d'architecture dans le monde égéen du VIe siécle av. J.-C. (Anatolica Varia vol. III)* (Paris), pp. 261–9.

Leighton, R. (1993) *Morgantina Studies, Vol. IV, The Protohistoric Settlement on the Cittadella* (Princeton).

Lyons, C.L. (1986) *Morgantina Studies, Vol. V, The Archaic Cemeteries* (Princeton).

Salomon, F. (1988) 'Indian Women of Early Colonial Quito as Seen through their Testaments', *The Americas*, 44, pp. 325–41.

Sjöqvist, E. (1973) *Sicily and the Greeks. Studies in the interrelationship between the indigenous populations and the Greek colonists* (Ann Arbor).

van Compernolle, R. (1983) 'Femmes indigénes et colonisateurs', in *Modes de contacts et processus de transformation dans les sociétés anciennes (Collogue de Cortone, 24–30 mai 1981)* (Rome). 1033–49.

Whitehouse, R. and J.B. Wilkins (1989) 'Greeks and Natives in South-east Italy: Approaches to the archaeological evidence', in T.C. Champion (ed.), *Centre and Periphery. Comparative studies in archaeology* (London), pp. 102–26.

7

Satyrs and Hetaerae: Looking for Gender on Greek Vases*

Matthew Fox

Introduction: the problem of ancient visual evidence for gender

In looking for gender on Greek vases, we seem to be in a comparatively privileged position: the highly decorated surfaces, the sophisticated techniques in painting and firing, the striving for realistic depictions of the human figure, the development of what seems like an aspiration towards the creation of beautiful objects; all would seem to suggest that we are dealing with a self-conscious art-form; a gift to the historian who wants to look inside the mind of an ancient civilization. What is more, the apparent realism of much vase-painting reinforces the belief that the realistic representation of the outside world was the main ambition behind such painting. As a result, vases have been put to use to illustrate the daily lives of the ancient Athenians.

When it is a question of reconstructing ancient technologies, such as weaving, or material objects, such as musical instruments or chariots, such an assumption is relatively unproblematic.[1] However, with the growth of interest in gender relations, the depictions of human figures on vases have come to be widely used as evidence for the social reality of Athenian society.[2] Generally speaking the results of covert assumptions that the vase represents the real world have been rather tamer than I suggest, but it is not difficult to deduce from recent scholarship the sense that vase images constituted a medium for self-representation at Athens, and that in looking at them, we have unmediated access either to the sexual practices or to the mentality of the ancients themselves.[3] In this chapter I want to question this approach, and to attempt to lay down some interpretative guidelines for those confronted with visual medium from an ancient culture who are interested in the application of gender as an analytical category.[4] I shall

Figure 7.1   Cup Boston Museum of Fine Art

Source: After Caskey.

suggest that vases did not offer possibilities for self-scrutiny, but that nevertheless, vase images can help us to understand gender relations in Athens if we are more careful about our critical procedures, and do not confuse our own need for information with the imagined responses of ancient vase producers.[5]

As a way of illustrating the need for rigorous critical criteria, and the snares inherent in an investigation of gender in vase images, I shall first discuss some images which seem to confirm precisely the opposite of what I have just been advocating: some vase images seem to demonstrate that our concern with gender has a close parallel in the interests of the ancients themselves; in other words, in looking for gender, we can find images that look at first sight like a self-reflexive comment upon sex-role definition, so confirming that our own interest in gender has an historical correlative. The cup in Figure 7.1 represents two different objects of sexual pursuit.[6] A man conventionally described as Zeus chases on one side of the vase a woman, and, on the other side, in a scene of symmetrical composition, a boy, usually thought to be Ganymede. It looks as though this vase is making a deliberate point about sexual preference. On the vase in Figure 7.2 we find three figures of a remarkably similar physical build, two of whom are male, one of whom is female.[7] The woman seems to be

Figure 7.2   Vase, Marlin von Wagner Museum, Wurzburg

Source: After Furtwangler-Reinhold.

fending off one of the men by stamping on his foot; she may even be prodding his genitals with her flute. Should we read her physique as in some way masculine, and further interpret her gesture and posture as giving an indication of women's power, albeit conceptualized in terms of assimilation to a male standard?

Another group of figures which seem to raise questions of gender definition, at least in relation to men, are the satyrs: semi-human figures, but with horses' tails and ears, and exaggerated phalluses. Satyrs occur on almost 10 per cent of our surviving vases, most often on those which are related by their shape to the symposium or drinking party; wine-cups and the various vessels used in the serving and mixing of wine.[8] They are often very close to men in the depiction of their physique, and are seen in various ways engaging in ordinary human activities; they can be shown as athletes, for example, or carrying armour.[9] More often their phallic nature is the subject of elaborate exploration; in Figure 7.3, on a wine-cooler, satyrs seem to suggest to the drinker new possibilities for the enjoyment of the symposium.[10] The symposium was, of course, a male environment, and the close parallel between the users of the vase and the images portrayed upon them seems to indicate that the painted surface of the vase was an arena for self-exploration, perhaps even for investigation into the nature of masculinity.

Reconstructing the gaze

These images rather startlingly suggest that the creators of vase images were thinking along very similar lines to ourselves. They seem to be interested, as we are, in definitions of gender, if we take that to mean definitions of appropriate behaviour for either sex. However, If we are to avoid casually forgetting about the historically specific nature of our material, we need to be more cautious, and to attempt to reconstruct the social background to the production, but perhaps more importantly, the use of Athenian vases. In other words, we want to find out about the original audience, and think in terms of reception. Now in this regard, in spite of the relative wealth of literary material, and in spite of the considerable number of Athenian vases to have survived to the present day, we are in a position which is not much more privileged than that of the prehistorian. A huge proportion of all these vases survived because they were exported to Italy and left in hordes inside Etruscan tombs; the record of their excavation can thus reveal nothing about the conditions of their production.[11] It is left to us to assume that in spite of their final resting place, it was the iconographical interests of the Athenian consumers that determined the repertory of images. In addition, we cannot be at all sure of the social status of vases; some regard them as cheap, popular substitutes in ceramic for expensive metal vessels;[12] others concentrate upon the finery of the techniques as

108

Figure 7.3 Wine Cooler

Source: Reproduced by kind permission of the Trustees of the British Museum.

manifestation of a social position more similar to works of art in the modern sense.

My own feeling is that vases were like household china today; their images could be read, but they were adjuncts to particular social events, nice to look at, but not produced primarily in order to be scrutinized in their own right. Such a view of the cultural context of vases, which must still be only guesswork, has implications for the way in which we interpret vase images: it reinforces the idea of vases as bearers of the imprint of gender values, rather than the arena for a conscious exploration. One is left with something of a paradox. Attic vases can, without doubt, be most finely worked, and meticulously decorated. Can these qualities be reconciled with a vision of consumption based upon their utility? What is needed is a model of cultural reception which unites the ordinariness of the object with the aesthetic pleasure of the decorated surface. If we can find such a model in this case, it could be of value for many other kinds of artefact.

One way of conceptualizing the visual perception of images nowadays is in terms of the gaze. This term has become particularly popular in film-theory, especially that with an interest in gender, and refers, in a film, to the way in which the camera encourages the spectator to focus his attention upon a particular area of the screen image.[13] I say 'his' because it is commonly argued that the gaze is the mechanism whereby films, particularly those made in the Hollywood tradition, work to reinforce relations of gender and power which are those dominant in our own economic situation – put bluntly, the objectification of women for the visual gratification of men, hinting at sexual domination.

Greek vases are miles away from the modern cinema, and there are many versions of the gaze that are more subtle than this bare outline. Nonetheless, the idea that visual representation is something which shares and reinforces the gender structures of a particular society is worth considering. We could, it follows, look for the reception of vases not by using the images themselves as a starting point, but rather, by using our knowledge of gender relationships to interpret the images. Looked at from another point of view, let us think of the normality of watching a film, and of the way in which we are drawn into the image, losing all consciousness of the mechanisms whereby the image is created. We then discover, reading film criticism, that our first response has not been a spontaneous, value-free, direct one, but one laden with social baggage, even one in which our sexual identity could be at issue. The disparity of these two ways of viewing can be transferred to our vases. Should we assume that variety of images is a manifestation of self-awareness and the exploitation of a visual medium for a particular social message? It seems more plausible to look outside the images themselves for the criteria for their interpretation. In looking for gender on vases, then, we may be better off looking at what conditions the viewer's gaze, rather than what that gaze actually fell upon.

The homosexual economy of representation

The work of the French feminist philosopher Luce Irigaray is seen as fundamental by many working in contemporary women's and gender studies.[14]
The concern of Irigaray's most widely known work, *Speculum of the Other
Woman* (1974), was to look at the discourses of patriarchy.[15] In detailed
readings ranging from Freud to Plato, Irigaray revealed how those attempting to define and describe human existence in terms of universal validity
were unwittingly reinscribing the exclusion of women, and confounding
humanity as a whole with men. She traces the way in which women
feature as variously deviating, absent, chaotic, meaningless, or insignificant
within those processes whereby the world is comprehended and society
defined. She has, as a result, been dismissed as an essentialist, which is, I
believe, a misrepresentation of her work; Irigaray is not aiming to root
women in a definition of their true nature, but is concerned rather to
uncover the extent to which women's position has historically been determined by the way in which she has been represented, and how this representation has always reinforced, in differing ways, the definition of woman
as not-man; as one whose identity, for men, was constituted merely by
default.

Within a discourse organized around male norms, woman becomes a
function of man's perpetuation of his own identity: drawing upon the logic
of Lacanian psychoanalytic theory, Irigaray's work allows us to stress the
double meaning of the word 'identity': it refers both to a definition of the
individual, as in the phrase 'personal identity', but also to the idea of sameness, as when we speak of 'identical twins'. The self is built upon its relations to others, in terms of difference from others, and thus, in terms of the
sameness, to itself; identity thus functions as a closed system, in which
meaning and order are continuously reaffirmed by returning to the point
from which they began. And what Irigaray also stresses is that in order to
maintain the social order, the process of signification whereby woman is
the other for the definition of man is not simply a given; it needs to be
constantly restated in order to maintain the edifice of patriarchal values
which have their corollary in the social position of women. It is this need
for continuous reassertion which links the discourses of phallocracy to the
social reality of women's lives, and which likewise gives a historical
dimension to Irigaray's thinking which extricates her from the trap of
essentialism.[16]

The relevance of Irigaray's work to the understanding of ancient
representation is this: what Irigaray suggests is that what is traditionally
representable is man, and that woman, where she is represented at all,
has hitherto only appeared in contrast to man. Representation thus takes
on a particular structure or organization, whereby man represents himself
to man. This is what Irigaray terms the 'economy of the same' or the

'homosexual economy'. When looking at visual representation, we must therefore bear in mind that the signification of an image will not take place in an area that is undefined, where there are no rules, and where anything is possible; rather, we should always look to the probability that norms in representation are masculine. Furthermore, where the aim of representation can be seen to be amusement, diversion, or visual pleasure generally, which I think is a tenable generalization for images on Greek vases, then the image will tend not to disturb the viewer's sense of identity. Vase images, then, viewed in Irigaray's terms, will reaffirm the position of the male as the subject of representation.

I have one favourite piece of ancient evidence that suggests that Irigaray's model of a homosexual economy may be particularly applicable to ancient Athens; here is a passage from the close of Thucydides' account of Pericles' great funeral speech:

> If I must also make some mention of feminine virtue, to those who will now be widows, I will say everything in a brief recommendation. If you are not inferior to your inherent nature you will acquire a great reputation, one which can belong to any woman who has the least fame among men, either in praise or reproach.[17]

Thucydides relishes the paradox that for women a great reputation (*doxa*) is to be obtained by possessing the smallest fame (*kleos*) – by being, in other words, least subject to the talk of men. It is a clear demonstration of the exclusion of women, not so much from society, but from the discourse and communication of men. They will be better women if they are not subject to verbal representation; to be absent from discussion will bring the highest praise. The question of how this praise could ever be communicated is not raised, but the picture of communication and evaluation as the sole prerogative of men in a well ordered society emerges unequivocally. Men's talk is directed to man, and it is best for women if it concerns itself only with men.

Returning to my remarks concerning the gaze, I hope the drift of this argument is becoming clearer. As background to the interpretation of vase images, the patriarchal monopoly on social signification will have a great effect on limiting the readings of a vase that can legitimately be regarded as historical. The conditioning of the gaze will tend not towards the exploration of the limits of masculinity, nor towards the unsettling of gender boundaries or the revelation of states of liminality and transgression. Unless we can find good reason for the contrary, it will be safer to assume that representation will itself be closely allied to the reinforcement of masculine norms.[18]

The implications can be most clearly demonstrated by looking back at satyrs. In these figures who are in part a parallel with men themselves, we can, I believe, stress similarity over difference. Man may be defining himself in terms of something other than himself, and perhaps this is something that Athenian men were rather prone to do.[19] But even more so than in Irigaray's description of woman, that something other is remarkably circumscribed in its potential. In fact, as an exploration of male identity, the satyr suggests that you don't have to go very far from man in order to reaffirm his identity. You may look at an Other, but see yourself reflected there, sometimes only very slightly distorted. And if we are thinking of vase-images as amusing and entertaining objects, then the affirmation of identity which this little excursion into otherness will grant will be sealed with a laugh, as the circle closes again in the perception of the male viewer.

Can we speak of women's gaze?

Irigaray states: 'Woman has no gaze, no discourse ... that would allow her to identify with herself [as same]. In Figure 7.4 we can see women who look very much as though they contradict this dictum.[20] These images look like

Figure 7.4   Wine Cooler, Hermitage Museum, Petersburg

Source: After Furtwangler-Reinhold.

representations of a female symposium. Conventional criticism responds by characterizing these women as hetaerae, the only possible female adjuncts to the male symposium. The flute player in Figure 7.2 is another possible hetaera; the boundary between a musical entertainer and a courtesan is supposed to be thin. Focusing on the question of identification misses a point, however, and reinscribes a patriarchal critical prejudice which clouds the issue. The exact character of the women is not open to question; for the male viewer, naked women enjoying themselves are unlikely to have a function outside reinforcing their own pleasure. Whatever external referent we propose, these women are caught in the language of visual representation, which is more probably concerned to stress their value as decorative features, amusing to the eye, than to set up an alternative world of women capable of self-sufficiency.

Although hetaerae can in no detailed analysis be conflated with satyrs, if we are looking at the significance of images for a broad understanding of Athenian gender relations, satyrs and hetaerae will have a certain amount in common. First of all, they are not men, but thereby tell us more about the construction of Athenian maleness; the enjoyment the hetaerae are displaying in their own entertainment is congruent to the sexual antics of the satyrs. Both are an invitation to the male drinker to approve the reflection of his own potency and sexual dominance, and to be reassured by aesthetic pleasure of the security of his social control. In the case of the hetaerae, this will be effected by the recollection of the availability to men of women's bodies. In the case of the satyr we can suspect a more complex interplay of the social control of men with their sense of self-control, as well as the possibility of unlimited licence to the phallus.[21]

There may, however, be places where vase images go further than the repetitive reinscription of male power by visual recreation. Once again, however, the criteria would seem to come more from the social background than from the images themselves. Maenads were women who worshipped Dionysus, and who had, unlike the satyrs, clearly creations of fantasy, a link with real religious rituals.[22] Maenads on vases are sometimes too no more than hapless victims to the lust of satyrs but sometimes we find them effectively repulsing sexual advances, and often they are depicted enjoying their own society, dedicated to the pursuit of their own pleasure. Their bodies are always concealed from the gaze of the male user. Perhaps such images give us an insight into those areas where men's power and dominance were more circumscribed: clearly in the world of religious rituals and festivals, women did have a public presence.[23] When Thucydides makes Pericles wish women out of the realm of discourse, he is doing so at a funeral, and has just pointed out the important role that women played in public funeral rites.[24] These two references to women in the context of Pericles' funeral oration set up a tension: a tension between the need for women's ritual involvement, and men's need for a monopolization of discourse. Pericles' words are to be imagined falling on the ears of an audience in which women have a prominent role. Perhaps there is a parallel in the representations of maenads; they can be appreciated and enjoyed, but they are not simply there as an amusing means to feeling good. The presence of maenads on vases designed for use at men's drinking parties could provide a fruitful avenue for discovering the limits of men's gaze, and even the possibility of women's.

Conclusion

I want to conclude by making some general points about the problem of looking for gender in historical artefacts generally; these points may be familiar, but nevertheless, some critical problems do not disappear with familiarity, and I think there is no harm in raising them.

Looking for gender is bound, I think, to result in a confusion of critical perspectives: I began by advocating caution concerning the reading of vase images as a transparent record of the time of their production, but subsequently I have adduced a model of reading and interpretation that equally clearly belongs firmly to our own day. Is one approach definitely better than another? Is one, in other words, able to bring us in any sense closer to the ancient Athenians who produced these images?

Such a quest for a reading with an historical basis is itself not as unproblematic as it sounds; it conceals an old-fashioned positivist belief that we should be aiming for a clear demarcation between critics and artefacts or texts; we should be disengaged from our objects of study and free from bias. Whether this is either possible or desirable needs to be examined; should we, as historians, be wary of substituting political commitment for the fundamental tenets of our discipline? Can we become new-historicists, and historicize our own critical practice together with our chosen discipline? This would, I suspect, be possible only if we undertook a fundamental revision of how we perceive historical periods, the uniqueness of particular bodies of evidence and, in particular, the scientific status of archaeological research. But this is only one of the many assumptions that the quest for the right approach to gender at Athens implies. Another major problem is the assumption that images, particular images with a material substance, are clear in meaning: we must remember not only that images are always open to a variety of interpretations, but more crucially that in the culture in which they are produced, questions of significance and signification would have been framed in wholly different ways. Perhaps, however, if we imagine the possibility of the trivial, insignificant or purely decorative image, we can liberate the historical enquiry from certain critical dilemmas; we might abandon the attempt at a reconstruction of the historical reception, focus instead upon imagery as a manifestation of social structures and the processes of signification. Not as some kind of self-conscious product, but as a discursive relic, one which is subject to the same problems of interpretation as any historical discourse. We will certainly need some kind of modern model to elicit the information that we desire, but perhaps we will end up by finding a way of looking at gender that responds to its historical context.

Notes

* I owe debts to Stephanie Bird, Lin Foxhall, Stephen Halliwell, Barbara Rasmussen, the University of Birmingham Gender seminar (who heard a previous version of the chapter), and the audience at Exeter. I gratefully acknowledge the assistance of the Library of the University of Birmingham and the Trustees of the British Museum for providing photographs and giving me permission to reproduce them.
1. Jenkins (1986).
2. A milestone was Dover (1978), who made extensive use of vase images in his detailed investigation of the mechanics and social ramifications of Greek homosexual behaviour. Very much in that tradition is Kilmer (1993) which *claims* to present a comprehensive catalogue of erotic vases; the curious distinction (p. 4) between fantastic and realistic representation used to justify the exclusion of satyrs from the book in my view invalidates this claim and encapsulates the book's methodological shortcomings.
3. See Sutton (1992), pp. 3–35.
4. Fundamental is Scott (1986), pp. 1053–75.
5. Osborne (1991), pp. 255–75, raises important questions about relating vase images to the real world; in this review of Bérard, *et al.* (1989), he assesses the work of Lissarague and his colleagues, largely responsible for questioning the use of the photographic analogy for vase painting. See also Lissarague (1990a), p. 196; Beard (1991), pp. 12–35.
6. Boston Museum of Fine Arts, 95.36 after Caskey.
7. Wurzburg, Martin von Wagner Museum, 507, after Furtwangler-Reinhold.
8. Satyrs have been the subject of elegant and fruitful research, see Lissarague (1990b), pp. 228–36, (1990d), pp. 131–50.
9. See Simon (1982), pp. 143–48, which gives ample illustrations of the wide range of satyric representation, although linked to the curious theory that satyr vases are often records of a particular theatrical occasion, rather than fantasy figures. For satyr athletes, see plate 34a. For a satyr with armour, see Boardman (1975), Plate 140.
10. British Museum; E768. Reproduced with the kind permission of the Trustees of the British Museum.
11. A judicious reassessment of the critical implications of the Etruscan excavations is given by Spivey (1991), pp. 131–50.
12. Vickers and Gill (1994). For the pre-history of the book and the critical reaction, see Osborne (1991), n. 1, p. 274.
13. For a critical introduction and bibliography, see Grosz (1992), pp. 447–50.
14. An accessible introduction and critique is Whitford (1991).
15. Irigaray (1985).
16. See Whitford (1991), pp. 9–25 for the debate on essentialism.
17. Thucydides, II. 45, my translation.

18. I have investigated the relationship of the gaze to the social background in more detail in Fox (1995).
19. Hall (1989); Cartledge (1992).
20. Leningrad, Hermitage Museum, 644, after Furtwangler-Reinhold.
21. I explore identification with satyrs and the vicissitudes of the Athenian male's sense of control in Fox (1995).
22. On 'real' Maenads, see Henrichs (1978), pp. 137–60. In spite of attested existence of ecstatic women's cults at a later period, one cannot rule out the element of fantasy in any description or depiction of maenads. Clearly as much as satyrs they represented society disrupted. However, vase maenads can be said to be less fantastic than satyrs, simply because they are characterized by external rather than anatomical attributes.
23. See Foxhall (1995).
24. Thucydides, II. 34.

Bibliography

Beard, M. (1991) 'Adopting an Approach II', in T. Rasmussen and N. Spivey (eds), *Looking at Greek Vases* (Cambridge), pp. 12–35.

Bérard, C. *et al.* (1989) *A City of Images* (Princeton).

Bérard, C. and C. Bron (1989) 'Satyric Revels', in C. Bérard, *City of Images* (Princeton), pp. 131–50.

Boardman, J. (1975) *Athenian Red Figure Vases: The Archaic Period* (London).

Cartledge, P. (1992) *The Greeks* (Oxford).

Caskey, L.D. *Attic Vases in the Boston Museum* ( ).

Dover, K.J. (1978) *Greek Homosexuality* (London).

Fox, M. (1995) 'The Fantasy and the Real in Attic Vase Painting', in M. Harlow and E. Marshall (eds), *In the Eye of the Beholder*.

Foxhall, L. (1995) 'Women's Ritual and Men's Work in Ancient Athens', in R. Hawley and B. Levick, *Women in Antiquity: New Assessments* (London).

Grosz, E. (1992) 'Voyeurism/Exhibitionism/The Gaze', in E. Wright (ed.), *Feminism and Psychoanalysis: A critical dictionary* (Oxford), pp. 447–50.

Hall, E. (1989) *Inventing the Barbarian* (Oxford).

Harlow, M. and E. Marshall (eds), *In the Eye of the Beholder* ( ).

Henrichs, A. (1978) 'Greek Maenadism from Olympias Messalina', *Harvard Studies in Classical Philology*, 82, pp. 137–60.

Irigaray, L. (1985) *Speculum of the Other Woman*, G.C. Gill (Ithaca) (originally *Speculum de l'autre femme*, Paris, 1974).

Jenkins, I. (1986) *Greek and Roman Life* (London).

Kilmer, M.F. (1993) *Greek Erotica* (London).

Kurz D. and B. Sparkes (1995) *The Eye of Greece*.

Lissarague, F. (1990a) 'Around the Krater: An aspect of banquet imagery', in O. Murray (ed.), *Sympotica* (Oxford), pp. 196–209.

Lissarague, F. (1990b) 'The Sexual Life of Satyrs', in D.M. Halperin, J.J. Winkler and F.I. Zeitlin (eds), *Before Sexuality* (Princeton), pp. 53–82.

Lissarague, F. (1990c) 'Why Satyrs are Good to Represent', in J.J. Winkler and F.I. Zeitlin (eds), *Nothing to do with Dionysus* (Princeton), pp. 228–36.

Lissarague, F. (1990d) *The Aesthetics of the Greek Banquet* (Princeton).

Osborne, R. (1991) 'Whose Image and Superscription is This?' *Arion*, 1(2), pp. 255–75.

Powell, A. (ed.) (1995) *Iconography as Evidence* ( ).

Rasmussen, T. and N. Spivey (eds) *Looking at Greek Vases* (Cambridge).

Richlin, A. (ed.) *Pornography and Representation in Greece and Rome* (Oxford).

Scott, J.W. (1986) 'Gender: A useful category of historical analysis', *American Historical Review*, 91, pp. 1053–75.

Simon, E. (1982) 'Satyr-plays on vases in the Time of Alschylers', in D. Kurtz and B. Sparkes (eds), *The Eye of Greece* (Cambridge).

Spivey, N. (1991) 'Greek Vases in Etruria', in T. Rasmussen and N. Spivey (eds), *Looking at Greek Vases* (Cambridge), pp. 131–50.

Sutton, R. F., Jr (1992) 'Pornography and. Persuasion on Attic Pottery', in A. Richlin, *Pornograph and Representation in Greece and Rome* (Oxford), pp. 3–35).

Vickers, M. and D. Gill (1994) *Artful Crafts* (Oxford).

Whitford, M. (1991) *Luce Irigaray: Philosophy in the Feminine* (London).

8

Food Preparation in Ancient Greece: Representations of Gender Roles in the Literary Evidence

John Wilkins

There are two high-grade restaurants in Devon,[1] *The Carved Angel* in Dartmouth and *Gidleigh Park Hotel* in Chagford. At the first at the time of writing, the head chef is a woman, at the second a man. This happy state of affairs is exceptional in the United Kingdom and in many other cultures. With some exceptions, in Britain and elsewhere high-status cooking of this kind is performed by men, while lower-status cooking, particularly in the home, is performed by women. A further contrast between the two establishments may be seen in the way in which staff are organized. At *The Carved Angel*, with the exception of the chef Joyce Molyneux, everyone in turn cooks and waits at table, while at *Gidleigh Park* a more authoritarian regime obtains under which young apprentices either wait at table or stay in the kitchen. Gender roles of this kind are remarkably distinct in British culture, at a domestic level as much as at the luxury end of the market. It is important for us to bear this in mind when looking at the ancient Greeks who to our eyes inhabited a culture which was overtly sexist and also slave-owning.

The Greeks are a suitable subject for investigation since they wrote extensively on many areas of life and also tended to set the cultural assumptions for the West for centuries and even millenia. If they did not set them, they often exemplify the trend. Thus in the case of food preparation, work in the kitchen was generally beneath consideration. In many texts, the consumption of food was of great social importance, but the food appears as if by magic; the people preparing that food are not mentioned. The same appears to be the case at some periods in two other early civilizations, China and Arab Babylonia.[2] When we are in the fortunate position of hearing about cookery in any detail, as in Arab Babylonia or Greece from 400 BC onwards[3] what we are offered tends to be recipes for dishes. But what of the food preparation itself? That is not appropriate for a written format, it appears. This, it seems to me, is a notable state of affairs, given that nearly all human beings eat prepared foods once, twice or three times a day.[4] The modern world, naturally, has a somewhat monolithic view of Greek culture, inevitably constructing the Greeks in its own terms. Tragedy, philosophy, democracy, art and architecture are admired, as are the fragmentary temples with their fine friezes, and the beautiful sculptures, now lost, of gods and goddesses that were housed in these temples. Less thought is given to the complexes of associated buildings in which worshippers ate together in the presence of the god, and less still about how that food was prepared, or how food was prepared on a domestic basis in buildings which have left negligible, if any, traces.

I wish to address four questions in this chapter. What do we know about food preparation in antiquity? If we know less than we might wish, is this because food preparation was in some sense not highly valued? Or is it because food preparation did not for some reason fit well into the system that recorded what was done? Is it perhaps because food was prepared by women and/or slaves (male and female) and was for that reason not highly valued?

From the perspective of the social anthropologist, the broad organization of food preparation is clear and predictable across cultures. Jack Goody has made the following observations, based on his study of the LoDagaa people of northern Ghana:

> The preparation of the meal, in Africa, as elsewhere, is often a long and time-consuming process ... The preparation of a meal normally takes a long time because the produce has to be transformed directly from its natural state ... The grinding [of the grain] is especially hard, and women sometimes try to lighten their work by singing songs and chatting amongst themselves ... Women queue up to have their grain ground into flour [by means of a diesel motor] ... The technology of food production, then, is complex, even in the simplest agricultural societies, and it lies largely in the hands of women ... The maintenance of fire is in the hands of women ... Like yeast, fire was one of the marvels passed down from hand to hand, the embodiment of communal living, difficult to start, easy to keep going, especially if one has kin and neighbours on whom to rely. And in certain respects, the women's world is more immediately dependent upon such cooperative activities than the man's.[5]

Goody continues:

> In his cross-cultural survey of the status of women, Whyte[6] notes that of all the 'economic' variables considered, it is only in the area of housekeeping that there is a definite bias towards one sex (i.e. the female one),

'while work outside the home tends to vary widely from one culture to another across the world, work within the home tends to be predominately done by women'. We can add a comment on the relation between cooking and gender … In human societies generally, cooking is seen as part of woman's role.[7]

Is this applicable to ancient Greece? Modern scholarship on women in ancient Greece makes clear that they were denied a political and legal voice, and that if they were citizen women, they lived indoors and not outdoors. What proportion, if any, of those indoor lives was spent on food preparation or cooking? Pomeroy (1976) has no index entry under food preparation. She has, in fact, far more to say about prostitution than food preparation.[8] This, we might note, reflects the interests of ancient male authors such as Athenaeus of Naucratis who devotes one of his 15 books on food and dining to prostitutes and courtesans, but none to food preparation. In Pomeroy's index, we find 'wine, drinking of', but not 'food, eating of' or 'food, preparation of'. Of such things are our images of antiquity fashioned. Pomeroy, it is true, has passing references to food preparation,[9] but it is not presented as an area in which women, especially lower-class and slave women, spent large parts of their lives. A typical entry is this:

> The preparation of ordinary food was considered exclusively women's work. During the seige of Plataea, when the city was evacuated, one hundred and ten women were left behind to cook for the four hundred and eighty[10] men remaining to defend the city.

Now this incident from Plataea, cited from Thucydides, II.78, implies that it was normal that women should prepare the food. Pomeroy is not concerned to take this any further – to ask, for example, what kind of food was being prepared. What was the status of the women: were they slave or free?[11] Was it a normal expectation that one preparer of food was needed for every 4.4 soldiers? How does military provision relate to that of everyday life? And most important, perhaps, was the preparation of ordinary food considered exclusively women's work? What was ordinary and what was not? Was any 'ordinary' food prepared by men of low status, slaves for example? Was any extraordinary food prepared by women?

In Pomeroy and other works[12] we are told that women were given[13] time-consuming tasks to perform, such as weaving. If ancient texts are full of references to women weaving, as indeed they are, then it is quite right that this should be reflected in modern studies. But we should also think of those other time-consuming tasks which women performed but which texts found less glamorous, and what women got out of them (if anything). Cooking and food preparation are not mentioned in Pomeroy's chapter 'Images of Women in Literature'. The present chapter aims to correct the omission, and to begin to clarify gender-division of roles in this area. Ancient literature *does* talk of women preparing food, but modern commentators have chosen to ignore it, for ideological or other reasons. Food preparation was undoubtedly part of most women's lives in antiquity, albeit it one of those parts that literature does not discuss at length. Here, as in many parts of ancient life, modern discussions tend to be confined within the limitations of the forms of ancient literature.

This may be because we have the same, similar or analogous problems with some aspects of women's work as the ancient Greeks had. Food preparation, after all, is a complex area, embracing practical, economic, social, emotional and psychological elements. In Britain, much purchase, preparation and serving of food continues to be performed by women, as has been demonstrated by many surveys. This despite the large increase in the proportion of women in paid employment. There are positive and negative aspects to this. Food preparation is hard work, and was much harder in a pre-technological age. It is at times laborious and repetitive. If some of that work can be avoided, or made easier, that option may be chosen. So technology is favoured in the modern home, and factory processing has made notable advances. On the other hand, some, including those with the power and the money to be able to choose, may opt to cook in a more traditional style, at least on some occasions, using fresh rather than processed ingredients. The traditional may be valued. Contemporary theories of good health, family bonding and psychological exchanges over a meal table may be preferred to TV meals and individual eating. The mother may try to bring up her children well, as she sees it, by serving a certain kind of food prepared in more than a minimal way. The children may on occasion reject such an approach and demand food processed in the factory rather than the carefully prepared dish. There are many interpersonal and gender-related complexities in this area.

Jack Goody made it clear that the milling of grain clearly was a time-consuming task. Was it therefore of low value? This need not be the case if the culture recognizes its dependence on processed flours. This was the case in ancient Greece in at least three respects:

1. The growing of grain was presided over by the goddesses Demeter and Persephone, in whose honour the citizen women of Attika performed festivals such as the Thesmophoria in order to promote the growth of cereal plants and children, both vital to the city state's survival.[14]
2. 'The life of the milled grain' was a term denoting the civilized life, the life of the farmer which succeeded the life of the hunter-gatherer.[15]
3. At marriage, women were given a barley-toaster,[16] a symbol of the work in the home to come: she would prepare the cereals for the family. Note that the Greeks described their food in terms of cereal staple and tasty addition (compare the modern pizza): this places a greater emphasis on

cereals than the 'meat and two veg' of Britain and other northern European cultures.

All ancient life, for men and women, was based on toil, except for the tiny élite who wrote all the literature. For most, it was the hard life of the subsistence farmer. The élite was composed almost entirely of men, who, when consuming food, reclined on couches at dinner and at the drinking party (*symposion*) which followed, apart from their wives, but with 'female companions' or *hetairai*, one of the categories of 'prostitute' discussed by Pomeroy.[17] Did wives prepare food for such dinners? It is most unlikely. Did they cook dinners for themselves and women friends? We have no information on this subject – a significant omission. It is very likely that such a wife supervised the preparation of food by servants and slaves, to judge from the extreme example of the wife of Ischomachos in Xenophon's *Oecononicus*, which is widely cited in the modern studies. The husband instructs his wife in household management in extremely patronizing terms.[18] He concentrates on how she should manage household stores and supervise servants and slaves; when food preparation is mentioned, it is strongly based on bread-making (kneading and baking), the most time-consuming of food processing.

For both sexes, status was important. Honorific preparation of foods might be performed, particularly for religious reasons. That is not to say that in every case the honoured person actually did the physical work. One area of food preparation had a special status, the killing and sacrifice of domestic animals in temples. At most festivals, food was eaten with the god: humans and gods were ritually sharing the meal. While there were many vegetarian rites, animal sacrifice was widespread, and at many periods was probably the only time much of the population ate meat.[19] While much food preparation was performed by women in ancient Greece, men came into their own in the case of meat. The slaughterer himself, the *mageiros*,[20] is less often mentioned than the chief officiants for whom he was the practical operative. It has even been suggested[21] that at the festival of the Thesmophoria, at which only women could be present, the pigs slaughtered to Demeter were killed by a man, so unthinkable was it that women should shed animal blood. The case is circumstantial, but if Detienne is right, this is an extreme illustration of the phenomenon.[22] Fiddes has much comparative material on meat and power relations between men and women.[23]

A second instance of honorific eating are the eating priests, the 'parasites',[24] who ritually prepared food for and ate with the gods, in a more restrictive gathering than the ritually shared meals mentioned above. We do not know whether in fact they prepared the food themselves, or whether preparation was actually the work of slaves. A certain case of priests preparing special religious foods themselves is that of the Vestal

Virgins in Rome, who prepared special salty cakes from ritually-pure grain.[25] A final honorific case: the most honoured friends and benefactors of the Greek city states were feasted at the city's expense at the civic hearth (*prytaneion*): benefactors, heroes, victorious athletes and particularly meritorious citizens. There is no mention of the servants who cooked this food, no special post of city chef, even though we know that food was cooked on the premises.[26]

Except in the shedding of blood in sacrifice, women appear to have been equal with men in religious honorific contexts, as far as priesthoods were concerned, and as likely (or not) to prepare the food offerings. When food was shared out afterwards, women had a share in some cults, everything in some others and no share in others.

Whether performed by women or men, we should not think of food preparation in terms of hot stoves in kitchens. Preparation was laborious and time-consuming, but cooking utensils small and technically simple. There may not have been dedicated kitchens as opposed to storage rooms in many houses. Storage is cited as within a woman's preserve much more often than cooking. That is not to say that there are many cooking processes possible on the modern stove that could not be matched in antiquity (apart from microwaving). The home could provide small braziers and ovens; larger ovens were available at community level.

A note on the archaeological evidence

Archaeological evidence is not the subject of this chapter. Some observations are however illuminating. In archaeology, a kitchen is identified by debris or more often cooking utensils. The Greek word for 'kitchen', while rare, is the same as the word for 'stove'. We may assume that cooking was conducted in a designated space indoors and/or outdoors. Archaeology has taught us much about many cooking pots and other utensils that have survived in quantity.[27] Some of the decorated pots portray scenes of food preparation. Those illustrating sacrifice and butchery are shown in Berthiaume[28] and Detienne and Vernant;[29] a scene of women preparing a wedding cake offers a further example of high-status food preparation.[30] Archaeology has also provided terracotta statues from various Greek cities, some of them of people preparing foods. These terracottas are a remarkable testimony.[31] Many, *but not all*[32] of the terracotta figures are female. The kneading and baking of bread and cakes is by far the most common activity portrayed: milling, mixing the dough, fanning the fire, putting loaves in the oven. There is cheese-grating, and one case of butchery. Taken with the evidence of Xenophon, we should consider bread-making to be a large part of women's lives. The terracottas show both small individual ovens being used, either in the ashes or in large pre-heated pots, and women working together at communal bakeries. The only commercial bakery we know about in early Athens is Thearion's bakery, which produced fine pastries at the time of Plato; Thearion was a man.

The terracottas are important, not only for their use as evidence in gendering food-preparation, but also as artefacts. If Boiotians, Rhodians or occasionally Athenians represented women making bread and so on in this art form, why were there not more representations in literature? Is the answer connected to Athenian sneering at the rusticity of the Boiotians? Or to the comparative agricultural wealth of Boiotia, which led them to this art-form on a large scale? Some of the methods of preparation illustrated are echoed in Athenian literature, but often in passing, and in a joking or metaphorical way. So, in the *Wasps* of Aristophanes, a cheese-grater is called from the kitchen to give evidence against a dog charged in an impromptu court with stealing a cheese, and in his *Clouds*, the heavens are compared with a domed bread cover for ash-bread, and humanity is said to be the charcoal under the dome. Kneading troughs, pestles and mortars, pots and pans can be added to the list, together with the breads, cakes and other finished products.

The literary evidence

Modern notions of men in ancient Greece are often constructed around their literature and power structures, with women, to a large extent separated from both.[33] An area related to literature that is often overlooked is the work song. As Jack Goody pointed out, food preparation is one of those areas of cultural activity in which women might combine two spheres, food preparation and singing (weaving was another). There is some evidence for work songs in antiquity, and the singing of women at work is important testimony to an aspect of their lives which was communal and shared. Men sang herdsmen's songs (Athenaeus, 619a–b), women winnowing songs (Athenaeus, 619a, Aristophanes, *Thesmpohoriazousai* B, fragment 352). There were songs sung while milling (Athenaeus, 618d), I presume by women since there is a women's milling song (milling barley) in Aristophanes, *Clouds*, 1358. Plutarch records a woman's work song, *Moralia*, 157e: 'I heard a foreign woman singing at the mill when I was staying in Ephesus: "Grind, mill, grind. Of course Pittakos used to grind when he was king of great Mytilene"'. 'Foreign' probably indicates slave status. Work songs were influential, both in bringing groups of workers together and in inspiring literary forms – comedy and pastoral both bear their traces. Some of the terracottas show women kneading bread to the sound of a pipe. They work in a row, side by side together. One of these is illustrated in West (1992),[34] who also mentions the working songs of each sex.[35]

In much literature, more is said about the presentation of food at table than the preparation of it in the kitchen. This reflects, I take it, the experience of rich men who most often saw their food only in a ready-cooked state and carried to the table by male or female slaves and servants. This use of literature is intended to be indicative and exemplary. It in no way sets out to be comprehensive or a strictly accurate report of the presentation of food and its preparation.

1 Homer

Men's work: preparing the meat

> When they had finished their prayer and thrown the barley grains, they first of all drew back the animals' heads, cut their throats and skinned them. They cut out the high bones and wrapped them in fat, making a double fold, and put raw meat on top of them. The old man burnt them over the firewood, and poured over a libation of fiery wine. The young men surrounded him, five-pronged forks in hand. When the thighs were burnt, and they had tasted the vital organs, then they carved up the rest, put them on spits, roasted them carefully, and then removed them from the fire. But when hey had finished their work and had set up the feast, they began to eat, nor was appetite lacking for the feast which gave equal shares to all. When they had satisfied their desire for drink and food, the youths filled to the brim with wine the mixing bowls, and distributed wine to all, having first made the ritual pouring into each man's cup. For the whole day the youths of the Achaeans appeased the god with song, singing a fine paean and hymns to Apollo the Far-shooter.[36]

Women's work: preparing the flour

> A woman grinding corn indoors uttered a word of omen nearby, at the place where the hand-mills were located for the shepherd of the people. Twelve women in all worked hard at these hand-mills to produce barleymeal and wheatmeal, which are the marrow of men. The other women were asleep, having ground their corn for the day, but this one had not yet come to the end and was physically the weakest. She stopped her mill and spoke a word, which was a sign for her master: 'may this be the last and final time that the suitors take their lovely feast today in the palace of Odysseus. They have made my knees weak with thus toil that pains my heart, grinding this barleymeal. May they now feast their last!'[37]

These extracts tell us much, not least that the description of food preparation was a feature of Europe's earliest literature. The all-male gathering for sacrifice and animal killing includes detailed dismemberment of the carcase.[38] It is a religious occasion (to appease Apollo), but any such occasion is a male occasion. Much stress is laid on the details of the preparation and how it differed for various parts of the animal, and that everyone then eats on an equal basis. There are many such sacrifices in Homer, and they are specially constructed to lend epic grandeur, particularly to the military world of the *Iliad*. The heroes eat an extraordinary amount of meat that aroused comment in later centuries.[39] There are no other grain-grinding passages. The slave-girl is mentioned not because of the importance of her task for the poet, but for her ominous uttering. Why is there so much meat in Homer and so little milling? The grain, after all, is important. It literally or metaphorically builds the marrow of men, we are told. Mortal men throughout the *Odyssey* are classified as 'grain-eating' to distinguish them from the gods and monsters who differ from the civilized Greeks in both their nature and their diet. These two passages demonstrate clearly the special world inhabited by literature. The date of the Homeric poems is disputed, but whatever the date, we may be quite sure that at that time most Greeks, male or female, were eating more grain than meat, and that more person-hours by far were devoted to grain as opposed to meat preparation. This privileging of meat preparation over cereal preparation is presented in an extreme form in Homer, but it may be only an exaggeration of the estimate of these categories of food in the wider culture. Meat is privileged over cereals in important respects in contemporary British society, though that position is now strongly contested, partly on grounds of gender.

2 Herodotus

The wreckage of the defeated Persian fleet after the battle of Salamis in 480 BC fulfilled a prophecy, according to Herodotus *Histories*, 8.96:

> The women of Kolias will do their roasting with oars

This bizarre prediction was made possible when oars from the Persian warships were washed up on the Attic beaches. The sentence clearly assumes that it is women and not men who roast, or rather toast, for in this case the reference is probably to the toasting of barley. The phrase 'the women of Kolias' indicates women of citizen status – slaves are less likely than in the Plataea incident considered above. It seems to be the case that the processing of cereals was in this culture largely women's work, whether slave or free.

3 Pherekrates

> Our wives wait for each of us, boiling a soup of pulses or lentils, and baking a solitary little bit of salt fish.[40]

This passage (an isolated fragment of a lost play) suggests that in this case poor women prepared food for their husbands (no one else at least is mentioned). Poverty is implied by the pulses and lentils and small amount of preserved fish, though all of these products were eaten by all classes. The speaker may be a soldier. The passage seems clear enough, but a comedy is not an unambiguous document.

4   Ovid

When the dwellers in heaven reached the little hearth, and bowing their heads, entered through the humble door, the old man showed them a seat on which to rest their limbs. Baucis, attentive to her guests, threw a rough piece of cloth over it, and raked the warm ashes in the hearth to revive yesterday's fire, feeding it with leaves and dry bark, and blowing on it with ancient breath to produce flames. She took down split wood and dried branches from the roof beams, broke them up and pushed them under her small bronze pot. Her husband had gathered some vegetables from his well-watered garden and these she trimmed of their leaves. He[41] lifted down with a two-pronged stick the smoky back of bacon which had been hanging from a beam, and from this long-preserved back she cut off a thin slice and cooked it in fiercely-boiling water. [The guests are given water for washing and are seated on a special couch. A table is brought.] She cleaned the table with mint leaves, and placed on it the two-coloured fruits of chaste Minerva [the olive] and cornel-cherries from last autumn preserved in a solution of wine-lees, and endives, radish, a piece of cheese, eggs lightly turned in ashes that were not too hot, all on terracotta. Then was brought a mixing bowl engraved in the same kind of silver as the rest, and cups of beech wood hollowed out and lined with yellow wax. After a short wait, the fire provided a hot feast and a wine of no great age was taken round again, and then put aside to make way for the dessert. Here were nuts, figs mixed with wrinkled dates, plums and fragrant apples in open baskets, and grapes just picked from the purple vines. A shining honey-comb was in the centre, and over all kindly faces and a welcome that was neither indifferent nor reduced by poverty.[42]

The textual problem noted above, and Ovid's introduction of the couple as having no master and no slave in the house makes any division of labour between the two entirely arbitrary. We cannot place any confidence in the fact that the woman stokes and revives the fire or that the man deals with the meat. That is not to say that there was no such division, simply that it is not operating here. There is much of the literary in Ovid, of the cosy moralist who approves of the worthy peasants; much too of the contrast between the tall visiting gods (who are looking for honest people before flooding the earth to kill the wicked)[43] and the humility of the old couple who have no fancy goods or rich tableware. They have foods that have been prepared for long-term storage, the ham and the pickled and dried fruits. The meat is boiled, but no bread is produced. Bread-making can be of literary interest, as can be seen in the similarly idealizing passage from the Pseudo-Virgil *Moretum*. This passage is in Latin, but draws on Greek and Phrygian influences for material and literary detail. It was written in the same metre as Homer and shares the fondness for detail, in this case taking pleasure in the contrast between the epic rhythm and the homeliness of the subject matter.

5   Pherecrates

In those days nobody had a slave, a Sambo or a Dinah, but the women of the household had to toil by themselves over all the housework. And what is more, they would grind the corn at early dawn, so that the village rang with the touch of the handmills[44]

I have retained Gulick's translation here, as a reminder of the power of modern preoccupations. Greek slave names have been transposed into American conventional slave names, despite the differences in cultures. The suggestion of the passage is that the grinding of the corn used to be women's work, but that now slaves (male and female) prepared the cereals. We might conclude from this that slaves (male and female) performed the tasks if they were available. This is reminiscent of the popularity of the diesel mill in Goody's investigations in Ghana. The preparation of cereals, to judge from this passage and the *Odyssey* passage in (1), is a tiring task that was performed only by the women of the house if they could not pass it on elsewhere, to a household slave. Conversely, passage (7) below shows a man grinding spelt, when he has a female slave at hand. Each literary form is manipulating the everyday task for its own purposes, and doubt may easily be cast on both the comic text and the pseudo-epic.

6   Crates

Speaker A: So no one will have a slave, male or female? Then each man, though old, will do his own chores for himself?
Speaker B: Not at all. I shall give everything the ability to walk.
Speaker A: How will that help them?
Speaker B: Each piece of furniture will advance when someone gives the order, 'Come over here, table! Get yourself ready.' 'Knead, my little trough!' 'Pour the wine, ladle!' 'Where is the cup? Go and wash yourself up!' 'Step up, barley cake!' 'The pot must disgorge the beet leaves!' 'Fish, walk! "But I'm not yet cooked on the other side."Can't you turn yourself over and sprinkle some salt and oil over yourself?'[45]

The chores here are a mixture of serving at table (see above) and preparing of food. This is one passage of a number cited by Athenaeus[46] in which food serves itself automatically in a kind of recreated golden age where toil is abolished and slaves are not required. In many of these passages, the serving of food, rather than cooking, is at issue. This strange and comic anticipation of our automated and robotic age is striking (the play dates to the late fifth century BC). We may note that male and female slaves are equally in mind. The speaker is a man: we might be surprised, if we believe that most labour-intensive food preparation was performed by women, to find that a man is interested in automatic catering. This may – and equally may not – reflect a dislike among poorer Athenians for their life of unremitting toil, of which food preparation may have been a notable example. The play is a comedy, demonstrating once again that this genre was considered particularly suitable for the presentation of items from the material world, in this case foods and their preparation.

7   Pseudo-Virgil

Then he called his two hands to the task, dividing the work between them; the left was dedicated to supplying the grains, the right to doing the work, turning in constant circular motion and moving the mill (the bruised grain fell through under the rapid blows of the stones). At times the left hand came to the aid of her weary sister and took her turn. Soon he began to sing a country song and ease his task with a rustic tune. At times he shouted to Scybale. She was his only help, African by race, her whole body bearing witness to her home country. Her hair was curly, her lips swollen, her colour dark, her chest broad, her breasts drooping, slimmer at her belly, her legs thin, her feet large and broad. Her shoes were split and cracked. He called her over and told her to put wood on the fire to make a blaze and to heat cold water over the flames.[47]

This passage, while literary, like the Ovid, appears to be more documentary. The man, an idealized peasant, here prepares the grain and sings his grinding song while his black slave and/or partner is told to see to the fire. The latter appears to conform with Jack Goody's findings, but is inconclusive as a single example. Written in the epic rhythm, the passage relishes the details of the milling and of the black woman's appearance. The poem is written in Latin, though probably derived from a Greek original. It is difficult to say whether this is serious evidence for grain-processing by men or a fiction designed to be charming and unusual. It is notable that the male subject and the black woman are not equal in status but that, notwithstanding, the man performs the arduous milling. There is some evidence for more milling by men in Rome than in Greece.

8   Dio Chrysostom, 7.66

So we went in and feasted for the rest of the day, we men lying on leaves and skins that made a high couch. The wife of the house sat beside her husband. A nubile daughter served our meal, pouring us sweet red wine to drink; the sons prepared the meat, and ate their own dinner after handing ours. I thought that these people were fortunate.

This is the scene in which one of the literary élite visits a poorer family and is impressed by their simple virtues. He is clearly distant from them. The passage illustrates the gender division further down the social scale into young males preparing and serving meat and the young female serving wine (the latter is served by men or women, according to context). There is, incidentally a parallel division in the elders, between the men who recline on the rustic couches and the woman who sits beside her husband. This feature appears to be almost universal among Greeks who used couches.

9   Menander

Chef, to me you seem most unsavoury. You've already asked me three times how many tables we are going to set. We are sacrificing one little pig. What's it to you whether we set one table or eight? Serve the dinner today! There are no foreign sauces to make, and none of the ingredients that accompany your recipes in that style, honey, fine flour or eggs. Everything is now reversed, you see. The male chef makes moulded cakes, bakes flatcakes, boils the bulgar wheat and brings it round after the salt fish, followed by savouries wrapped in a fig leaf and a bunch of grapes. The female worker, on the other hand, takes up her station opposite him and roasts little pieces of meat and thrushes for dessert. Then the diner expecting main courses gets him dessert, and when he has anointed himself with myrrh and has put on his garland for dessert he gets main courses of honey cakes and thrushes.[48]

This fragment is quoted by Athenaeus (172a–c), who gives other evidence for female kitchen workers as distinct from male chefs, but also adds cases of male kitchen workers. The fragment belongs to a category of comedy in which a boastful chef is given a scene to display all his overblown skills. The present speaker counters such bombast with satirical comment on current eating habits which have blurred the division between courses. This is luxurious eating, the equivalent of the modern restaurant, and gives the kitchen workers a rare voice. There is an implied hierarchy in which the chef stands much higher than the female worker. There are no known cases of female chefs (compare n. 22).

10   Aristophanes

Praxagora: I will demonstrate how women are better than us in their conduct. To start with, they dye wool with hot water, according to ancient custom. All of them. And you won't see them introducing any changes either. By contrast, the city of Athens, if it has any institution that is doing fine, it does not look after it, unless some new light on it can be devised. The women sit down to roast their barley, just as they used to. They carry things on their head, just as they used to. They celebrate the Thesmophoria festival, just as they used to. They bake flatcakes just as they used to. They worry their husbands to death, just as they used to. They have lovers in the house, just as they used to. They buy themselves little things on the side, just as they used to. They like their wine neat, just as they used to. They enjoy sexual intercourse, just as they used to. Therefore, gentlemen, let's not drone on about handing the city over to them, and let's not bother to enquire what it is they propose, but simply let them run things.[49]

This is a passage from Attic Old Comedy, a rumbustuous and lively form, written by men, probably for an exclusively male audience of over 15 000.[50] From this male perspective, various things are imagined of women, and women tend to conform to these stereotypes when they are female characters in the plays (played by male actors). These stereotypes include a large appetite for sex and wine. It will be seen that the whole passage, spoken by a vigorous female character who is disguised as a man, stresses the conservative nature of women and their consequent suitability for running the city. Their traditional attributes include cereal preparation (barley-roasting) and baking: if these were not regularly women's tasks, they would not make sense in this context. Citizen women are meant here, not slaves, and presumably not aristocratic women, since the personnel of comedy tends to be drawn from humbler citizens.

While treatises on bread-making[51] and other techniques of food preparation have not survived from antiquity, it can be seen that literature does throw important light on this area of work, an area which brings material objects into literature, in which gender implications are likely to be present, and which can be evaluated profitably when set beside the archaeological record and comparative material from other cultures. I have concentrated on what might be termed heavy-duty food preparation at the expense of 'cooking' in the modern sense, which featured in passages (3) and (9). There are many literary passages like passage (9), in which a male chef prepares something pretentious for a dinner party.[52] These passages tend to be used for satirical and moralizing purposes, attacking the fantasies of the chef and the gluttony of the employer. They stand in clear contrast to passages (4) and (7) which concentrate on simplicity and honest toil and show a marked absence of rich sauces and other luxuries. Carefully-garnered fruits, preserved fruits and meat, and cereals signify rustic integrity, with all hints of grinding poverty kept at a distance. At the same time, here is in this kind of literary presentation a note of humour or patronizing surprise at how wholesome the food of the poor can be.

Notes

1. Four stars in *The Good Food Guide* (1994).
2. On Islamic culture, see Marín and Waines (1989), p. 123; on China, they refer to Chang (1977), pp. 85–192, chapters on the T'ang and Sung dynasties by

E.H. Schafer and M. Freeman. The picture is more complex for China, since there were cookery books in the early period (see Bottéro in Wilkins, Harvey and Dobson (1995). The detail includes the preparation of bread by a woman.
3. See Wilkins and Hill (1994). For example: Archestratus, fragment 23 (pp. 59–60)

> Whenever you stew fish within the sides of a hollow cooking pot, do not add water or wine vinegar, but pour on only oil and dried cumin together with fragment leaves. Stew it over the heat of the charcoal without bringing it too close to the flames, and stir often in case it burns without your noticing.

4. Those human beings (if any) who subsist exclusively on a diet of raw or wild foods are too few to upset significantly this generalization. A partial diet of raw or wild foods is another matter, and was in fact a feature of the ancient Greek diet.
5. Goody (1982), pp. 69–71.
6. Whyte (1978).
7. Further comparative studies may be seen in Segalen (1983), pp. 78–111 and in Arnott (1975), pp. 251–337.
8. Pomeroy (1976).
9. Pomeroy (1976), pp. 30, 72, 191, 200–1.
10. Pomeroy (1976), p. 72; Pomeroy's text reads 'four hundred', ignoring 80 Athenian troops in attendance.
11. A question asked by Gomme (1956), p. 212.
12. Lefkowitz and Fant (1982); Just (1989); Cameron and Khurt (1983).
13. Note the passive voice.
14. For a description of the festival, see Burkert (1985), pp. 242–6.
15. Compare Lacey (1994), pp. 99–113 and Waines (1987), pp. 255–63 (Based on Mesopotamia). For the phrase 'the life of the milled grain', see Amphis the comic poet, fragment 9.1–2.
16. *Phrygetron*: see Pollux 1.246.
17. The division of the sexes in dining at formal meals is discussed in a comparative study by Visser (1992).
18. This may have been accentuated by age differentials at marriage, men tending to be about 30, women 14 or 15.
19. Detienne and Vernant (1989).
20. This term also embraces our 'butcher' and 'chef'. See further Berthiaume (1982).
21. Detienne and Vernant (1989).
22. He may not be right. He appears to be supported by a passage from a comedy by the poet Pherecrates (fragment 70): 'Whoever has ever seen a female *mageiros* or a female fish seller?', but we cannot tell whether or not this is a joke.
23. Fiddes (1991), pp. 144–62.
24. On these priests, see Bruit (1995).
25. For the Vestal Virgins, see Scullard (1981), pp. 149–50. It is less clear who prepared, for example, the phallic cakes at the Thesmophoria or the fig pastry carried in the procession bringing Athena her new robe (Burkert (1985) pp. 243, 228.
26. See Miller (1978). A fragment (300 KA) of the comic poet Cratinus says '... they roast the barley [at the prytaneion]'. But the subject could be masculine or feminine.
27. See, for example, Sparkes and Talcott (1970).
28. Berthiaume (1982).
29. Detienne and Vernant (1989).
30. By the Eleusinian painter, St Petersburg, Hermitage St., 1791.

31. Many of them come from Boiotia, the territory of the city of Thebes to the north of Attika. A number are listed in Sparkes (1962), (1965), pp. 132–7.
32. For example, Berlin, Staatliche Museen, 6674, a Boiotian terracotta of the early fifth century BC, is of a male figure testing the heat of a fire for cooking. This appears to show that women did not control exclusively the home fire in Greece (see Goody, 1982).
33. With certain notable exceptions such as the poets Sappho, Corinna and Praxilla, and the literary wife of Perikles of Athens, Aspasia.
34. West (1992), Plate 8.
35. West (1992), Plate 28.
36. Homer, *Iliad*, lines 458–74.
37. Homer, *Odyssey*, 20.105–19.
38. Contrast the practice of the Spanish region of Estremadura where men kill the pig, but women prepare and dress it: see Pitt-Rivers (1971), pp. 84–7. I am grateful to Dr Tim Rees for drawing my attention to this practice.
39. See Plato, *Republic*, 404b–c; Athenaeus, 8f–25e.
40. Pherekrates the comic poet, *Fugitives*, fragment 26 KA.
41. The manuscripts are divided between *illa* (she) and *ille* (he) in line 647. For a discussion on literary grounds see Griffin (1991), p. 55. He argues '*ille* gives Philemon his fair share of the work and it also seems more appropriate that the man should lift down the heavy piece of pork'.
42. Ovid, *Metamorphoses*, 8, lines 637–78.
43. In a Graeco–Roman version of Noah's flood.
44. Pherekrates the comic poet, *Savages*, fragment 10 KA, trans C.B. Gulick (1929), III, line 183.
45. Crates the comic poet, *Wild beasts*, fragment 16 KA.
46. 267e–270a.
47. Pseudo-Virgil, *The Moretum*, lines 24–38.
48. Menander, *The false Heracles*, fragment 518K.
49. Aristophanes, *Assembly-Women*, lines 214–32.
50. On the evidence for and against women in the theatre audience, see e.g. Pickard-Cambridge (1968), pp. 263–5, Henderson (1991), pp. 133–48.
51. We know of a lost treatise on breadmaking by Chrysippus of Tyana, some of which is preserved by Athenaeus at 647c–648a. He gives recipes for breads and cakes, to be made once the flours have been prepared.
52. A series of these are quoted by Athenaeus at 290b–293e.

Bibliography

Arnott, M.L. (1975) *Gastronomy: The anthropology of food and food habits* (The Hague).

Berthiaume, G. (1982) *Les rôles du Mágeiros* (Leiden).

Bottéro, J. (1995) 'The Most Ancient Recipe of all', in J. Wilkins, D. Harvey and M. Dobson, *Food in Antiquity* (Exeter).

Bruit, L. (1995) 'Ritual Eating"The case of the parasite', in J. Wilkins, D. Harvey and M. Dobson, *Food in Antiquity* (Exeter).

Burkert, W. (1985) *Greek Religion* (Oxford).

Cameron, A. and A. Khurt (1983) *Images of Women in Antiquity* (London).

Chang, K.C. (ed.) (1997) *Food in Chinese Culture* (New Haven, Conn.), pp. 85–192.

Detienne, M. (1989) 'The Violence of Wellborn Ladies', in M. Detienne and J.-P. Vernant, *The Cuisine of Sacrifice among the Greeks* (Chicago).

Detienne, M. and J.-P. Vernant (1989) *The Cuisine of Sacrifice among the Greeks* (Chicago).

Fiddes, N. (1991) *Meat: A natural symbol* (London).

Gomme, A.W. (1956) *A Historical Commentary on Thucydides* (Oxford), p. 212.

Goody, J. (1982) *Cooking, Cuisine and Class* (Cambridge).

Griffin, A.H.F. (1991) 'Philemon and Baucis in Ovid's *Metamorphoses*', *Hermathena*, CLI, p. 55.

Gulick, C.B. (1929) *Athenaeus: The Deipnosophists* (Cambridge, Mass. and London), III, 183.

Henderson, J. (1991) 'Women and the Athenian Dramatic Festivals', *American Journal of Philology*, 121, pp. 133–48.

Just, R. (1989) *Women in Athenian Law and Life* (London).

Lacey, R.W. (1994) *Hard to Swallow* (Cambridge).

Lefkowitz, M.R. and M.B. Fant (1989) *Women's Life in Greece and Rome* (London).

Marín, M. and D. Waines (1989) 'The Balanced Way: Food for pleasure and health in Medieval Islam', *Manuscripts of the Middle East*, 4, pp. 123–32.

Miller, S.J. (1978) *The Prytaneion: Its function and architectural form* (Berkeley).

Pickard-Cambridge, A. (1968) *The Dramatic Festivals of Athens*, 2nd edn (Oxford), pp. 263–5.

Pitt-Rivers, J.A. (1971) *The People of the Sierra* (Chicago), pp. 84–7.

Pomeroy, S. (1976) *Goddesses, Whores, Wives and Slaves* (London).

Scullard, H.H. (1981) *Festivals and Ceremonies of the Roman Republic* (London), pp. 149–50.

Segalen, M. (1983) Love and Power in the Peasant Family, Eng. trans, S. Matthews (Oxford).

Sparkes, B.A. (1962), (1965) 'The Greek Kitchen', *Journal of Hellenic Studies*, 82, pp. 121–37; 85, pp. 162–3.

Sparkes, B.A. and Talcott (1970) *The Athenian agora, XII, Black and Plain Pottery* (Princeton).

Visser, M. (1992) *The Rituals of Dinner* (London).

Waines, D. (1987) 'Cereals, Bread and Society', *Journal of the Economic and Social History of the Orient*, 30, pp. 256–85.

West, M.L. (1992) *Ancient Greek Music* (Oxford).

Whyte, M.K. (1978) *The Status of Women in Pre-industrial Societies* (Princeton).

Wilkins, J., D. Harvey and M. Dobson (1995) *Food in Antiquity* (Exeter).

Wilkins, J. and S. Hill (1994) *Archestratus: The life of luxury* (Totnes).

Part III
Gendered Symbolism in History

9
Glamour and Glory: The Symbolic Imagery of Women on Paper Money

Virginia Hewitt

Important influences on our thinking and understanding may come from the least expected sources, everyday objects which we take for granted. Few people would think of looking at banknotes for clues to the status of women, assuming that they would offer only atypical figureheads, of monarchs or heads of states, and these mainly male. Yet for over 200 years paper money across the world has been adorned with an extraordinary range of images of women, including neo-classical allegories, glamorous cotton-pickers, smiling tractor-drivers and Nobel prize-winners. The aim of this chapter is to examine briefly why images of women have been chosen for notes, how they have been used to convey particular messages, and how this in turn might affect our perception of women.[1]

To understand the purpose of female images[2] on paper money, we must first consider the general function of note design. Because paper has no intrinsic value, the successful circulation of banknotes depends on confidence. The graphic design of notes must therefore impart dignity to the currency and make it easy to use by establishing the authority issuing the note, identifying its value and deterring forgery. To achieve these goals the design must attract attention, and while landscape, architecture and abstract pattern have all been used to this effect, human figures have a particular power to capture our interest, for we are readily drawn to another of our own kind.

But why have women so often been chosen to symbolize good qualities on currency? Men, children and mixed groups are also depicted on notes, but they are outshone by the variety and vitality of the images of women.[3] Yet this is rather ironic, for authoritative female allegories preside on notes of the eighteenth and nineteenth centuries, when women had limited control over money in either public or private life.[4] Even today, while an increasing number of portraits of women appear on national currency, banking remains very much a male-dominated profession, and in many homes men still assume control over the family finances. It is striking, too, that the characteristics required of a successful bank or state treasury, such as strength, stability and rationality, are not those which have been stereotypically associated with the female temperament. It is, however, in the conception of woman as mutable and elusive that part of the answer may lie. From pre-history to the present day, in many cultures, the female form has served as a symbol of such universal and disparate concepts as life and death, agriculture and commerce, justice and law. These mythic associations have long since ceased to be consciously acknowledged, at least in western societies, but their legacy pervades our iconography, and those who design banknotes, no less than anyone else, must be influenced by such traditions. These may be illustrated quite explicitly: for example, a German note of 1915 juxtaposes a male labourer with rolled-up shirt sleeves, looking directly at the viewer, with a woman whose head is bowed in sleep against a backdrop of moon and stars – an archetypal distinction between man as embodiment of daylight, work and reason, and woman as emblem of night, mystery and intuition[5] (Figure 9.1). Allegorical figures of women are often accompanied by animals, especially lions. These creatures are no doubt intended to suggest power, majesty and patriotism, but they are also a reminder that many female deities have been identified with wild animals, affirming woman's mythological affinity with the untamed forces of nature. In this regard it is interesting to speculate on the mixed messages of a Brazilian note of 1907 in which a rather sulky personification of Law, the ultimate attribute of civilized society, dangles her hand companionably in a lion's fur (Figure 9.2). Those who choose such imagery for note designs are unwittingly acknowledging a debt to ideas deeper and older than they may realize; they may be aware only of adopting a common visual language in which certain representations of women will be readily accepted, albeit seldom analyzed and imperfectly understood. Indeed, the sharpening distinction between sacred and secular, mythology and science, imagination and fact, may even encourage the use of female forms as emblems of supposedly 'unfeminine' traits for, in fantasy, anything is possible.[6]

How, then, have these images been used? In addition to unconscious psychological influences, banknote designs are above all dictated by practical considerations such as the nature of the institution to be advertised, be it nineteenth-century private bank or twentieth-century state treasury; contemporary trends in graphic design; and the limitations or opportunities given by the available printing technology. Inevitably there have been changes over time – broadly speaking, a shift from allegorical figures to imaginary but naturalistic scenes of women in everyday life and, most recently, portraits of renowned women. However, all these have been

Figure 9.1   Symbolic opposites: man and woman on a 20-mark note, Germany, 1915 (actual size)

Source: Reproduced by kind permission of the Trustees of the British Museum.
British Museum, 1994.

Figure 9.2   The personification of Law with a majestic lion on 10-million reis note, Brazil 1907

Source: Reproduced by kind permission of the Trustees of the British Museum. British Museum, 1994.

employed across boundaries of time and place, and rather than present a strictly chronological account, I intend to look at the characteristic images which have recurred on notes as symbols of financial prosperity, economic well-being and national glory, focusing particularly on allegories, lifelike representations, and portraits.

Allegorical female figures[7] on paper money date back at least to 1694, when the Bank of England decorated its first notes with a small vignette of Britannia seated beside a pile of coins. Neo-classical images with attributes borrowed from Greek and Roman mythology are sometimes still found on present-day issues, but enjoyed their heyday on eighteenth- and nineteenth-century notes, conforming to the iconography of contemporary art and architecture. As might be expected, they appear mainly on European and western currency. Though many permutations are possible, allegorical women on notes fall into two main types: those representing ideas of authority, such as personifications of a state, or institutions such as Justice and Law; and those which embody the means of production and exchange which create wealth, such as agriculture, industry, trade and communications. The figures of authority are particularly interesting because, other than heads of state, they are almost the only form in which women are shown on notes in positions of power. It is noticeable that, while clearly female, their womanly curves are often encased in masculine armour: Justice generally has her traditional attributes of sword and scales, while personifications of countries may be protected by helmet, spear, shield and breastplate[8] (Figure 9.3). The significance of these figures is therefore ambiguous, for on the one hand their inversion of conventional 'femininity' may simply point up the muted status of real women; while on the other, they may give a message, however veiled, that women can attain power.

Female allegorical figures representing wealth, abundance and fertility have been enduringly popular, woman's maternal role as bearer and sustainer of life appearing as a perennial symbol of the means by which wealth is first generated, then distributed. On nineteenth-century notes they often appear as goddesses of agriculture, holding sheaves of corn, or corn-ears and a scythe, emblem of harvest and death followed by rebirth. Here the imagery correlates woman's reproductive cycle, the agricultural seasons and fluctuations in economic wealth. Other figures are less specifically defined, being endowed with a range of attributes such as industrial cogs, agricultural tools, horns of plenty, ships' anchors, and often sheep, so that they represent industry, agriculture and trade (Figure 9.4). Compared with the allegories of authority, these women are much more feminine, with demure expressions, gentle demeanour and soft, flowing draperies. Often they are depicted with one or both breasts exposed, symbolizing fecundity and nourishment. Personifications of countries or of Liberty are also sometimes found with exposed breasts, suggesting perhaps the maternal authority of the state on the one hand, and political freedom and autonomy on the other. As with the women personifying powerful, male-dominated institutions, these nude figures are evidence of how the fantastic and imaginary nature of allegories allows them to display ideas and characteristics which might in reality be hidden or denied.

The symbolic affinity between women and economic wealth has continued in note designs of the twentieth century. Sometimes these still employ neo-classical allegories: for instance, a note from Martinique in the 1940s shows a young woman in billowing robes with a plump healthy baby; between them is a basket so full of grapes (themselves symbolic of life and immortality) that the well fed baby is tossing them around like toys (Figure 9.5). It is also common, especially on colonial issues, to see lifelike images of indigenous women surrounded by lush vegetation and ripe tropical fruits. Over time such obviously stylized imagery has given way to more naturalistic scenes of women at work in fields and factories, though it should be stressed that time is not an absolute frontier. Traditional allegorical emblems are often incorporated into realistic images – as, for example, on a note of Czechoslovakia, circulating from 1960 until 1993, on which a peasant woman carrying a sheaf of corn stands next to a male labourer, their heads framed by conjoined semicircles composed of a corn-ear and a

Figure 9.3   Britannia with helmet, spear and shield beside Justice with sword and scales on 5-dollar note of the Farmers' Joint Stock Bank, Canada, 1849 (size 3/2)

Source: Reproduced by kind permission of the Trustees of the British Museum. British Museum, 1994.

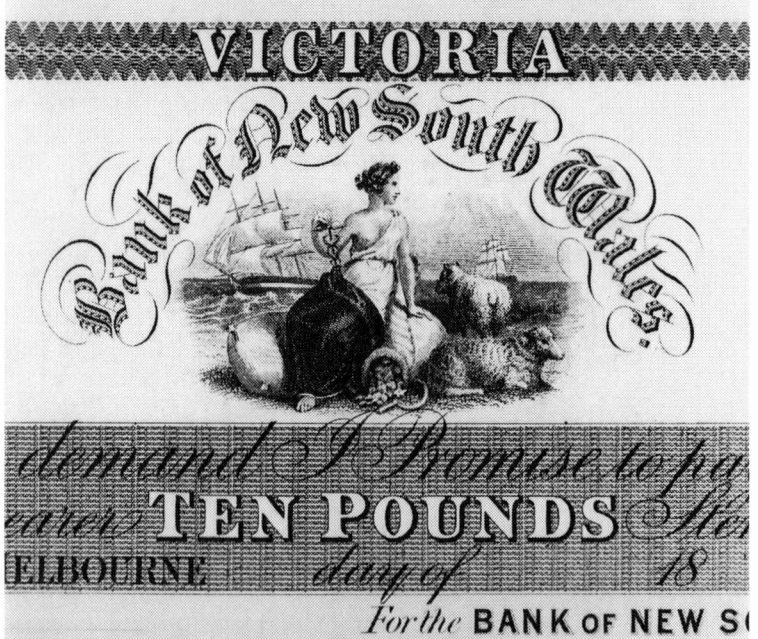

Figure 9.4   Female allegory with myriad emblems of trade and a culture on a 10-pound note of the Bank of New South Wales, Australia, ca. 1850–60 (actual size)

Source: Reproduced by kind permission of the Trustees of the British Museum. British Museum, 1994.

Figure 9.5   Burgeoning life and plenty symbolized by a woman and child with grapes on a 100-franc note, Martinique, 1942 (actual size)

Source: Reproduced by kind permission of the Trustees of the British Museum. British Museum, 1994.

cogwheel, respectively (Figure 9.6). Conversely, views of women working in everyday tasks are also found on nineteenth-century notes, especially those issued by local banks in North America.[9]

These everyday scenes merit attention precisely because they appear straightforward. It is easy to accept the images at face value, but in fact the women thus portrayed are still symbols – of economic growth, national prosperity, or cultural identity – and any interpretation should allow for that intended effect. Moreover, the discrepancy between image and reality can operate in different ways: for example a Swiss note of 1923, superficially showing three women sewing quietly at home, probably represents the three communities who formed the original Confederation of Switzerland, and the peaceful coexistence of different cultures in one country (Figure 9.7); in contrast, a note circulating in China since 1960 proclaims progress and equality by showing a smiling young woman with overalls and short windswept hair driving a tractor, distracting attention from a regime of domestic oppression.

Figure 9.6   Symbolic figures associating woman with agriculture and man with industry against a background of factory chimneys on a 100-korun note, Czechoslovakia, 1961 (length 162 mm)

Source: Reproduced by kind permission of the Trustees of the British Museum. British Museum, 1994.

Figure 9.7   Domestic harmony on a Swiss 500-franc note, 1923

Source: Reproduced by kind permission of the Trustees of the British Museum. British Museum, 1994.

Interior domestic scenes are rare, perhaps because they seem too intimate and informal for national currency. The few that do occur are often metaphors, equating happiness at home with a contented country: the Swiss note just mentioned, for example, or a Brazilian note issued in 1989 which commemorates the centenary of the Republic by reproducing a detail from a painting in which a mother and her family are sewing the Republican flag, thus symbolizing national unity and freedom. Not surprisingly, men are not shown in domestic situations, except very occasionally as fathers in symbolic family groups. A striking instance of gender stereotypes reflecting good order is found on Chinese notes printed in Shanghai around 1900: tiny vignettes of women in traditional feminine roles – teaching children, going for gentle walks – form a decorative frame for long extracts from classical texts on leading a virtuous life, written by male scholars. But all these are exceptions: working women on banknotes are almost invariably employed in important areas of the country's economy, such as cotton-picking in Syria and Mali, gathering roses for perfume in Bulgaria, or harvesting rice in paddy-fields in Vietnam (Figures 9.8, 9.9). The images are generally romanticized – a teacher with one eager pupil, or

Figure 9.8   Cheerfully laden woman harvesting roses for perfume on a 50-leva note, Bulgaria, 1951 (actual size)

Source: Reproduced by kind permission of the Trustees of the British Museum. British Museum, 1994.

Figure 9.9   Women working in paddy-fields on a 100-dong note, Vietnam, 1985 (actual size)

Source: Reproduced by kind permission of the Trustees of the British Museum. British Museum, 1994.

a woman plucking cotton as though it were a rose in a garden – and may be used to advertize economic development, as with scenes of textile factories in Albania or computer screens in Macedonia (formally part of Yugoslavia), both predominantly agricultural nations.[10] Even on very modern notes, however, the women are usually engaged in traditional areas of female employment, such as agriculture, textile manufacture, teaching or nursing. The press release accompanying a note issued in Zimbabwe in the early 1980s demonstrates how the designs are chosen to give a particular image of a country: cultivated fields with modern fencing symbolized progress, while women grinding maize in the traditional manner, in front of traditional huts, represented the maintenance of national culture and heritage.

At first sight these images may seem quite distinct from female allegorical figures, but they still perform a symbolic function, associating woman's life-giving and nourishing nature with economic growth, which is in turn used as an indicator of national glory and identity. National characteristics have become a more prominent feature of note design during the twentieth century, as the right of issue has increasingly been reserved for central authorities. Flora and fauna, landscape and agriculture are all used as badges of cultural identity, but in non-western countries ethnicity is often represented by human figures, usually female. Women are frequently shown wearing distinctive national costumes: a girl in traditional Tibetan headdress and earrings on a note from China in the 1920s; a woman in an embroidered dress on an Estonian note of 1940 (Figure 9.10); ceremonial costumes worn by the king's daughters on a note from Swaziland, 1974. Men are rarely depicted in local or national costume and, if they are, it is usually as part of a wider context; when the costume is itself a focal point, it is invariably modelled by a woman. In this respect, consciously or not, note designs reflect the practice in many societies today where, in the face of encroaching westernization, it is the women rather than the men who retain their traditional dress, especially for public occasions. Displays of ethnicity may be both attractive and innocent, or they may be a palatable key to political status, as is particularly evident on colonial note issues of the 1930s and 1940s. Here it is common to find both mother country and colony personified as female figures, but they are seldom sisters under the skin, for the mother country generally appears as a western allegory, fully

Figure 9.10   Woman in national costume with traditional symbols of the harvest on a 10-krooni note, Estonia, 1940 (actual size)

Source: Reproduced by kind permission of the Trustees of the British Museum. British Museum, 1994.

draped, while her subject is a native woman, often semi-clad with exposed breasts. Sometimes the design suggests harmony and affection between ruler and ruled, as on a French West African note depicting a black native woman with a white European allegory, her fingers clasped by the native woman's baby. In other cases the balance of power is all too obvious; thus a note of Angola under Portugal's rule in 1947 shows a clothed allegorical woman giving guidance to a bare-breasted black girl kneeling quietly by her side. (Figure 9.11) From a late-twentieth-century perspective, such images are blatantly exploitative, but caution is needed here, for figures of indigenous women are also used on notes of independent countries, where, presumably, no cultural condescension is implied – the joyful, bare-breasted girls seen performing a traditional dance on the note from Swaziland mentioned above are a good example. Nonetheless, the iconography of colonial note designs, revealing the imposition of western concepts on non-western cultures, invites further study. In the context of this chapter I would stress the equivocal message in the dual images of women – that is, authority is vested in the imaginary allegorical woman, while the lifelike woman represents the subservient colony.

Political authority and economic success, however desirable in themselves, are also routes to achieving national power and greatness, and

Figure 9.11   Allegory of authority with indigenous woman on a 50-angolares note, Angola, 1947 (actual size)

Source: Reproduced by kind permission of the Trustees of the British Museum. British Museum, 1994.

rather than illustrating the sometimes dubious means used to attain such goals, many countries nowadays advertize the resulting glory on their banknotes with portraits of national figures. Indeed, this is probably the sort of female image on notes with which most people are familiar. I am not so concerned here with portraits of monarchs, heads of state, or political leaders; although they do, of course, reflect the fact that women can attain such positions in some societies, they appear by virtue of their office, not their gender. Rather I want to consider the women of personal achievement and renown who have been chosen to represent their country on banknotes. Once again, this is not a new feature of note design; for example, an 1864 issue of the Confederate States of America carried a small vignette of Lucy Pickens, wife of the Governor of South Carolina, acclaimed as the very model of Southern virtue, elegance and authority. But larger-scale portraits, often filling a third to a half of the face of a note, have become a regular characteristic of note design in the second half of the twentieth century. This is partly a response to practical requirements in deterring forgery – distinctive portraits are easily recognized by the public, and the very fine engraving is hard to copy – but there is also a psychological element. Vivid portraits can bring warmth and personality to notes issued by increasingly impersonal institutions; furthermore they comply with the value many modern societies place on individual attainment, and it is becoming common for note-issuing authorities deliberately to portray women as well as men on their currency.

Despite this recognition, the fact remains that portraits must conform to the traditional function of note design – that is, they must bring dignity and authority to the currency. This inevitably has implications for the note-issuer's choice and our interpretation of those depicted: the women (or men, for that matter) who are chosen become ambassadors for a country, their personal success translated into national honour. Invariably the individuals portrayed are historical figures: their status is established, often woven into the country's heritage, and there is less risk of controversy than would occur with living people. This may help to explain certain patterns which emerge in the professions of the women whose portraits appear on notes. The arts, especially literature, are well represented, and while this may partly be because art, rather than science, is more readily ascribed to a particular country or culture, it no doubt also reflects the fact that women have traditionally had more opportunities in the arts than in science and technology. It is noticeable, too, that many of the women are celebrated for their work in human welfare. Florence Nightingale, who reformed the atrocious barracks hospital at Scutari during the Crimean War and established professional training for nurses in Britain, is familiar from the Bank of England 10 pound note of 1975–93. Modern Italian notes feature Maria Montessori (1870–1952) who developed the educational method which bears her name (Figure 9.12), and the

Figure 9.12   Portrait of Maria Montessori (1870–1952), who developed the Montessori method education, on 1000-lire note, Italy, 1990 (size 3/2)

Source: Reproduced by kind permission of the Trustees of the British Museum. British Museum, 1994.

10 dollar note issued in Australia in 1993 features Dame Mary Gilmore (1865–1962), a poet and active campaigner for the rights of the poor and disadvantaged – including women. All of these women must have kicked hard against prevailing customs, but it may be questioned whether, in the context of national currency, they are honoured as much for their rebellion as for their compassion and tenderness, both conventionally regarded as feminine traits. In their role as symbols of national greatness, the message given by these women may be just as ambiguous as their allegorical predecessors of the eighteenth and nineteenth centuries.

Throughout the history of paper money images of women have been a major element of note design. It is only possible here to survey the predominant themes but I hope to have demonstrated that this functional and highly specialized branch of graphic design has a wider symbolic significance. These female forms, from allegory to portrait, are chosen to meet the needs and constraints of banknote design, and to project the desired public image of the issuing authority. They are not chosen for what they say about women, but this is part of their legacy. Inevitably, the views presented of women are conservative, idealistic and only partially, if at all, true – yet they are given a spurious validity by the official nature of currency, which is a powerful and unsuspected source of propaganda, used by millions of people every day. But we must not draw too cynical a conclusion along the lines of deliberate manipulation: those who select the designs for paper money cannot help but be influenced by unconscious associations; furthermore, to maintain confidence they must choose images which will be recognizable and acceptable to the public. It is in the most commonplace objects that we may find clues to our identity; thus the symbolic women on paper money both reflect and reinforce our own conflicting perceptions of women and their place in different societies.

Notes

1. For a fuller discussion, see Hewitt (1994) published to accompany an exhibition of the same title held at the British Museum.
2. In this chapter I am looking only at images of women, and not at other symbolic female forms, such as the phoenix, which have appeared on notes.
3. It is perhaps worth pointing out that the ways in which women and men are shown on notes are not always in direct contrast. I hope to do more work on a comparative study and, in particular, on images of men and women shown together.
4. There are a few instances of women involved in running private banks in Britain, but they are rare – as, indeed, are women in senior management in banking today.
5. It has also been suggested to me that, given the date of the note, the woman may be praying for peace and the safety of her menfolk, while the man rolls up his sleeves in preparation to fight. This interpretation would also reflect popular gender stereotypes.
6. See Baring and Cashford (1993) for a compelling account of the emergence and suppression of goddess mythologies and the cultural consequences; and Warner (1987) for an excellent survey and analysis of female images used as metaphors.
7. In a sense all images of women on banknotes are allegorical, in that they are symbols of other meanings. Here I am using the term 'allegorical' to refer specifically to neo-classical personifications and goddesses.
8. See Warner (1987), pp. 124–5, on the analogy between these figures and Athena, goddess of war.
9. See, for example, Tyler (1994) and Doty (1995).
10. It is noticeable that the notes issued in industrialized countries seldom depict people at work, favouring more romantic views of landscape, architecture or national heroes.

Bibliography

Baring, A. and J. Cashford, (1993) *The Myth of the Goddess. Evolution of an image* (London).

Doty, R.G. (1995) 'Surviving Images, Forgotten Peoples: Native Americans, Women and African Americans on United States obsolete bank notes', in V. Hewitt (ed.), *The Banker's Art. Proceedings of the conference held at the British Museum 1994* (London).

Hewitt, V. (1994) *Beauty and the Banknote. Images of women on paper money.*

Hewitt, V. (ed.), (1995) *The Banker's Art. Proceedings of the conference held at the British Museum 1994* (London).

Tyler, F. (1994) 'The Angel in the Factory: Images of women workers engraved on ante-bellum bank notes', *Imprint. Journal of the American Historical Print Collectors Society*, 19 (1) (Fairfield, Conn.).

Warner, M. (1987) *Monuments and Maidens. The allegory of the female form* (London).

10
The Gendering of Artistic Labour in Mid-Victorian Britain[1]

Tim Barringer

In contrast with earlier periods when work was considered to be an activity commanding low social status (such as classical Greece and feudal Europe), post-Reformation Europe, especially during the industrial revolution, saw the idea of work become highly charged with religious and moral significance. A long debate inaugurated by Max Weber in his essay of 1904–5, *The Protestant Ethic and the Spirit of Capitalism*, and continued by R.H. Tawney[2] and others has problematized the intellectual and ideological roots of this cultural formation, acknowledging that the duty of work came to occupy a central position in ethical as well as economic theory and behaviour. However, the central role of gender in discourses of work has been largely overlooked. Focusing on British middle-class and artisan culture of the nineteenth century, this chapter examines ways in which work came to be associated predominantly with masculinity. This is not to say that women did not work in the nineteenth century; on the contrary, the employment of women in industry was on a massive scale. Domestic service was predominantly carried out by women, and, as Davidoff and Hall (1987) have shown, many middle-class women were involved in business enterprises.[3] Nonetheless, across a wide range of representations and ideological forms, from the novel to painting, from political debate to journalism and philosophy, work was perceived and presented as an essentially masculine activity.

The relationship between art and work constituted an important moral preoccupation of the mid-Victorian period. While the work of the artist undoubtedly held a higher cultural value during the nineteenth century than in many preceding periods, the creation of art – often conceived of as the play of genius – could be seen as work's other, and the life of the artist as constructed by the Romantics could pose a radical threat to a social order in which a Protestant work ethic played a central role. The stereotypical lifestyle of the artist – exemplified by Byron, Haydon or Rossetti – could be understood not only as not respectable, because not related to approved forms of labour, but also as not conforming to socially approved conceptions of the masculine, as effeminate. Representations of modern life produced during the mid-Victorian period are shot through with an anxiety to counter these notions with an image of the artist linked with both work and masculinity. This chapter addresses these issues through close readings of two mid-Victorian representations of labour, and the role of the gendered body within them. In the light of this analysis I shall examine the tensions which surrounded the idea of the work of the artist within the gendered account of labour dominant at this time, and indicate the importance of visual representations to the formulation and articulation of these ideas.

The historiography of Victorian Britain may reasonably be thought of as one of the ancestral homes of gender studies. Partly as a result of our continuing and deeply problematic ideological inheritance from this period, a great deal of intellectual activity has been focused on the social and legal position of women in Victorian Britain:[4] women's historians, drawing initially on textual sources such as the novel and the advice-book literature of the early and mid-nineteenth century, have identified a strong and relatively coherent body of ideology concerning the segregation of men and women into 'separate spheres' of 'public' and 'private' life. In this cluster of beliefs, largely middle-class in origin, medical and moral discourses were intertwined with social and behavioural prescription and proscription in the production of essentialized accounts of masculine and feminine sexuality and sexual difference.[5] It is essential to acknowledge that this cultural construction of 'separate spheres' does not provide an adequate, or even necessarily a useful, device for an historical understanding of the social functioning of gender in the nineteenth century. As Linda Kerber has suggested, rather than allowing ourselves to assume a deterministic relationship between a body of texts and social realities, in examining this material we should instead examine the languages used and identify the specific discursive strategies deployed.[6]

This applies to images – visual texts – as much as to their verbal counterparts and especially to visual representations which, while claiming to be descriptive, are in fact prescriptive. Lynda Nead (1988) and others have shown that visual representations were important in shaping and reinforcing the rhetorical construct of 'separate spheres'.[7] George Elgar Hicks' watercolour *The Sinews of Old England* (1857)[8] pictures an idealized, respectable working-class couple literally on the threshold between male and female spheres. A manual labourer bearing a pick-axe as the emblem of his trade, stares into the outside world with a determined expression, a declaration of intent directed towards his place of work. His wife, identified with the imagery of wholesomeness, fecundity and passivity signalled by an abundance of flowering and climbing plants, clearly belongs to the domestic region which opens up behind her. A young boy signals his future labour power and will to work through the spade he is holding (Figure 10.1). Hicks' image – which is manifestly highly inflected and idealized – enshrines the investment of gender characteristics through labour: the male becomes masculine through working and being seen to work, the female, feminine through abstaining from work in the public sphere, but (under some social and economic circumstances) performing domestic labour.

Women artists were certainly not exempt from these restrictions. While Deborah Cherry's book *Painting Women* (1993) has demonstrated the multiplicity of artistic production by women during the nineteenth century, institutional constraints on their activities at the time were severe. Bodies such as the Royal Academy, which at its foundation in 1768 had two women members, elected no women members during the Victorian period; the Victorian Academy was indeed an exclusively homosocial environment, operating both as a gentleman's club and an assertive professional interest group.[9] At the same time an increasingly conventionalized language of art criticism, also employed in artistic biographies which were often written by women, firmly situated art as a masculine practice. Sketching was encouraged as an accomplishment for ladies, but female artists with professional ambitions were restricted by the market and the institutions which served and defined it. To be a professional artist was of course to work and, in theory at least under the doctrine of separate spheres, middle-class women were prohibited from working. A combination of demand in the marketplace and social convention determined that women artists tended to produce small-scale paintings of domestic subjects, interiors and flowerpieces, representations of the domestic sphere. Examples such as *A Coming Event* by Jessica Hayllar (1886), which plays out a complex narrative concerning a coming wedding, indicate what accomplished women artists were able to achieve within these limitations. A fierce irony surrounds the fact that, although as I hope to show, artistic work for men occupied an ambivalent position in relation to debates around labour and masculinity, the artistic profession was nonetheless firmly regulated to exclude female protagonists.

It is these debates surrounding labour and masculinity to which I now want to turn, before considering the status of the male artist within them. The most conspicuous, and certainly the most elaborate, representation of labour to be produced in mid-nineteenth century Britain is *Work* by Ford Madox Brown (Figure 10.2). I am unapologetic in concentrating on a painting on which so many words have already been spilled, because a re-reading of it is demanded by the emergence of gender as a primary category of analysis.[10] The analysis of gender as socially constructed and thus historically variable,[11] in particular, occasions a reappraisal of what I want to describe as a visual text which is dominated by naturalized representations

Figure 10.1   George Elgar Hicks, *The Sinews of Old England*, watercolour, 1857; private collection

Source: Reproduced by courtesy of Sotheby's.

Figure 10.2   Ford Madox Brown, *Work*, oil painting, 1852–65

Source: Reproduced by courtesy of Manchester City Art Gallery.

of the gendered body. Madox Brown's *Work* is the polar opposite of Hayllar's small interiors, representing and directing itself to the public and not the domestic sphere: large in scale, rhetorical in tone, it is a painting which, I suggest, centrally thematizes the masculinity both of its protagonists and its creator. I shall read *Work* as a visual text which is a contribution to discourses of work and sexuality, and not a reflection of mid-nineteenth century social life, in spite of the claims to realism pressed by the artist's technique. The painting posits an absolute identification between masculinity and work, and in a corollary form, between middle-class femininity and non-work. This is achieved through the presentation of specific and readily-identifiable body types. Under this representational regime, the gendering of the individual subject is achieved through the inscription on the represented body of visual signs of labour or occupation, or the absence of these signs. The central group of navvies, similar in physique and dress to Hicks' idealized workman in *The Sinews of Old England*, digging a trench for the placing of a new water system in Heath Street, Hampstead, forms a paradigm of masculinity, hard at work. The *Illustrated London News* acknowledged Brown's success in identifying the navvy's central – and essentially masculine – role in the national mission of industrialization and progress:

> Bravo! Mr Brown, we would at once exclaim for the boldness of representing as your principle that potent agent in the work of British civilisation, the excavator or 'navvy'.[12]

Brown's painting and his long explanatory essay about it ascribe positive value in both aesthetic and economic terms to the physique of the working men: he describes the muscular navvy shovelling soil as being 'in the pride of manly health and beauty'.[13] These figures become the visual archetypes of a concept of work which emphasizes what were, and still are, powerful signifiers of masculinity: muscularity, exposure to the sun and assertive action.

The composition enforces the idea of separate spheres: the navvies, at centre stage, are juxtaposed with their polar opposites in the shade at the back and ranged down the left-hand side of the painting; ladies who do not work, archetypes of middle-class femininity, and a shady figure at the front, the barefoot and vagrant flowerseller, whose 'effeminate' disposition Madox Brown himself noted.[14] Described in the catalogue as the 'ragged wretch who has never been taught to work', this figure, identified in one popular book on Victorian art as a woman, lacks the characteristics of muscularity, active posture and gesture and exposure to the sun which identify the workers as real men.

In this image, then, value is attributed to particular forms of labour through the representation of the active male body. Compelling as this idea was in terms of contemporary discourses of gender, it presented problems in relation to the realities of middle-class work, the work of the patron group and that of the artist himself. The middle classes, by definition, did not indulge in manual labour: artists, businessmen and the new professional classes lived by their heads, not by their hands. Madox Brown's painting claimed to be simultaneously realistic and metaphorical, to function at once as both reportage and allegory: yet its metaphorical scheme, based on reading off value from body types, closed off mental as opposed to manual labour from honorific representation. The composition emphasizes an antithesis between the central group and the two figures of middle-aged men on the right. These are portraits of Thomas Carlyle, the historian and man of letters, and the philanthropic Anglican clergyman and Christian Socialist, Frederick Denison Maurice. The eccentric appearance of the diminutive preacher and the sneering prophet, with their drab clothing and stooped bodies, suggests that they fail to live up to the criteria of masculinity, physical activity and assertiveness, which identify the workers. Carlyle's major work *Past and Present* (1843), declared that 'there is a perennial nobleness, and even sacredness, in work',[15] removing work from the sphere of necessity and instrumentality and giving it instead a defining role not only in the earthly status but in the ultimate divine judgement of an individual. For Carlyle, work was the means of access to the grace of God: 'Blessed is he who has found his work: let him ask no other blessedness.'[16] Yet Carlyle agonized privately about not following his father's honest profession as a manual labourer. Even the intellectuals felt that mental labour was somehow lacking, a lack which was constructed in gendered terminology as effeminacy and impotence. What, then, of Madox Brown's own status as an artist?

If the painting seems to discount Carlyle and Maurice as working protagonists, their position in the composition is nonetheless clearly significant. Carlyle's gaze out to the right of the viewer, and Maurice's absorption in events, imply that they are interpreters, a part of the painting's expository strategy, our guides to the scene before us. Evidence from the painting's development indicates that the position they occupy in the composition is an important one. An earlier watercolour version shows a sketchily depicted *flâneur*-like figure in the place later to be occupied by Carlyle and Maurice, which can be identified from Brown's diary as the image of the artist.[17] This spectral self-image was worked out as a more prominent signifier of the artist's presence in the smaller *Hayfield* (1855).[18] Here, Brown incorporated a portrait of the artist with his tools and technologies, positioned in the corner as a mediator between the scene of labour before him and the viewing public behind him, outside the frame. The artist here is not only a virtuoso technician of visual representation, but also an interpreter, mediating the truths of nature and labour for the viewers as Carlyle and Maurice do in *Work*. Yet in spite of his pivotal role as creator and interpreter, the artist still appears to be inactive: his body is languid and lacks those signs of masculinity which identify the real workers before him: he is beyond labour rather than central to it.

The solution Madox Brown finally settled upon for his *magnum opus*, *Work*, is more sophisticated: in the final version the artist's body is erased, but his presence remains through the signs of his own labour. The first thing the viewer notices about *Work* is the amount of work the artist has put into it, the elaboration of detail and the hard-won verisimilitude. I suggest that his anxiety to be seen as performing valuable work himself, an anxiety intimately linked to his concerns over his own masculinity as voiced in his diary, precipitated his retreat, as a represented body, from the canvas. Passages in the diary indicate that it was not so much the finished result of *Work* but the process of designing and manufacturing it – the work which went into it – which Madox Brown valued so highly. Thus on 3 January 1855:

> Worked at the designe [*sic*] of the Hampstead picture called Work. Whenever I set to at designing I feel in the most ethereal and extatic state possible. I do not hurry with it because it is such enjoyment.[19]

The strategy was successful: contemporary critics perceived the signs of this extensive and extended labour in the surface of the painting and in its conceptual structure.

> It is to be hoped, then, that Mr Madox Brown's 'Work' may be received with all the approval its most conscientious performance entitles him to, and that it may be admitted as one accepted example of the dignity of labour, as well as a pretty strong assertion that he is well entitled to give his opinion of what constitutes hard work.[20]

Reading the physical elaboration and intellectual rigour of the image as signs of Brown's own labour, the critics incorporated this into debates on labour and masculinity, allying Brown's artistic labour with the manly physical endeavours of his main protagonists:

> Mr Ford Madox Brown in his very cleverly-painted picture intended to illustrate the dignity of labour, appeals quite as eloquently in his own behalf to show the effects of industry as in that of the robust type he presents and describes as 'the British excavator or navvy ...' whose well-developed physical strength, and rich glow of complexion, consequent on the healthful exercise of it, if it suggest the benefit of such employment, as, of course, it is meant to do, may also evoke something like a feeling of envy from those whose vocation does not conduce to those advantages.[21]

Madox Brown's own labour as an artist is here acknowledged as being the equal in terms of masculinity of that of his muscular protagonists. The *Athenaeum* critic adopted a Carlylean register of language, describing *Work* as:

> So impressive, so manly and so nearly complete, and above all, so originally and so powerfully treated ... Brilliant, solid, sound, studied with extraordinary earnestness, elaborate and masterly, the vigour of 'Work' will astonish those who do not know what the artist has done before.[22]

By remaining absent from the text but figuring himself in terms of his own labour as an artist, Madox Brown was able to circumvent the critique of artistic labour as non-masculine and to assert his mastery over the social scene.

My second short case study addresses a quite different aspect of the same problem of artistic labour and gender. At exactly the same time as Madox Brown was agonizing over *Work*, an industrial smith in Blackburn, James Sharples, was busy producing a painting and engraving which represented the scene of his own labour as an ironworker.[23] Applauded by John Ruskin and other critics when it emerged in 1859, Sharples' engraving, *The Forge* (Figure 10.3), is unusual if not unique in being a working man's representation of the scene of his own labour. Unlike Madox Brown contemplating navvies or haymakers from the position of a bystander, Sharples' image carries with it the authority of a protagonist, an authority inscribed in the careful delineation of tools, processes and practices comprehensible only to one with the specific skills and knowledges of an insider. In terms of debates over gender and labour, Sharples' image presents intact the unmistakable identification of work with masculinity. There are no women or girls present in his image, an absence which commemorates the success of the Amalgamated Society of Engineers, to which Sharples belonged, in prohibiting both female and unskilled male labour from competing with the more costly skilled labour of its members. We are looking at a closed shop.

Here, as in Madox Brown, the workers are seen in action, marked out by rhetorically heightened gesture and posture, their skin exposed to a brilliant source of light. Once again labour is presented as heroic and muscular, here with many of the figures arranged along a single plane like the Greek athletes of a classical frieze. Yet this powerful cultural formation of masculinity and work does not easily accommodate Sharples' work as an artist. The duality in Sharples – blacksmith and artist – raises important issues concerning class status: bound together in an uneasy dialectic within one man were the artist, typically a middle-class figure and the skilled workman and union member, who by definition belonged to the working class. This dichotomy also returns us to the anxieties raised by the gendering of artistic labour problematized in Madox Brown's image. Nineteenth-

162

Figure 10.3   James Sharples, *The Forge*, engraving, 1859, detail; this is a late impression incorporating some revisions made after the initial publication of the engraving

Source: Reproduced by courtesy of the Victoria and Albert Museum.

century commentators on *The Forge* agonized over the relative value of the labour which the image represented compared with the labour of producing the representation: was art labour, or labour's other? Was honest toil the equal of the fruits of genius? Could one man accomplish both? Industrial production and artistic production were thrown into an immediate and dramatic juxtaposition.

Although John Ruskin admired the engraving and purchased 12 impressions, the key contemporary commentator on Sharples' work was the polemicist Samuel Smiles. In 1860, Smiles included an account of Sharples' life in a revised edition of his homiletic volume of brief lives, *Self-help: Illustrations of Character and Conduct*.[24] Smiles is ambivalent about the rival claims of Sharples as blacksmith and as artist. Receiving a photograph of Sharples (Figure 10.4), the author was delighted to see not the typical image of an artist – at lesiure surrounded by the paraphernalia of the studio – but that of an industrial smith. Smiles wrote to Sharples:

> I am much gratified that you appear in it in your working garb. I like your face: it is so sturdy and honest – as you have proved yourself to be. I will have you hung up beside George Stephenson and Robert Burns.[25]

Sharples is here incorporated into a pantheon of manly men whose achievements are industrial and not artistic, a distinction onto which could be mapped a significant gender polarity. Yet his story was inserted into the chapter on artists, whose rags-to-riches life histories included those of Turner, the barber's son who became a Royal Academician, and Sir David Wilkie, the impoverished Scottish minister's son who became painter to the king. Smiles surely implies that Sharples, in his thirties when *Self-Help* appeared, would follow Turner and Wilkie up the social ladder. Yet if the artist in him left the blacksmith behind, what then of sturdiness and honesty?

A coda to these debates can be found in the biography of Sharples published in the year of his death, 1893, by a local journalist in Blackburn, Joseph Baron. Sharples had never repeated the success of *The Forge* and remained a blacksmith until ill-health forced his retirement. Baron's account is once more permeated with discourses of labour and gender, but he partly inverts Smiles' paradigm, writing:

> There are people living today who will tell you that *The Forge* was not a success, simply because the profits arising from it did not put the author in a villa residence, – did not enervate him for the rest of his life.[26]

In Baron's account Sharples continued his active and manly work as a blacksmith rather than risk the effeminate state of enervation supposed to be typical of the fashionable artist. By the 1890s, artistic practice had come,

Figure 10.4   R.A. Grigson, photograph of James Sharples. Blackburn, 1860

Source: Reproduced by courtesy of Mrs Marion Sharples, on loan to Blackburn City Museum.

in *avant-garde* circles, to be regarded as the polar opposite of work; it was this very issue on which turned the Ruskin–Whistler trial of 1878.[27] Baron accordingly presented his local hero, Sharples, as the honest negation of effeminate metropolitan sophistication. James Sharples, he tells us 'commenced life with no other fairy gift than his Northern grit'; moreover,

he could not, with his sensitive nature, have sat in bar-parlours glorifying himself; nor, with his independence, have submitted to patronage; nor, with his industry, have lived a life of namby-pambiness.[28]

By the 1890s, moralized links between labour, art and masculinity had been superseded. The Ruskinian and Carlylean moment, in which self-consciously manly artists laboured after a hard-won realism and produced so many morally charged representations of labour, had passed.

Notes

1. This chapter derives in part from research conducted for my doctoral thesis, 'Representations of Labour in British Visual Culture, 1850–75' (1994), which is currently in the process of revision for publication. I would like to acknowledge the constant support and inspiration provided by my supervisor, Marcia Pointon.
2. Tawney (1922).
3. For a survey of the literature, see Joyce (1992); Davidoff and Hall (1987).
4. See Vickery (1993), pp. 383–414.
5. See Weeks (1989), pp. 24–38 for an interpretation which situates this period in the history of discourses about sexuality. For a specific study of the medical treatment and representation of women, see Poovey (1989), esp. pp. 24–50.
6. Kerber (1988), pp. 9–39.
7. Nead (1988), pp. 12–47.
8. Private collection; see Allwood and Treble (1982), p. 22.
9. Hutchinson (1986), pp. 109–32.
10. Scott (1986), p. 91.
11. Foucault (1979); see also Mort (1987).
12. 'Exhibition of Mr Madox Brown's Works', *Illustrated London News* (18 March 1865), p. 266.
13. F.M. Brown, *An Exhibition of WORK and other paintings by Ford Madox Brown at the Gallery, 191 Piccadilly.*
14. *Ibid.*
15. T. Carlyle, *Past and Present*, p. 189.
16. *Ibid.*, p. 190.
17. Collection: Manchester City Art Gallery; see Surtees (1981).
18. Collection: Tate Gallery, London.
19. Surtees (1981), p. 113.
20. *The Builder* (18 March 1865), p. 186.
21. *The Builder* (18 March 1865), p. 186.
22. *Athenaeum* (11 March 1865), p. 353.

23. There is no modern account of Sharples' work. The most accessible analysis is Klingender (1947). (A revised edition of this work, edited by Arthur Elton in 1968 materially distorts Klingender's text.) A study of Sharples' work for the Amalgamated Society of Engineers can be found in C. Müller's PhD thesis (1978). The contemporary accounts are S. Smiles, *Self-Help* and Baron (1893).
24. See also Travers (1985).
25. Samuel Smiles to James Sharples (28 June 1860), Sharples Family Papers, on loan to Blackburn City Museum.
26. Baron (1893), p. 3.
27. Merrill (1992).
28. Baron (1893), p. 9.

Bibliography

Allwood, R. and R. Treble (1982) *George Elgar Hicks: Painter of Victorian life* (London).

Athenaeum (11 March 1865).

Baron, J. (1893) *James Sharples: Blacksmith and artist* (London).

Barringer, T. (1994) 'Representations of Labour in British Visual Culture, 1850–75', PhD Thesis, University of Sussex.

Brown, F.M. (1865) 'An Exhibition of WORK and other Paintings by Ford Madox Brown at the Gallery, 191 Piccadilly (opp. Sackville St) (London).

The Builder (18 March 1865).

Carlyle, T. (1912) *Past and Present* (London).

Cherry, D. (1993) *Painting Women: Victorian women artists* (London).

Davidoff, L. and C. Hall (1987) *Family Fortunes: Men and women of the English middle class, 1780–1850* (London).

Foucault, M. (1979) *History of Sexuality*, vol. 1 (Harmondsworth).

Hutchinson, S. (1988) *The History of the Royal Academy, 1768–1986* (London).

Illustrated London News (18 March 1865).

Joyce, P. (1992) 'Work', in F.M.L. Thompson (ed.), *The Cambridge Social History of Britain*, vol. 1 (Cambridge).

Kerber, L. (1988) 'Separate Sphere, Female Worlds, Woman's Place: The rhetoric of women's history', *Journal of American History*, LXXV, pp. 9–39.

Klingender, F.D. (1947) *Art and the Industrial Revolution* (London).

Merrill, L. (1992) *A Pot of Paint: Aesthetics on trial in Whistler v. Ruskin* (Washington).

Mort, F. (1987) *Dangerous Sexualities: Medio–moral politics in England since 1830* (London).

Müller, C. (1878) 'James Sharples und das Zertifikat der Amalgamated Society of Engineers: Studien zur Bildkultur der Britischer Gewerkschaften', PhD thesis, University of Hamburg.

Nead, L. (1988) *Myths of Sexuality: Representations of women in Victorian Britain,* (Oxford).

Poovey, M. (1989) *Uneven Developments: The ideological work of gender in mid-Victorian England* (Chicago).

Scott, J.W. (1986) 'Gender: A useful category of historical analysis', *American Historical Review*, 91.

Smiles, S. (1859) *Self-Help: Illustrations of character and conduct* (London) (revised edn London, 1860).

Surtees, V. (1981) *Diary of Ford Madox Brown* (New Haven).

Tawney, R.H. (1922) *Religion and the Rise of Capitalism: A historical study* (London).

Travers, T. (1985) *Samuel Smiles and the Victorian Work Ethic* (New York).
Vickery, A. (1993) 'Golden Age to Separate Spheres? A review of the categories and chronology of English women's history', *Historical Journal*, 36(2); pp. 383–414.
Weber, Max (1991) *The Protestant Ethic and the Spirit of Capitalism* (London).
Weeks, J. (1989) *Sex, Politics and Society* (London).

11
Posters and Images of Women in the Great War[1]

Helen Sims

By the early twentieth century, posters were an established means of communication: in entertainment, in the marketing of consumer goods and also in a political context, in the suffrage campaign. However, they were to assume a new importance when the war, which began in the summer of 1914, did not, as was hoped, end by Christmas. The First World War required a far greater mobilization of national resources than earlier conflicts, so that posters became just one element, but a very considerable element, of a growing home propaganda front; print runs of 40 000 were not unusual, and re-prints frequent.[2]

Promoters included not only government agencies like the Parliamentary Recruiting Committee and the National Service Department, but private sponsors too, including major charities such as the Red Cross, with contributions from patriotic individuals such as the commercial poster designer John Hassall and the artist Frank Brangwyn. However, despite the gradual evolution of government propaganda agencies (emerging as the Department of Information in 1917), the production of posters appears to have been a haphazard affair, often facilitated by personal contact (via business or political networks) and suggestions from printers' own in-house designers.[3]

Posters were ubiquitous in the Great War, in a society where there were far fewer visual images than today. They adorned railway stations and tram stops, public buildings, shop windows, theatres, cinemas, hotels and boarding houses (there were even seaside campaigns in the holiday season), with smaller versions on tram windows and pillar boxes, etc. Despite the apparently unsystematic (though nonetheless effective) methods of manufacture, it is possible to find common themes and shared social values within the posters, even where they originate from a variety of designers and institutions. Our perception of the Great War tends to be dominated by images of the front line, but war posters also constitute important representations of this period. As historical documents, they reveal much about the politics, particularly the gendered politics, and social attitudes of the time. Although propaganda is used to shape beliefs, it must accord with popular social values to be effective, even though the nature of the message may be subtle and not fully understood.

Michele Shover's review of the representation of women in First World War posters of Europe and America (1977) reveals basically two themes or objectives concerning women's roles in wartime,[4] which I will examine in greater detail with reference to British posters and the British context. The first objective was aimed at securing the participation of women in the war effort, including recruiting them to work in support of, and even alongside, men in the Services. But there was also an anxiety to preserve traditional, passive, 'feminine' roles (perhaps in the wake of the suffrage campaign), forming what Shover refers to as a 'neat and revealing contradiction'.[5] This resulted in the representation of women's war work in the reassuring mode of 'service, support and sacrifice'.[6] This was clearly no great departure for femininity. The second position sought to exploit an idealized image of womanhood to legitimize and justify the waging of war. Quite simply, women were used to 'sell' the war.

The first objective, securing the cooperation of women in the war effort without transgressing accepted feminine ideals, is evident in the text of posters to recruit women into the newly formed Women's Services. A Women's Army Auxiliary Corps (WAAC) poster appealed for 'Cooks, Waitresses, Clerks, Driver Mechanics, All Kinds of Domestic Workers and Women in Many Other Capacities'.[7] However, the references to 'Cooks' and 'Domestic Workers' are the most striking, since they are outlined in red (against black print elsewhere). This declaration that there was 'Fit Work for Every Fit Woman' is replicated in a Women's Royal Airforce (WRAF) poster.[8] Although the theme is 'modern', with a backdrop of aeroplanes, and a 'ripping' young woman with bobbed hair in the foreground, the vacancies are for clerks, waitresses and cooks, while 'experienced' motor-cyclists are relegated to the small print.

Like dutiful wives and daughters, servicewomen's mission was to support men; as non-combatants, their military status did not supplant their image as homemakers or domestic servants, even when some of their number took on male-identified skills like carpentry and motor mechanics. As if to emphasize the point, posters appeared towards the end of the war urging women to return to domestic service. Servicewomen had a duty to care for servicemen; as one VAD poster (by John Hassall) declared, 'You can help *him* in one hundred ways'.[9] Thus, the *Glasgow Herald* extolled the virtues of WAAC canteens for the men in France: 'To be asked by a nice, clean girl in a nice, clean apron, whether one would have tea or coffee was just like heaven.'[10] The 'Angel of the Hearth' image may also have been promoted to reassure the parents of recruits. It became necessary to deny publicly rumours of heterosexual and homosexual 'immorality' in the Women's

Services which were circulating at the time – rumours which, incidently, had little foundation in fact and could often be traced back to servicemen.[11] Lest service life (particularly overseas) should appear too dangerous for well-brought-up young women, a family image was carefully cultivated. One recruiting poster featuring Britannia keeping a proud but watchful eye, and a protective but controlling arm around a young WAAC and 'Wren'.[12] Publicity material for the women's Services portrayed administrators ('officer' would have been too military) as motherly, watching over their brood of WAACS, WRAFs or WRNS with firm but kindly discipline.

Even the recruitment of nursing auxiliaries (a sphere which did not apparently offend feminine ideals) was influenced by the concern to emphasize women's traditional roles. In a Voluntary Aid Detachment (VAD) posters, designed by a serving VAD, Joyce Dennys (one of only two women designers of war posters I came across),[13] nursing heads the appeal for volunteers, but the emphasis is still domestic, with motor drivers last on the list (Figure 11.1). This domestic image, together with the resemblance of the women in the centre to well behaved parlour maids offsets the romance of travel at the top of the poster. It was not possible to discover the details of the original commission, but as Joyce was working in the publicity department at VAD headquarters in Devonshire House at the time, it is probably safe to assume she was in touch with current Red Cross concerns regarding the type of woman they wished to attract.[14] One could also speculate whether the domestic theme of the poster was a deliberate ploy to discourage the 'lady adventurer' who was said to have irritated the Military when she packed up her dubious reputation with her nursing kit to rush off to the Boer War.[15] However, that was only the military (and press) version of events.

Other tasks, too, were designated suitable occupations for women: the Ministry of Food ran a recruiting campaign for clerical workers which declared 'The Food Question Is A Woman's Question'. Not surprisingly, posters aimed at preserving the nation's food reserves were also usually addressed to women, who were regarded as responsible for all things domestic. Even those which featured images of sailors or sinking ships implied women's responsibility for male death – once women's duty to manage the nation's food had been established.

Another example of the 'feminizing' of war work can be traced in the recurring healthy image promoted wherever women were urged to 'join up' for the war effort. One might have expected this in agricultural posters, which echoed the rural idyll of green landscapes, sunshine, fresh air and the bracing outdoor life (with the addition of a baby animal or two to appeal to a Land Girl's supposed motherly instincts). However, one can also detect the health theme in munitions and factory posters (Figure 11.2). Bright golden sunshine streams in through open doors and windows, in spacious, spotless surroundings, an ironic representation of munitions work in view of the yellow skin many TNT workers developed.[16]

Figure 11.1 VAD Poster, by Joyce Dennys

Source: Reproduced by kind permission of the Imperial War Museum.

Figure 11.2   Munitions Workers, Poster by Septimus Scott

Source: Reproduced by kind permission of the Imperial War Museum.

The Women's Services, too, reflected this image of the healthy outdoor life; another poster by Joyce Dennys (for the WRNS) exploited their marine connections (although, with the exception of one woman 'manning' a small motor boat, they never went to sea),[17] to produce a bracing and robust image of womanhood (Figure 11.3). The flourishing cow parsley in the foreground represents another symbol of physical health, and perhaps even suggested sexual innocence. There are also echoes here of nineteenth-century advertising for patent medicines, which often used 'the seaside girl type' to express youth and vigour.[18] Women's Services' publicity often stressed the benefits of camp life and medical care for physical and mental well-being. This theme of physical fitness had its roots in the changing image of nineteenth-century femininity, which demanded a healthy physique for childbearing, and now operated in a war context where the slaughter of so many young men increased eugenic concerns for the nation's stock.

Only white women featured on recruiting posters; it was not eugenically acceptable to recruit non-white women to work alongside white men. Racist imperialism went unquestioned, even when there was a desperate need for nurses in the Indian Army – particularly for Mesopotamia. Asian and mixed race women were barred,[19] and Army regulations made this explicit in 1927. There was even an attempt to influence the class mix; a Women's Land Service Corps poster asked for 5000 'educated' women, which was probably another reflection of anxieties about sexual immorality.[20]

The second theme aimed to exploit women's image to legitimize and 'sell' the war. Women were presented as helpless victims,[21] often with children clinging, passive and vulnerable, and even sexually suggestive (usually of rape). These images were presented in a context of press stories of atrocities supposedly committed by the German Army. Since women were noncombatant, men were urged that they had a duty to protect 'their' women (implying women's status as sexual possessions). The somewhat unsubtle poster which demanded (in large script) 'Have You Any Women Worth Defending?'[22] also issued the challenge 'Remember The Women Of Belgium' – a reference to stories of rape. As this was a poster aimed at the Irish market, 'Belgium' also neatly side-stepped English – Irish politics. On the mainland, men were addressed by bills which declared:

> BRITAIN is FIGHTING
> not only for the
> FREEDOM of EUROPE
> BUT TO DEFEND
> YOUR MOTHERS
> WIVES & SISTERS
> From The Horrors Of War
>
> We Must Crush This Idea
> Of 'GERMANY OVER ALL.'[23]

The references to sexual possession and sexual violation are clear.

Figure 11.3   WRNS poster, by Joyce Dennys

Source: Reproduced by kind permission of the Imperial War Museum.

The creation of this passive image had further repercussions for women. Although they themselves were firmly defined as non-combatant, women were manipulated by the government to shame men into enlisting, or to themselves take up war work to 'free' men for the front. It is sometimes argued that all women entered into this with enthusiasm, citing the 'white-feather movement' or the encouragement the Women's Social and Political Union gave to the war effort. But not all in the suffrage movement were a party to this – a significant women's peace movement existed in opposition,[24] while the white-feather movement was begun by a man (Admiral Penrose), and was originally a 'masculine' metaphor, referring to bad breeding in a game bird. However many women were swept up in this appeal, it in effect rebounded upon all women. The male war literature betrays a distinctly misogynistic streak, displayed in the writings of Richard Aldington and D.H. Lawrence, for example. Wilfred Owen originally entitled one famous war poem 'To Jessie Pope', and then, 'To a certain Poetess' before finally settling upon '*Dulce Et Decorum Est [Pro Patria Mori]*', an ironic reference to Horace.[25]

Many recruiting posters (aimed at both men and women) added to the impression that women were not merely patriotic, but war-mongering too. A WAAC poster urged: Every Woman Employed Releases a Man for the Firing Line.[26] Although some men did eventually accept the presence of women in uniform behind the lines, they initially ostracized the women and committed acts of sabotage around their work, to create the impression that women were incompetent. They also spread rumours that the women were immoral and were responsible for the high incidence of venereal disease in the lines of communication.[27] Not surprisingly, men did not appreciate being 'freed' for the front when women arrived to replace them in their (relatively) safe jobs at the rear. Women at home, too, were used in the campaign. One of the most familiar posters of this genre, 'Women of Britain Say Go!',[28] depicts both mother and wife waving from a window while the young men go off to war. Female children, too, were not exempt. The famous words, 'Daddy, what did you do in the war?'[29] are spoken by a little girl in the poster, yet the original idea was conceived by a printer who was deeply concerned as to how his little son would regard his father's 'war effort' in later years.[30] For the purposes of propaganda, the child had changed sex.

Flesh and blood images of women were seemingly not quite enough to sanitize and legitimize the waging of war. Allegorical images were also mobilized to strengthen the cause. These ranged from angelic or Madonna-like nurse figures, to classically draped matrons representing War, Victory, or Britannia. Unlike suffrage classical figures, which were intended to demonstrate the virtues women could bring to politics, ordinary women, as non-combatants, could not identify with the grand scale of the war goddesses (who were often armed); allegorical figures of this kind provided no direct role models.[31] Noticeably, Joan of Arc, with her suffrage connotations, did not figure very much in British tableaux; she was more popular in France, where her associations were nationalist rather than feminist.

The symbol women could most easily aspire to was that of the nurse-icon. The folk-memory symbol of women's contribution in the First World War appears to be the nursing VAD, and wherever women feature on war memorials (a rarity), it is as the nurse rather than the munitionette, the WAAC or the Land Girl. Jane Marcus's, drawing from Virginia Woolf, points out that the state needs women to make war, and casts them in the two crucial roles of nurse and mother,[32] which are neatly combined in Alonzo Foringer's 'Greatest Mother' – a somewhat controversial figure. (Figure 11.4) Originally produced in the United States, it crossed the Atlantic in both world wars, and was enormously popular in Red Cross fund-raising campaigns. As a depiction of both the Virgin and Child, and Mary with the body of Christ, with the statuesque Virgin towering over the diminutive soldier on a stretcher, it has been described as a powerful figure for women,[33] but I share Jane Marcus' reservations with regard to this interpretation. Rather than an icon of strength, I feel she presents a passive figure of suffering and sacrifice (all 'feminine' characteristics). She reminds women of their 'natural' destiny of motherhood, and even the power of the mother is doubled-edged, since it requires selfless devotion from women, while the power of the Madonna is wielded through intercession rather than directly. Her image demands perfection from women,[34] and her association with the nurse sanctifies nursing as a vocation, which effectively detracts from professionalism – and the payment of a proper financial reward. The image of nursing may be the stuff of saints and angels, but the real power in the hospital setting is (as it was then) held by the mainly male medical profession.

If the image of First World War posters still brings to mind only the pointing finger of Alfred Leete's 'Kitchener', this must be in part because the literature of war posters focuses largely on the male point of view. Yet an examination of posters which feature (or address) women has much to contribute to the history of the attitudes and discourses of the time. Although large numbers of women were drawn into war work, sometimes in occupations previously defined as male and even serving alongside the military, poster images reveal a determination to represent them in traditionally 'feminine' mode, as passive, nurturing and still (wherever possible) involved in tasks of a largely domestic nature. Represented as vulnerable victims and the sexual possessions of men, or viragos goading men to enlist, they were perceived as responsible for male death; while avenging allegorical figures offered too-distant unattainable roles, or re-stated woman's 'natural' destiny of motherhood and selfless devotion to men. As Shover has also demonstrated, women were still cast in the roles of 'service, support, and sacrifice'.[35]

Figure 11.4   'Greatest Mother' poster, by Alonzo Foringer

Source: Reproduced by kind permission of the Imperial War Museum.

Notes

1. The scope of this chapter is limited to Britain. While there is an extensive litera-ture on the posters of the combatant nations of the First World War, references to women (and particularly to posters addressed to women) are at best only brief. It became apparent that I would have to examine every nation's national archives to do justice to an international perspective, and so I had to be content with a search of British collections. Fortunately, an extensive record of British poster campaigns of the Great War are held in the Imperial War and Victoria and Albert Museums, to which I owe my thanks. I have also drawn from two articles which offer a femininist analysis of the roles and images constructed for women in wartime: Shover (19); Marcus (1989).
2. Dutton (1989).
3. Dutton (1989), p. 45; Haste (1977), p. 53.
4. Shover (1977), pp. 469–86.
5. Shover (1977), p. 469.
6. Shover (1977), p. 473.
7. Imperial War Museum Art Department, PST5476.
8. Imperial War Museum Art Department, PST0357.
9. Victoria and Albert Museum, E2322–1918, author's emphasis.
10. Undated extract from *Glasgow Herald*, cited in Crosthwait (1986), p. 167.
11. Crosthwait (1986), pp. 172–3; Gould (1987), pp. 114–25.
12. Imperial War Museum Art Department, PST3942. The three main women's organizations attached to the men's Services were the Women's Army Auxiliary Crops, (WAAC) the Women's Royal Airforce (WRAF) and the Women's Royal Naval Service (WRNS). But women were never enlisted – they remained civilians. All three organizations were disbanded after the war.
13. Imperial War Museum Art Department, PST3268. Joyce Dennys trained at the London art school of the noted poster designer, John Hassall, before joining the Voluntary Aid Detachment (VAD). VADs were trained in first aid and simple nursing skills, but in practice were more often involved in domestic tasks than nursing. A few (already trained drivers and mechanics) were able to become ambulance drivers. The records of the Red Cross Archive at Barnet Hill indicate that Joyce was transferred to Headquarters at Devonshire House, London, to work on publicity. She was therefore familiar with Red Cross recruiting policy, although the original instructions for the design of the poster have yet to be found. An archive of Joyce's very eventful life is held at the Fairlynch museum, Budleigh Salterton, Devon.
14. An interesting letter from VAD headquarters to the National Service Department (marked 'private and confidential') indicates just how careful was 'the selection of only suitable women' for VAD work. Each applicant was required to provide four references, including one from 'a lady who had known her at least five years as to character' (Public Record Office, NATS/11267).
15. Summers (1988), p. 198.
16. Woollacott (1994), p. 81 (the title of this monograph is taken from a poster aimed at munitionettes).
17. Imperial War Museum Department of Photographs, Plate Q19727 shows Mrs Gerard Barnes, WRNS motor-boat driver, with her dog. The pair make an eye-catching publicity photograph.
18. Richards (1990), p. 241.

19. Imperial War Museum, Department of Sound Records (9523/3) interview with Eunice Lemere-Goff, who nursed in India and Mesopotamia.
20. Bayes, W.J., Victoria and Albert Museum, E885.
21. Gallo (1989), p. 134; Shover (19), p. 484.
22. Imperial War Museum Art Department, PST0357.
23. Imperial War Museum Art Department, PST5084.
24. Tickner (1987).
25. Gilbert (1987), pp. 197–226. Although some of Jessie Pope's poetry could be interpreted as jingoistic, she was by no means the only writer in this vein – many men also wrote with patriotic fervour.
26. Imperial War Museum Art Department, PST6240.
27. The Report of the Commission of Enquiry appointed by the Ministry of Labour, Women's Army Auxiliary Corps in France (1918) not only exonerated the women, but identified disgruntled male soldiery as the source of the slander.
28. Imperial War Museum Art Department, PST2763 Paret *et al.* (1992) describes this tactics as 'the mobilisation of shame' (xii).
29. Imperial War Museum Art Department, PST311.
30. Darrocott (1974).
31. Shover (1977), p. 64.
32. Shover (1977), p. 477 emphasizes the power of the woman's figure over the helpless man. Marcus (1989), p. 64, contests this and Jones and Howell (1972) even refer to the Greatest Mother as a 'monstrous damp figure of useless compassion' (p. 119).
34. Warner (1976).
35. Shover (1977), p. 473.

Bibliography

Primary sources

Archives of:
Fairlynch Museum, Budleigh Salterton, Devon – Joyce Dennys Archive.
Imperial War Museum, Art Department (Poster Collection), Department of Sound Records (Eunice 'LeMere Goff, 9523/3), and Department of Photographs.
Public Record Office, NATS 1 – archive of National Service Department.
Red Cross Society Archive, Barnet Hill, Surrey.
Victoria and Albert Museum, Print Room.

Secondary sources

Crosthwait, E. (1986) 'The Girl Behind the Man Behind the Gun: The Women's Army Auxiliary Corps, 1914–18', in L. Davidoff and B. Westover (eds), *Our Work, Our Lives, Our Words: Women's history and women's work* (London), pp. 161–81.
Darrocott, J. (1974). *The First World War In Posters* (New York).
Dutton, P. (1989) 'Moving Images? The Parliamentary Recruiting Committee's poster campaign, 1914–1916', in *Imperial War Museum Review*, 4 pp. 43–58.
Gallo, M. (1989) *The Poster in History* (New Jersey).
Gilbert, S. (1987) 'Soldier's Heart: Literary men, literary women', in M.R. Higonnet and J. Jenson (eds), *Behind the Lines: Gender and the two world wars* (London), pp. 197–226.

Gould, J. (1987) 'Women's Military Services in First World War Britain', in M.R. Higonnet and J. Jenson (eds), *Behind the Lines: Gender and the two world wars (London)*, pp. 114–25.

Haste, C. (1977) *Keep the Home Fires Burning: Propaganda in the First World War* (London).

Jones, B. and B. Howell (1972) *Popular Arts of the First World War* (London).

Marcus, J. (1989) 'The Asylums of Antaeus. Women, war and madness: Is there a feminist fetishism?', in E. Meese and A. Parker (eds), *The Difference Within: Feminism and critical theory* (Philadelphia), pp. 49–83.

Paret, P. *et al.* (1992) *Persuasive Images: Posters of war and revolution* (New Jersey).

Report of the Commission of Enquiry appointed by the Ministry of Labour, Women's Army Auxiliary Corps in France (HMSO, 1918).

Richards, T. (1990) *The Commodity Culture of Victorian England* (California).

Shover, M. (1977) Roles and images of Women in World War I Propaganda', *Politics and Society*, 5(3), pp. 469–86.

Summers, A.(1988) *Angels and Citizens: British women as military nurses 1854–1914* (London).

Tickner, L. (1987) *The Spectacle of Women* (London).

Warner, M. (1976) *Alone of all her Sex: The myth and the cult of the Virgin Mary* (London).

Woollacott A. (1994) *On Her Their Lives Depend: Munitions workers in the Great War* (London).

Part IV

Dress and Gender Identity in Modern History

12

The Case of the Hidden Consumer: Men, Fashion and Luxury, 1870–1974[*]

Christopher Breward

'I always hold in having it if you fancy it!' sang the music hall star Marie Lloyd in the final decade of the nineteenth century, a clarion call to an unapologetic and popular consumption of luxury commodities that appears to illustrate precisely the claims made for new forms of consumer behaviour by recent investigations into the nature of late nineteenth-century consumer culture. The character of both the evidence and much of the analysis surrounding Victorian shopping practices, however, also suggests that both consumer choice and consumer pleasure were prioritized and enforced for one half of the population and either stigmatized or ignored by the other. Fashion consumption in particular has been presented by historians and social commentators as an activity defined and divided through gender difference;[1] from the late eighteenth century through to the mid-twentieth century it has been generally assumed that women consumers held the prerogative as far as choice and style in clothing and related 'luxury' commodities were concerned.

The later half of the nineteenth century presents a particularly fruitful area for research based around the construction and formation of gendered identities within the marketplace. It encompasses several areas that have been isolated as pivotal moments in a perceived history of 'mass consumption' – the rise of the department store,[2] the establishment of an organized couture and ready-made clothing industry,[3] and the culmination of a system of publicity and advertizing that redefined the role played by gender in patterns of consumption.[4] However, recent histories of late-nineteenth-century consumption have tended to concentrate on the effects any changes might have had on new constructions of metropolitan femininity.[5] The role of men as consumers within this new arena of shopping and acquisition has not yet been studied in its own right, presumably because the majority of men are assumed to have been absent from this particular sphere of activity. In the course of this chapter I therefore propose to present an overview of historiographical material drawn from a wide range of critical disciplines which offers a variety of possible methodologies that might be used to begin an analysis of historical masculine consumption habits, leading towards a tentative discussion of those areas of late-nine-teenth-century cultural and material production that describe the position of those lost Victorian men 'who shopped'.

Initially it may be worth indicating the reasons for the marginalization of masculine consumption habits by recent historical enquiry. Undoubtedly it is primarily through the discourse of 'separate spheres' that many histori-ans have attempted to structure and explain the social roles taken by men and women during the nineteenth century, defining the processes of pro-duction and consumption as, respectively, masculine and feminine. Davidoff and Hall, in their influential work *Family Fortunes: Men and women of the English middle class 1780–1850* (1987), trace the formation of separate feminine and masculine, private and public spheres which, they suggest, came to symbolize the foundation of middle-class morality, family struc-tures and domestic economy from the late eighteenth century onwards. Through their work it has become generally accepted that a concept of domestic and decorative femininity was informed by the rise of a particu-larly vehement non-conformist Protestantism which disregarded the com-plexities of a female position compromised by the mounting pressures of changing business practices and the growth of suburban segregation in favour of a simplistic spiritual vision of a pure angelic womanhood. This model, it is claimed, was enforced on the middle classes by an uncritical press until the late 1850s. Within its dictates there arose a central contra-diction between the transcendental innocence of the model wife and mother, and the demands of material display made of the domestic, fem-inine sphere by the public, masculine world.

A perceived shift in the popular construction of middle- and lower-middle-class femininity, which occurred through the 1860s as a result of changes in the structure of publishing, advertizing and retailing industries, alongside reflective renegotiations of public morality in legislation relating to areas such as divorce and prostitution, and a decline in the influence of evangelical religious strictures, suggests a refocusing of the relationship between public and private spheres.[6] The concurrent expansion of a metro-politan department-store culture, backed by advertizing and magazines, has led many recent commentators to make claims for a new feminized public sphere, revolving around the act of acquiring fashionable goods.[7] This has not necessarily involved any inference that an increased female engagement with the world of fashion magazines, advertizing hoardings, and department-store counters implied an equal sense of social and political emancipation. Indeed, Thomas Richards (1991) argues that such constructions, rather than signifying a relative freedom, enforced the division of sexual labour in which women acted as ciphers for consuming men:

Advertising managed to establish a female model for consumption without ceding the activity entirely to women. Advertisers defined consumption as an extension of the sexual division of labour enshrined in the Victorian household. Shopping was an errand to be run rather than a choice to be made, and advertising was eager to avoid identifying itself too closely with the needs and desires of women. So consumption became something that women undertook on behalf of men.[8]

Nevertheless, the pioneering selling policies of West End establishments such as Dickins and Jones, Swann and Edgar and Debenham and Freebody, building on the innovations of eighteenth- and early-nineteenth-century retailers, together with the increased availability of women's magazines to consumers other than the élite, offered a new arena of acquisition based on display and spectacle directed specifically towards women, which has been picked up by commentators such as Rachel Bowlby (1985) and Rosalind Williams (1982). The visual world of the department store, like the world of the magazine, was one that did not necessarily rely on the rationality of the market system, or predominant social and cultural ideals, and authors dealing with the circumstances and implications of its rise, while rejecting the empirical narratives of earlier writers, tend to emphasize its fantastic and other-worldly character, which sets off balance any attempt to define the material nature of consumer demand. Elaine Abelson (1989), in her work on Victorian shoplifters, states:

Women had to walk a tightrope between real needs, defined by practical use, and simulated wants created by a suggestive ambience ... confusion about what was in fact a real need or a symbolic one was encouraged.[9]

Similarly Rachel Bowlby (1985) in her study of an emergent feminized consumer culture in the late nineteenth-century novel, provides a useful analogy with the myth of Narcissus in order to explain the subjective and beguiling nature of the promotional image:

The consumer is equally hooked on images which she takes for her own identity, but does not recognise as not of her own making ... The private solipsistic fascination of the lady at home in her boudoir, or Narcissus at one with his image in the lake, moves out into the wordly public allure of *publicité*, the outside solicitations of advertising.[10]

An interpretation such as this, which aims to elucidate the commodification of fashionable images and items, draws the rhetoric of fashion into a new arena, one explicitly concerned with consumption and the burgeoning links between the definition of femininity and a new world of goods. A link that, while allowing for a degree of escapism and the forging of imagined identities, also strengthens the problematic notion of a clearly demarcated sexual division of labour driven by the engines of capitalism.

So, while historians have been relatively successful in establishing models for new forms of feminine consumption and its representation, the repercussions for an understanding of masculinity within the market place are accordingly not so positive. It is perhaps ironic that Bowlby's psychoanalytical method should take the male figure of Narcissus as a metaphor for the construction of nineteenth-century female consumption patterns, when the feminization of shopping in the nineteenth century succeeded in relegating and stigmatizing the act for men. Nowhere in the secondary literature is there any discussion of physical divisions or gender-specific activity in shopping spaces beyond the act of looking. What is required is knowledge of such basic minutiae as the amount of floor space devoted to male- and female-identified goods, the respective roles and status of men and women employed as shopwalkers, window dressers and cashiers, or the exact proportion of female to male customers. Eve Kosofsky Sedgwick (1985) proposes a series of questions arising out of the 'separate spheres' debate that begin to place the problem of the mis-placed male in focus:

> In the recent give and take between Marxist and radical feminism an important crux has been the issue of priority – chronological priority, explanatory priority or functional/teleological priority – between industrial capitalism and the male dependent family household. The following questions, coarsely formulated as they are, are among the immediate, practical feminist issues at stake in this discussion of priority. Is it men as a group, or capitalists as a class, that chiefly benefit from the modern sexual division of labour? How close is the fit between the function of the gendered family and the needs of capitalism? Is the gendered family necessary for capitalism? Will changes in one necessarily effect changes in the other and if so how?[11]

In more recent evaluations of such priorities, it is becoming increasingly important that assumptions surrounding the symbiotic relationship between men and capitalism be subjected to an analysis as equally incisive as that formerly applied to the domestic role of women. One of the ways in which such assumptions have been questioned has been through the study of the role of men within the family and the household. Margaret Marsh, for example, in her study of suburban men and masculine domesticity in late-nineteenth-century America (1990) has usefully illuminated the manner in which suburbanization, rather than simply entrapping and separating women off into an enclosed domestic sphere, also served as a forum in which men could enact some of those largely domestic and patriarchal virtues described under the Victorian notion of 'manliness', while allowing for an element of escapism and fantasy not so dissimilar from women's espousal of magazine romance and material aspirations during the same period:

> The concepts of masculine domesticity and 'manliness' were in many ways more complementary than antithetical: One might hypothesize that men, as their behavior within the family became less aloof or patriarchal and more nurturing and companiable, would develop a fantasy life that was more aggressive. The rage for football and boxing, and the reading of adventure novels, might have provided that vigorous fantasy life, masking but not contradicting masculine domesticity.[12]

In the same way, the growing importance of home decoration, household maintenance and gardening to the new suburban classes could describe a sense of traditional masculine duty, while allowing for processes of taste, choice, discrimination and discernment more commonly associated with those supposedly 'feminine' skills employed during the execution of shopping activities. Such approaches, which aim to uncover those areas of masculine experience obscured by the 'separate spheres' discourse, should not however, be read as competing with, or overturning, the groundbreaking work achieved by feminist historians. On the contrary, much of the work on masculinity shares the same preoccupations. For example, there has been a long-standing interest in historical attitudes to the physical body and its relationship to political and sexual power over the past 20 years;[13] Sara Delamont and Lorna Duffin (1978), in their pioneering work on the physical world of nineteenth-century women, used existing feminist theory to move beyond a simple model of male oppression as an explanatory device in women's history, arguing:

> that studies of the position of women frequently illustrate how women are placed in an inferior category in the predominant system of a given society compared to the men of the society. However, even after the relative position of women in the structure has been documented and established, there is another fruitful area for research. This is the whole topic of the unclear, vague and probably repressed theories which women have about the world, and perhaps even more interesting, about themselves.[14]

This kind of approach can be extended in conjunction with recent work on the structures of masculinity, itself arising from, and in part reacting to, the reductive but politically necessary agenda of first-wave feminism, which suggests a more problematic and negotiated reading of 'masculinities' rather than 'a monolithic understanding of men as agents of domination'. The notion of patriarchy is held up for scrutiny by historians such as Michael Roper and John Tosh in their collection of essays, *Manful Assertions: Masculinities in Britain since 1800* (1991) as an unhelpful explanatory term which promotes an overunified and a historical notion of masculinity as a construct, unproblematized by internal tensions, transgression and notions of difference. Similarly Jonathon Rutherford in the book *Male Order: Unwrapping masculinity* (Chapman and Rutherford, 1988),[15] although postulating a problematic understanding of patriarchy as an absolute, unchanging identity, sustained by its capacity to remain beyond question and out of sight, reveals its strategy of creating a notion of 'other' through policies of misogyny, racism and homophobia, which enslave men as well as women. Rutherford goes on to use Barthes' definition of 'myth' to explain the continuing ability of masculinity to pass itself off as natural and universal, 'free of problems', which may be useful for any attempt to define its representation and wider circulation through material goods and practices:

> Myth does not deny things, on the contrary, its function is to talk about them; simply it purifies them, it makes them innocent, it gives them natural and eternal justification, it gives them clarity which is not that of explanation but that of a statement of fact.[16]

However, to lay the blame for a marginalization of masculine material culture wholly at the door of recent cultural and gender theory would be unfair. It is undoubtedly difficult to gain access to the sorts of sources that have inspired much of the work on nineteenth-century feminine culture and consumption that relate exclusively to the consuming activities of men. Men's magazines of the same period, alongside more general family journals which included the promotion of masculine sartorial choice and presentation, remain unthumbed and untheorized, if indeed they ever existed in quantities large enough to compare with the contemporary explosion of women's magazines and catalogues. The representation of Victorian masculinity in popular periodicals, when it has been addressed, has tended to include only the 'respectable' examination of formations of empire,[17] public school education,[18] religion and sport,[19] precisely because these were the images that presumably carried the greatest currency for publishers and male consumers. Male dress and objects associated with grooming or the cultivation of a personal identity have, as a result, been overlooked, subsumed in the assumption that a discourse of separate spheres, whilst constructing display and dress as innately feminine pursuits, enforced a model of masculinity in which overt interest in clothing and appearance automatically inferred a tendency towards unmanliness and effeminacy. Such simplistic interpretations have been used to explain the rise of those ultra-conservative, non-expressive male dress codes that prioritized the uniformity of the city suit as a model for the respectable middle classes for most of the nineteenth and twentieth centuries. What they cannot do is explain the ways in which men also consumed fashion. Whilst the *Flâneur* of the 1850s, the Aesthete of the 1880s and the Dandy of the 1890s have received particular historical scrutiny from art history, fashion history and literary criticism through to gay studies,[20] the more typical consumption patterns and aspirations of the middle- and lower-middle-classes male have yet to receive adequate attention.

As a form of suggestive conclusion, it may be useful to indicate those areas of cultural and material production around which it should be possible to begin a deconstructive procedure equal to that lavished on femininity and fashion consumption (though much of that work remains to be completed and is outside of the remit of this chapter). As stated, evidence of masculine shopping habits and attitudes is perhaps difficult to come by; fashion magazines aimed at a general, rather than an aristocratic male readership did not begin to attract publishers interest until the 1920s at least, and then only in a very limited sense. Trade journals such as *The Tailor and Cutter* and *The London Tailor*, alongside shop and wholesalers' catalogues, do provide useful evidence of a broad choice in terms of style and display, but can give little information regarding consumption patterns or domestic readership, and those popular-interest periodicals directed towards a broad male audience such as *The Field, The Illustrated Sporting and Dramatic News, The Idler*, and catering to the labouring classes, *The British Workman*, tend towards either highly specific representations of sporting and hunting attire, generalized caricatures of formal and day wear or a didactic religious condemnation of any interest in clothing whatsoever. It is little wonder then that this lack of comparable concrete material, and the overriding attention paid to feminine consumption and its representation, has in part led to a general inference that men abdicated all involvement in the world of material, fashionable pleasure to wives, mothers and daughters. However, in contrast to such claims, *carte de visite*, portrait and street photographs throughout the second half of the century betray a self-conscious and highly individual interest in cut and style by male sitters of all classes, and the advertizing columns of journals and newspapers are filled with the accoutrements of male grooming, from shaving brushes to shoe polish. That public interest in fashion and its acquisition was not wholly the preserve of women is also communicated through the pages of novels, diaries, etiquette guides and tourist literature, which indicated the best shopping streets and clothing suppliers to those travelling up from the country.

To focus on the rich seam of commentary surrounding respectable working- and lower-middle-class culture, it has also been established that between 1860 and 1930 the comics and artistes of the music hall provided a loud-checked, bowler-hatted and bewhiskered icon of self-satisfied, belligerent masculinity for the 'masher' or young man around town. H.G. Wells' upwardly mobile shop-boy Kipps, for example, discovers the promise inherent in the art of dressing:

> His costume ... began to interest him more; he began to realise himself as a visible object, to find an interest in the costume-room mirrors and the eyes of the girl apprentices. In this he was helped by counsel and example. Pearce, his immediate senior, was by way of being what was called a masher, and preached his cult. During slack times grave discussions about collars, ties, the cut of trouser legs, and the proper shape of a boot toe, were held in the manchester department. In due course Kipps went to a tailor, and his short jacket was replaced by a morning coat with tails. Stirred by this, he purchased at his own expense three stand-up collars to replace his former turn-down ones. They were nearly three inches high, higher than those Pearce wore, and they made his neck quite sore, and left a red mark under his ears.[21]

At the same time the neatly trimmed, tightly suited and primly booted bon-viveur offered an alternative model of 'swelldom' to the rising sons of newly affluent districts such as Holloway and Peckham, satirized most memorably by the figure of Lupin in the Grossmith's 'Diary of a Nobody', published periodically in *Punch* magazine during the 1890s as a lampoon on the pretentions of suburban North Londoners. Peter Bailey in his study of the music hall swell song, describes the precise but multiple attractions that figures like George Leybourne's 'Champagne Charlie' conveyed to such audiences from the late 1860s onwards. On the one hand, the appearance of the performer often verged on caricature:

> Dress and bearing were of central importance. The stage swell paraded all the apparatus of genteel apparel, though variation and distortion were common where the object was parody. Thus Arthur Lloyd often performed in bizarre dress and make up, sporting a coat with exaggerated lapels, an outlandish silk choker and a forty Cardigan power moustache. In his song the dancing swell, Harry Liston was reported as wearing 'a pair of unmentionables [trousers] which no one outside of Hanwell [an asylum] would think of putting on ... ' trousers were inherently comic, particularly where their incumbent suffered for fashion's sake. 'How did you get those trousers on and did it hurt you much?' sang George Leybourne in his Comet of the West.[22]

Whilst on the other hand Bailey suggests that the very physicality of music hall spectacle, combined with the emulative appeal of many of the songs, encouraged an attention to sartorial presentation amongst the predominantly male audience:

> The music hall was in one respect quite literally the mirror of fashion. From its early days the music hall had made extensive use of mirror glass, a feature inherited from the gin palace. As well as providing a greater illusion of space and comfort, the mirrors made for an increased self consciousness of bearing and appearance. 'All round the hall', remarked a review of the refurbished Middlesex in 1872, 'handsome mirrors reflect the glittering lights, and offer abundant opportunities for self admiration.' As the lion comique paraded his fashionable self on stage, members of his audience could with a sidelong glance decide how their image matched up to that of their hero.[23]

It is perhaps no coincidence that these are physical descriptions which tally closely with contemporary representations of department-store ambience in their emphasis on qualities of luxury and display, more usually identified with spaces for female as opposed to male consumption.

Such suggestive work shows how it is possible to begin to prise a notion of self-conscious, popular, masculine fashionability from the dress codes and architecture of elements of organized, indeed commodified working-class and lower middle-class culture. The middle-class male arguably faced a more problematic discourse of fashionable masculinity, which while focusing on the external healthiness and physical glory of the male body, demanded a rigorous attention to structures of self-denial, difficult to maintain in an arena of expanded consumer choice. Advances in the science of tailoring, coupled with a proliferation of cheap, machine woven, wool cotton mixes, sweated labour and a system of modern retailing typified by the replacement of old slop sellers with new clothiers and outfitters adept at the latest advertizing skills, offered a growing market the prospect of increasingly sophisticated ready-made suits alongside a continuing emphasis on British bespoke tailoring. A wide range of subtly varying styles were available for consumption with an almost fetishistic attention to detail and differentiation in terms of trimming, texture, colour and cut, and a finish indicative of modernity and the luxury of an industrial age. The adoption of occasion-specific styles ranging from the severe frock coat through to the loose, unwaisted paletot or lounge jacket, to the box-pleated and back-belted Norfolk, by a variety of middle class consumers besides the rich, the young and the cosmopolitan, do not lend much weight to explanations which prioritize the self-denying aspects of nineteenth-century manliness, but suggest the existence of a carefully honed, highly detailed sartorial rhetoric around which men were able to construct individual, yet conventional identities, adapted for the office, workshop, sports field, theatre and sea front. H. Dennis Bradley presented a typically rigid, though self-consciously modern guide for fashionable dressing in his catalogue for the Bond Street tailoring firm Pope and Bradley:

> Worn alike by all classes, the necessity of having one's lounge suits well cut is obvious. The subtle details which elevate the expert cutter to a plane above the lesser lights of his profession are never more pronounced than in this important garment … For Town wear it is always advisable to have a fairly well-shaped coat with the waistline defined without being in anyway accentuated. Tweeds for country and knockabout wear should have a more négligé effect. Any extreme fashion is entirely out of keeping with the character and term of a 'lounge' [see Figure 12.1].[24]

It may not be too far-fetched to suggest that such a reading can traverse barriers of work and pleasure to incorporate a gendered appreciation of the qualities of tailoring; Davidoff and Hall (1987), for example, imply that certain areas of leisured cultural activity such as collecting, labelling and classifying, were prioritized for men in the sphere of the connoisseur and curator, whilst being demoted for women to the realm of the domestic chore or trivial hobby.[25] A hidden language of clothing demanding the 'connoisseur's eye' may have released male fashion from accusations of effeminacy, a closer examination of its grammar and meaning would certainly allow for a more searching and innovative investigation of the status

Figure 12.1   'The Lounge' suit, c. 1895

Source: Drawn by S. Rouillard.

of male clothing as a socially constructed 'object', producing shared meaning between men, than the culturally simplistic explanations offered by traditional dress history. If anything, rather than signifying the much quoted 'great masculine renunciation', or male rejection of style change and sartorial expression, the self-denying rhetoric of tailoring journals and etiquette manuals actually reveals a rigorous attention to rules and details of dress which in itself constitutes an alternative fashion system. E. Cheadle, writing in 1872, suggests that behind the silence often associated with discussion of men's fashion, lies a wealth of hidden information:

> of course it will be thought that there cannot be much to say about the toilets of gentlemen, since they are supposed never to think about dress, nor talk about it, and rarely to change their fashions. I have said very little about them yet it is true, but the subject is by no means a barren one ... I could write pages to show how in every age the art of dress has been one of the leading studies of the masculine mind.[26]

Similarly, the author of 'Clothes and the Man' implies that whilst a slavish devotion to fashionable detail is the unmanly concern of the fop, all men owe some responsibility to the unwritten, but complicated rules of restrained fashionable deportment:

> Some men object to having their clothes made well and fashionably, partly because they consider that to dress badly is a sign of intellectual superiority, and partly because they think that they show their independence by refusing to conform to the laws of fashion. They might as well go in for a course of commandment breaking, and then think they have done something original.[27]

Nevertheless, research in the social and cultural formation of masculinity has stressed the pressure which models of ideal manhood placed on Victorian men, and which may have countered a less complicated relationship with the acquisition and display of fashionable dress. Graham Dawson (1991), in his work on images of the exotic and formations of masculinity in the inter-war years, has suggested ways in which ideal role models, communicated through the fictions of popular literature, painting and film can have a very concrete effect on the material choices and attitudes that men take up, and vice versa, proposing a relationship between masculinity and its models that is apparently much more self-fulfilling and much less imposed from without than feminine equivalents:

> Masculine identities are lived out in the flesh but fashioned in the imagination ... an imagined identity is something that has been 'made up' in the positive sense of active creation but has real effects in the world of

everyday relationships, which it invests with meaning and makes intelligible in specific ways. It organises a form that a masculine self can assume in the world (its bodily appearance and dress, its code of conduct and means of relating) as well as its values and aspirations, its tastes and desires.[28]

The two central ideological models that underpinned official nineteenth-century attitudes to masculinity, were the historically based concepts of platonism and chivalry. Through recourse to the justifying power of historical precedent, concepts as diverse as the supremacy of 'pure' male friendship over heterosexual marriage, the spiritual beauty of the exercised male physique, codes of chivalric behaviour intended to protect and nurture the frail and feminine, muscular Christian exhortations to celibacy and crusading concepts of imperial might, could become embedded in popular definitions of manliness through such institutions as the public school, the church, the army and the club. The figure of the knight and the athlete constantly recur in elements of Victorian culture, both high and low.[29] The power that such concepts held in maintaining the status quo both undermined and supported attitudes towards fashionable masculinity, pathologizing an 'unseemly' personal interest in appearances as evidence of inversion, especially after the Wilde trials of 1895, the sensationalist reporting of which, combined with concurrent attempts by the medical and legal professions to define the distinctiveness of sexual behaviour, has been shown by historians following Foucault, to have branded on the public consciousness stock images of masculine normality and perversion.[30] At the same time, ironically, supposedly normative forms of masculinity celebrated a culture of shared power through what Eve Kosofsky-Sedgwick (1985) would term 'homosocial kinship', which laid emphasis on the physical body through a rhetoric of sportsmanship and the purity of health. A pamphlet of 1877 delivered to the Victoria Street Church Young Men's Literary Society, Derby, makes the contradictions explicit:

> Manliness is not an affair of patent leather boots, or of fine clothes, or of tight fitting kid gloves, or of exquisite beard and moustache ... Conventionalism is not manliness, foppery is not manliness ... Manly character is the grandest thing beneath the stars. And the day will dawn upon this sorely confused world of ours when the highest places will be filled by men, and the only nobility will be the nobility of manly character ... It is the thing of greatest worth in God's sight. It is the temple in which he dwells.[31]

However, as in the complicated relationship between the reactionary and the hallucinatory in accounts and representations of nineteenth-century women's fashion consumption, the lectures of clerics, headmasters and editors should not be read as a literal reflection of the actual consumption habits and aspirations of all nineteenth-century men. There is just enough evidence, though most of it has not been properly digested, to suggest a thriving, though problematized engagement with notions of a mainstream masculine fashionability. The resounding silences and denials proffered by both trade publications and moralizing pamphlets in themselves speak of a vigorously contested arena of sartorial choice. Hopefully a more sophisticated reading of representational material, combined with a wider investigation of the material context of menswear production and retailing, will help to flesh out the aspirations, tastes and opinions of those men who, against the odds of all those received notions concerning the place of masculinity within consumer culture and a family based economy, might have agreed with Marie Lloyd's proposal that 'a little of what you fancy does you good'.

Notes

I would like to thank John Styles, Madeleine Ginsburg, Deborah Sugg, James Ryan, Tim Barringer, Louise Purbrick, David Peters Corbett, Naomi Tarrant, Penny Sparke and Frank Mort for comments, suggestions and support received during ongoing research into clothing and nineteenth-century masculinity.

1. Veblen (1899).
2. Adburgham (1981), pp. 137–48.
3. Levitt (1986).
4. McCracken (1990); Campbell (1987).
5. Williams (1982).
6. Trudgill (1976).
7. Wilson (1991), pp. 58–60.
8. Richards (1991), p. 206.
9. Abelson (1989), p. 35.
10. Bowlby (1985).
11. Kosofsky-Sedgwick (1985), pp. 135–6.
12. Marsh (1990), p. 122.
13. Gaines and Herzog (1990).
14. Delamont and Duffin (1978).
15. Rutherford (1988).
16. Barthes (1972), p. 143.
17. MacKenzie (1984).
18. Mangan (1981).
19. Mangan and Walvin (1987).
20. Steele (1988); Gagnier (1987), pp. 67–95.
21. Wells (1993), p. 37.
22. Bailey (1986), p. 59.
23. Bailey (1986), p. 61.
24. Bradley (1912), p. 22.
25. Davidoff and Hall (1987), p. 443.
26. Cheadle (1872), p. 84.

27. Major (1900), p. 18.
28. Dawson (1991), p. 118.
29. Girouard (1981); Turner (1981).
30. Sinfield (1994).
31. Crosby (1877), p. 14.

Bibliography

Abelson, E. (1989) *When Ladies go a Thieving: Middle class shoplifters in the Victorian department store* (Oxford).

Adburgham, A. (1981) *Shops and Shopping 1800–1914* (London).

Bailey, P. (1986) 'Champagne Charlie: Performance and ideology in the music hall swell song', in J.S. Bratton (ed.), *Music Hall: performance and style* (Oxford).

Barthes, R. (1972) *Mythologies* (London).

Bowlby, R. (1985) *Just Looking: Consumer culture in Dreiser, Gisssing and Zola* (London).

Bradley, H.D. (1912) *Vogue* (London).

Campbell, C. (1987) *The Romantic Ethic and the Spirit of Modern Consumerism* (Oxford).

Cheadle, E. (1872) *Manners of Modern Society* (London).

Crosby, W. (1877) *Manliness: An address delivered to the Victoria Street Young Men's Literary Society*, Derby (London).

Davidoff, L. and C. Hall (1987) *Family Fortunes: Men and women of the English middle class 1780–1850* (London).

Dawson, G. (1991) 'The Blond Bedouin', in M. Roper and J. Tosh, *Manful Assertions: Masculinities in Britain since 1800* (London).

Delamont, S. and L. Duffin (1978) *The Nineteenth Century Woman: Her cultural and physical world* (London).

Gagnier, R. (1988) *Idylls of the marketplace: Oscar Wilde and the Victorian public* (Aldershot), pp. 67–95.

Gaines, J. and C. Herzog (1990) *Fabrications, Costume and the Female Body* (London).

Girouard, M. (1981) *The Return to Camelot, Chivalry and the English Gentleman* (New Haven).

Kosofsky-Sedgwick, E. (1985) *Between Men: English literature and the homosocial desire* (Washington, DC).

Levitt, S. (1986) *Victorians Unbuttoned* (London).

MacKenzie, J.M. (1984) *Propaganda and Empire: The manipulation of British public opinion, 1880–1960* (Manchester).

Major of 'Today' (1900) *Clothes and the Man, Hints on the Wearing and Caring of Clothes* (London).

Mangan, A. (1981) *Athleticism in the Victorian and Edwardian Public School* (Cambridge).

Mangan, A. and J. Walvin (1987) *Manliness and Morality: Middle-class masculinity in Britain and America, 1800–1940* (Manchester).

Mardh, M. (1990) 'Suburban Men and Masculine Domesticity 1870–1915', in M.C. Carnes and C. Griffen (eds), *Meanings for Manhood: Constructions of masculinity in Victorian America* (Chicago).

McCraken, G. (1990) *Culture and Consumption* (Indianapolis).

Richards, T. (1991) *The Commodity Culture of Victorian England: Advertising and spectacle 1851–1914* (London).

Roper, M. and J. Tosh (1991) *Manful Assertions: Masculinities in Britain since 1800* (London).

Rutherford, J. (1988) 'Who's That Man?', in R. Chapman and J. Rutherford (eds), *Male Order: Unwrapping masculinity* (London).

Sinfield, A. (1994) *The Wilde Century: Effeminacy, Oscar Wilde and the queer moment* (London).

Steele, V. (1988) *Paris Fashion* (Oxford).

Trudgill, E. (1976) *Madonnas and Magdalenes* (London).

Turner, F. (1981) *The Greek Heritage in Victorian Britain* (New Haven).

Veblen, T. (1899) *The Theory of the Leisure Class: An economic study in the evolution of institutions* (London).

Wells, H.G. (1993) *Kipps* (London).

Williams, R. (1982) *Dream Worlds: Mass consumption in late nineteenth century France* (California).

Wilson, E. (1991) *The Sphinx in the City* (London).

13
Dressed to Kill: Clothes, Cultural Meaning and First World War Women Munitions Workers*

Angela Woollacott

Clothing has much to offer as a subject for cultural analysis. Clearly used by humanity as a language of symbolism and communication beyond its practical and economic purposes, clothing allows us to read what people want to tell others about themselves as well as what culture, social systems and eroticism elaborate. The very words 'to clothe' and 'clothes' have become a pervasive metaphor for both value systems and collusion to mask them, the latter often through the particular metaphor of 'the emperor's new clothes'. For the historian, clothing presents a tantalizing dilemma: scholars who have written about fashion insist that changes in fashion cannot be simply and directly read as representing historical events such as war,[1] but, as a form of cultural, artistic and social expression, clothing is too good a subject matter not to mine for cultural history. Elizabeth Wilson (1987) has asserted that 'Fashion is obsessed with gender, defines and redefines the gender boundary.'[2] My interest here is mostly not in fashion but because, like fashion, clothing itself is a cultural marker of the gender boundary, I want to investigate the coexistence of multiple cultural and historical meanings of the clothing of one cohort of women, and thus to discover what we can learn from them.

In this chapter I wish to suggest that for British society in the First World War, the public discussion of and debate over women munitions workers' clothing was a forum in which anxieties over the destabilizing effects of the war, particularly in terms of gender and class relationships, were expressed. Women's clothing became a culturally agreed-upon subject about which people could identify changes caused or accelerated by the war and ways in which women were transgressing against class-specific ideals of femininity.

Mary Louise Roberts (1994) has asserted in relation to late-war and post-war France that:

> Debate concerning gender identity became a primary way to embrace, resist, or reconcile oneself to changes associated with the war … [T]o make these changes comprehensible, [French men and women] focused on a set of images, issues, and power relationships that were both familiar and compelling. For many French men, it was simpler to think about the dramatic shifts in their wives's [*sic*] behavior or in women's fashion than it was to seek to understand something as abstract as the fall of the franc or the decline of the middle class.[3]

In Britain, I submit, focusing on women munitions workers' clothing was a simple and direct way to seek to circumscribe women's wartime autonomy and the potential changes that women with a desire for skilled or semi-skilled industrial work, higher wages and greater physical and social freedom could herald for post-war society. Besides the discourse surrounding women workers' clothing, I want to focus on how women workers themselves generated various meanings from their uniforms; the wartime significance of boots; what the public censure of women's increased expenditure on clothing represented and how women workers identified its political meanings; and finally what we can make of women's propensity to steal each other's clothes.

Uniforms

British women munitions workers' uniforms became, during the First World War, emblems of their direct involvement in the war effort. It was not only that trousers represented gender transgression; the very fact of women participating in the making of war transgressed notions of war propagation as a masculine activity.

At a time of war, uniforms carried enormous social prestige and symbolism.[4] A war-related uniform was an immediately recognizable emblem of patriotic engagement, of dedication to the nation's cause.[5] To wear such a uniform was a statement at once political and moral. But uniforms were also readable in multiple ways as signifiers of gendered behaviour and were integral to ways in which at least some women were perceived as becoming more like men.[6] The ubiquitous, publicly heralded uniform of the nurse and VAD with crisp white apron, starched headdress and red cross were emblems of patriotic dedication that represented the quintessentially feminine work of the healer and nurturer. Later in the war the uniforms of the women's paramilitary organizations, the WAAC, the WRNS and the WRAF, challenged traditional gender assumptions by signifying women's attachment, albeit in service positions, to the armed forces (see also chapter 11 in this volume). Earlier in the war other occupations had similarly represented gender transgression: the much-noted trousers of the Women's Land Army,[7] and the blue uniforms of the newly created women police, which included skirts but were otherwise so like policemen's uniforms that they were immediately identifiable as the women patrolled streets and public places claiming official authority in matters of public order that had previously been a male preserve.

Wartime uniforms allowed for various sorts of gender transgression. The English woman who cut her hair, donned 'an absolutely correct military aviator's uniform', found a plane, and flew in chase of a squadron at Dijon 'so that she might serve France like all her compatriots' captured national publicity for her overt challenge to the exclusion of women from the armed forces.[8] Similarly Flora Sanders, by attaining the rank of Sergeant-Major in the Serbian army and adopting a male officer's uniform, became one of the highly visible cross-dressers of the war.[9] Certainly there must have been other cases of cross-dressing.[10] We know of one at least among munitions workers. The fact that Charles Brian Capon, wireworker, was really Ellen Harriet came to light only when Capon/Harriet turned 18 and was called up. The fact that Capon was walking out with a young woman, as was stated in *The Times'* new story, compounded the gender confusion by adding an issue of sexuality.[11]

Munitions workers' uniforms were not tailored and completely lacked spit, polish and militaristic regimentation. In use they quickly became dirty but even clean they were loose and baggy as is evident in Figure 13.1. Nevertheless these garments conveyed multiple and contradictory gendered meanings. They were recognizably the garments of women workers because they included feminine caps or headcoverings and because they usually included waisted smocks. Yet contemporary commentators noted and some condemned the ways in which uniforms undercut women's femininity. For one thing many women workers, depending at which factory they worked and what their occupation was, wore trousers or puttees (cloth bound round the legs).[12] The very fact of women wearing trousers, even under loose-fitting kneelength smocks or overalls, constituted transgression against femininity that was satirized in the pages of *Punch* and objected to by women (such as the few women workers who refused to wear them)[13] and men alike. G.F. Wilby, an ambulance driver in East Africa, harangued and threatened his fiancee Ethel in his letters home to her, about the unwomanliness of doing munitions work especially in trousers:

I hope you don't wear trousers on your job, Sweetheart, – I think its [*sic*] so disgusting. – & I hope you will never put such things on, anyway if you do, don't ever let me see you in them, take them off before you come into my sight. – otherwise I shall pull them off you, & I shan't be at all gentle about it neither. & whatever you do, don't lose your

Figure 13.1 *The Munition Girls*, by Stanhope A. Forbes. This painting, depicting women forging 4.5 inch shells at the Kilnhurst Street Works of John Baker & Co. Ltd, Rotherham, was commissioned by the company in 1918 in honour of the women workers, each of whom was presented with a framed lithographic copy.

Source: Reproduced by courtesy of the Science Museum, Science & Society Picture Library, London.

womanly little ways or nature, – I Love you because you are such a perfect little woman, & the only reason why I wanted to keep you out of Munition-work was because I thought you might develop [*sic*] coarse, manly ways, – You were my ideal of a Loveable little woman when last I saw you, & I want to come back & find the same ideal little woman that I left behind.[14]

Even when they did not include trousers, munitions workers' uniforms transgressed gender boundaries. As emblems of women's direct engagement in the propagation of war (and munitions workers were immediately involved in the war effort through their manufacture of weapons and ammunition), munitions uniforms represented women's status as belligerents. The public face of this female participation in a domain gendered masculine included the celebration of munitions workers' contributions in the press, in ceremonies such as the frequent royal visits to munitions factories, and the awarding of medals to munitions workers wounded or killed at work. The munitions worker's uniform was so widely represented in the press that it became a recognized cultural icon.[15]

But there was a private dimension to the meaning of munitions workers' uniforms, as symbolizing patriotic effort and group identity, as well. Two munitions workers' weddings illustrate the pride which they took in their uniforms and the meanings of shared effort and loyalty with which they were invested. In December 1916 a worker married her soldier in her munitions overalls while a party of her workmates also wore theirs to the wedding.[16] In September 1918 a munitions worker bride was attended by 24 of her workmates all in their 'white smocks and trousers' who 'pulled the taxicab from the church to the bride's home', a feat which demonstrated not only their pride in their uniforms but their obvious pride in their patriotic work and their physical strength.[17]

Coexisting with these public and private symbolic meanings of uniforms as recognizable artifacts were the ways in which women workers subverted the very uniformity of their uniforms. The fact that there was a great range of colour, design and style among women munitions workers' uniforms was commented on by most observers of factory life. The variety was in part that of the range of possibilities among which factory managers and welfare supervisors could choose; given the number and geographical distribution of munitions factories around Britain, it is hardly surprising that there was variation. Moreover, within any factory variation of style and colour was deliberately used to indicate differences of rank,[18] different tasks and belonging to different work units within the factory. For example at the Phoenix Dynamo Manufacturing Company in Bradford, where the welfare supervisors apparently consulted the women workers in choosing their factory uniforms, one shop voted for trousers and tunic in sage green, whereas another chose the same design but in blue drill with red piping on their matching cap.[19]

But transposed on the planned variations were the ways in which women workers wilfully subverted their uniforms. It became one of the oft-noted facts of the war that women adapted their uniforms to their own whim or choice. The workers at this same company could apparently turn the same cap into what a journalist called 'many bewitching forms', due to their 'feminine individuality':

> one girl, with thoughts upon some occupant of the trenches, dons it
> with a stiff and formal military set, and struts. The coquette gives the
> brim an upward curl, adjusts it to her head at a provocative angle, and
> invites your approval.[20]

The fact that some women chose *not* to wear their protective caps was often cited as the reason for industrial accidents, particularly women being scalped when their hair caught in the machinery. Their reluctance to button up their overalls to a tight closure at the neck, to wear their caps properly and to wear face masks when provided was often claimed to be part of the reason for the pervasiveness of the TNT poisoning which injured and killed many women. But their adaption of their uniforms was also noted in less serious contexts: journalists frequently commented on their desire for colour and adornment (particularly with flowers)[21] and their fashionable touches of style. Arnold Bennett admired the projectile factory workers in 'peg-top trousers', calling them

> piquant creatures [who] start with two minute points near the ground, and very often finish near the top with an elaborate white lacy corsage or a flowing, glowing scarf;

he was especially taken with the

> girl-checker delicately rolling a nine-inch shell over with her fashionable glacé-kid boot that peeped out beneath the yellow overall.[22]

The cumulative impression from such accounts is of a wilful cohort of women who resisted the uniformity of their factory garb and asserted their choice of style as far as they could.

Style was not always a matter of individualism, however. One way in which women workers proclaimed their group loyalty to their workmates in their own shed, factory, or work process, was through mutually agreed-upon styles of clothing or adornment. For example at the Georgetown Filling Factory outside Glasgow, the workers in the 'Disintegrating House' opted for wearing white stockings whereas the 'ladies of the I.G.A.' chose diamond-checked hose.[23] Similarly women workers claimed their group of shift loyalty through the lyrics they made up for the songs they frequently sang as they worked, such as the shell-filling workers who sang:

> If you want the powder girls/Hard at work you'll find them; But if you want the assembling girls/I'm hanged if you can find them.[24]

This group or unit loyalty, forged through proximity and shared shifts, was not unlike the sense of cohort that soldiers evinced. For women workers, many of whom were new to the massive work environments of wartime factories, creating fashions which identified themselves as belonging to a recognizable group may also have been, as Elizabeth Wilson (1987) has suggested about one role fashion plays in modern industrial society, a form of social connection and identity in response to fears of loneliness or annihilation.[25]

What we can learn from these various aspects of women munitions workers' uniforms is that they held various meanings for the women themselves, for those who observed them, and for British wartime culture. Uniforms held no one overarching gendered meaning, but rather were the vehicles for multiple enacted and coexisting meanings, exemplifying Judith Butler's (1990) notion of gender itself as performative, consisting of 'articulated and enacted desires'.[26] In this context, clothes simultaneously signified that women were performing work previously considered men's, and producing munitions of war essential to its propagation; that factory welfare supervisors were providing women with uniforms to protect them from work processes, in one dimension of an innovative female-specific industrial welfare programme; that at least some women workers were wearing trousers and thus overtly adopting a masculine appearance; and that women were wont to trim and adapt their uniforms for personal adornment and group identity.

Public censure of women workers' spending on clothes

The powerful symbolism of uniforms was probably the inspiration for a fashion among women of high-topped boots during the war. Boots were the subject of much wartime commentary. Partly this was because boots and shoes were very expensive items for workers' budgets; poor people, especially children, in pre-war years had often gone barefoot. The marked rise in the standard of living in poor neighbourhoods during the war was often measured by the fact that workers' children were far better shod than before the war.[27] Women workers commonly used their increased earnings buying shoes or boots for themselves.[28] But the style of high-legged boots was not just a product of newfound income, it was also a wartime fashion that was linked to the shortening of skirts and to the high boots which were part of military uniform.[29] This fashion consisted of boots that were 10–15 inches from the heel up, and led to many women asking bootmakers to affix extra inches of leather or fabric to boots they already had. The expense of high-legged leather boots meant some women chose fabric ones instead.[30]

The manufacture and sale of high-legged boots for women were banned in early 1918 by the Army Council in order to control the supply of leather and other materials. While this was no doubt a practical measure, it had the effect of outlawing a militaristic and therefore masculine fashion which women had adopted; it can therefore be read as an attempt to control gender transgression. When *The Times* reported the news of the Army Council order, it editorialized that this

> will affect only a certain number of women who cannot expect much sympathy, as the object of their high boots, worn all through the summer, was obviously vanity rather than warmth.

'The price of these high leather boots', the paper continued

> has steadily increased. Those that reached almost to the knee have been sold for the most part in a class of shops which has sprung up since the war, like similar shops for the sale of showy blouses and ready-made costumes.[31]

Women workers were often publicly censured for the clothes and jewellery they bought during the war with their newly adequate wages. One writer noted that: 'many incline to satin and *crêpe de Chine* of vivid hues, white kid boots, ostrich plumes, and no gloves.'[32] Another observer decried the situation in Birmingham:

> many thousands of girl-workers have poured into the district since the war began from the Black Country, and even from so far away as the Channel Islands; and mere children, straight from school, can draw wages which two years ago would not have been paid to girls of eighteen ... And they are not buying *sham* jewellery; they are buying *real*; real furs, also.[33]

The public censure against women workers became so commonplace that by the end of the war a shorthand for this indictment emerged: it became enough to refer to 'munitions workers in their fur coats and jewellery' for readers or listeners to understand the full complaint about women's higher wages, their gaudy tastes which revealed their lack of respectability and their cheeky flaunting of their new-found income which was tantamount to a statement that they did not care what the middle and upper classes thought, nor were they going to be subservient and return immediately to the domestic-service positions they had left in droves. The challenge to class boundaries of women workers' higher quality clothes is represented in Figure 13.2 by the 'munition girls' who in 1919 recognize a friend in Stanhope Forbes' painting at Burlington House, a sanctuary of high culture. The political subtext to the censure was especially obvious during the process of demobilization, when references to public protests by women munitions workers against their firing often included the recognized discourse about fur coats and flashy dressing in such ways as to convey both returning men workers' sense of outrage that women might be continuing to hold jobs that they considered their preserve, and middle- and upper-class anger that women workers were not showing an immediate desire to return to the domestic-service positions where their social superiors wanted them.[34]

The censuring of women munitions workers for their spending on clothes constituted a wartime discourse that ought to contain the

206

Figure 13.2   Recognition at Burlington House: *The Munition Girls'*, *The Bystander* (21 May 1919), p. 463. Stanhope Forbes' painting *The Munition Girls* was exhibited at the Royal Academy summer exhibition in Burlington House in 1919. I am indebted to the Science Museum for the reference to this cartoon which they exhibit underneath the painting. However, their mistaken contention that the cartoon depicts 'a couple of society girls' who recognized two of the figures in the painting as 'studio models' is very telling; they have been misled by *The Bystander's* representation of these two 'munition girls' high standard of dress. The apparent contradiction between the relatively expensive clothing and the women's class status (given away by their speech) is due to the cartoon's subtext of the public censure of women workers' extravagance on clothes that was so pervasive in the demobilization period. The woman on the left seems to be shown wearing the high-legged boots so fashionable during the war.

Source: Reproduced by courtesy of *The Tatler*.

challenges mounted by women in relation to both the class and the gender order. While there was a wartime sensibility that any kind of extravagance was at odds with the national mood of sacrifice, women workers were criticized by women and men of the upper- and middle-classes for buying and wearing clothes supposedly inappropriate to their social station, both because they were relatively expensive and because they did not accord with the tastes of their social superiors.[35] Reformers and welfare supervisors who worked with women maintained a constant stream of advice as to how they should dress. Typically they emphasized plainness and modesty of style and colour. The religiously motivated magazine *The War-Worker* ran a column of advice to women workers on clothing, which included such admonitions as that only tortoiseshell haircombs should be worn during the daytime and imitation diamond ones left for the evening; and that 'High white leather boots, black velvet boots, or any very theatrical high boots are really vulgar'.[36] Yet women workers were also criticized for wearing old and shabby clothes. A journalist seeking to describe the contrast in the scene outside a particular munitions factory between the six days of the week when the regular workers were there and the weekends when middle- and upper-class women came in to do relief shifts put it this way:

> The imitation fur coats, shabby from long wear, and the hats be trimmed with feathers out of curl from exposure to all weathers are replaced by useful travelling coats cut on severe lines, and beaver hats or dark-coloured felts plainly trimmed with a band of ribbon.[37]

While charges of extravagance were laid against workers of both sexes, charges of women workers' extravagance centred on their bodies. Critics seemed to fear that women workers' acquisition of more expensive clothing threatened subversion of the social order, as workers wearing the clothing of the bourgeoisie would blur the demarcation of class. Moreover, as Mariana Valverde (1989) has discussed for the Victorian period, charges of women workers wearing 'finery' clearly implied sexual promiscuity; the wartime terminology and implications echoed the older discourse's contention that women of the working class who loved dress too much were on a downward path.[38]

The singling out of women workers' clothing for public discussion, reform efforts and censure occurred in a longer-term historical context in which fashion had evolved with the capitalist economic system. By the mid-nineteenth century fashion had become gendered feminine as men had eschewed fashion and opted for a limited, more slowly changing range of clothing styles (but see Chapter 12 in this volume).[39] The nineteenth-century equation of fashion with bourgeois women meant that women of the working class were measured against middle-class norms, and were thus easily judged to be either disreputably at variance with accepted styles, or as reaching for personal adornment above their social station. Some women workers, at least, recognized the political dimensions to the criticism and advice to which they were subjected. They fought back by naming it and pointing out how unreasonable, and indeed illogical, it was. A woman who signed herself 'A Munition Girl' expressed her 'Self-Defence' thus:

I am not in ignorance of all the censure which is levelled at me by some people for what is called my reckless extravagance in dress ... Perhaps it is a very discreditable thing to long for pretty clothes. If so, the whole race of womankind is imbued with discreditable longings ...

Those who point the finger of scorn at me seem to be utterly without imagination. Let them put themselves in my place. Let them realise what it means, after a life of soul-suffocation, to find oneself suddenly able to breathe free air, to see the walls of one's prison house gradually crumbling, to feel the shackles of tyranny loosening from one's feet, to taste a tiny bit of ambition realised. Ambition is the same power in every walk of life, whether it aims at world dominion or the possession of a small article of flesh-coloured crêpe de Chine ...

If I were to put every penny I make into war certificates there would still be those who considered it unseemly that I should be in the position to make such an investment. It is the old autocratic spirit, struggling in its death throes to make a last endeavour to assert itself. The same spirit which my efforts in war work are supposed to be helping to crush.[40]

The struggle here not only related to the class order, but also carried clear gender implications. Part of what commentators found so problematic is that women workers were exhibiting autonomy; they were enjoying and taking advantage of incomes which rendered them relatively free of fathers and husbands.[41]

Mary Louise Roberts (1994) has identified the *femme moderne* as the figure in French wartime and post-war culture who represented changes in women's dress and social behaviour that became equated with the destructiveness of the war itself, particularly through her sexual assertiveness, and her desire for physical and social liberation.[42] In Britain the comparable figure was the 'flapper', the trope used in the 1920s to represent the socially and sexually active young woman, particularly in the debate leading up to the equalization of the suffrage in 1928.[43] But during the war the term 'the flapper' became pervasively used to represent very young women who behaved assertively, even aggressively, in public and, most significantly for my purposes, could be immediately identified by their dress. For example in 1917 one outraged commentator railed at 'the young girls called "flappers"… with high heels, skirts up to their knees, and blouses open to the diaphragm, painted, powdered, self-conscious, ogling'.[44]

Valerie Steele has demonstrated that the shifts in fashion often associated with the flapper and the 1920s, and seen as being caused by the war, had in fact appeared as early as 1908 and were the result of the determination of Paul Poiret and other Parisian designers to challenge the importance of the corset and the narrow waistline. But, Steele points out, it is also true that there were important fashion shifts during the war, particularly shorter skirts, and the much more general acceptance of looser fitting and one-piece dresses.[45] While the causal role of the war and women's work in industry and other areas of the economy in changing dress styles is debatable, one shift from the *fin-de-siècle* period to the 1920s that has its fulcrum during the war is clear: whereas the ideal figure at the turn of the century was the mature woman with a very full bust, by the 1920s the ideal of feminine beauty was a slim, boyish figure clearly correlated to youth and emphasizing physical liberation.[46] Given this generational swing in the ideal of feminine beauty, the criticism of women workers for their wartime expenditure on clothing may well also have been partly the resentment of an older generation toward a cohort of women who were dominantly in their teens and twenties, who were daily demonstrating their physical fitness and suppleness in their work, and who therefore could be seen to represent the new feminine ideal that had begun to be valorized.

Stealing: clothing as a vehicle of self-representation

Perhaps most intriguing and difficult to interpret of the cultural meanings of women workers' clothing is what it meant to workers themselves as symbolic property. Throughout the war women workers were charged and tried for petty theft from factories and hostels. They were charged with stealing all kinds of items from money, to canteen cutlery, to the products of the factories such as cartridges and cordite.[47] But many of the cases were of stealing clothing from each other, including coats, boots, shoes, 'costumes' and even underwear.[48] One commentator noted that 'the working-girl's worst fault' was pilfering, particularly 'annex[ing] articles of clothing and adornment from one another'.[49] This practice of petty theft needs to be seen in the context of widespread comparable pre-war theft, as well as wartime theft by others such as the stealing that was notorious among soldiers at the front.[50]

But even if women workers were not alone in carrying out petty theft their particular practice of it is significant. It was physically possible for them to steal from each other in munitions factories because of the extremely crowded changing rooms or cloak rooms where the shift coming off and the shift going on were crammed in, in near succession, to change from street clothes to factory uniforms or vice versa. Commentators noted that the intense struggle of changing in these conditions meant that workers commonly lost track of their own possessions just due to the scrum;[51] some who where accused of stealing claimed that their own coat or shoes had been taken so they just took another's.[52] But purposeful theft flourished in these crowded conditions, even after women police were hired by munitions factories to check workers both on the way in and on the way out.

Fashion and style must have been strong incentives for theft, but I suggest that because clothing was an essential indicator of class and respectability for women, taking and wearing items of clothing was a way of experimenting with self-presentation and indulging in fantasy to relieve the monotony of their lives.[53] Even with their heightened wartime earnings, there was a limit to what they could afford in clothes, hats, shoes, coats and jewellery. Early in the war and in some less well-paid areas of unskilled work, poverty was a real cause of coveting another's clothing. Not uncommonly, women would turn up at (or near) work soon afterward, wearing the stolen item.[54] While it is difficult to reconstruct women's thinking about their chances of being caught or otherwise when they wore a stolen item back to the factory where they had taken it, we can at least deduce that clothing held great appeal even – or perhaps especially – when another's.

For women of the working class, clothing was the most obvious vehicle through which to express their aspirations for respectability, social status and style. For men the attainment of skilled worker status, the possession of, for example, a motorbike, physical prowess at sport or in fighting, popularity at the pub or success at gambling, were all potential indicators of social attainment. But for women clothing and personal adornment constituted the most obvious means of self-expression, respectability or social status. Clothing was the public vehicle through which they could seek self-betterment,[55] or could make themselves attractive to the men who were their avenue to the marital status which was the only form of mature achievement allowed them. With limited clothing of their own, others' coats, hats and dresses must have been extremely tempting objects all too close at hand. As Carolyn Steedman has argued in her explication of her mother's working-class Conservatism, political analysis does not yet allow 'the desire for a New Look skirt ... as a political want, let alone a proper one', nor has 'unfulfilled desire' for material goods been seen as belonging to political struggle by those who are dispossessed.[56] Perhaps the women who wore stolen clothing back to the factory from where they had taken it were acknowledging that they could not for long pretend it was their individual property; perhaps they were in a sense insisting on sharing around the items of clothing of which the women of their class had so few in comparison to those who were better off.

If on a systematic cultural level we can see clothing as related to political economy and class structure,[57] to communication, ritual, performance and art, on an individual level we can see it as related to pleasure, to fantasy, to self-expression and artistic expression. Elizabeth Wilson (1987) has suggested that fashion and clothing represent our desires, even the irreconcilable, and illuminate our dilemmas about our bodies, daily life and behaviour.[58] Perhaps for the women workers whose desires and fantasies went well beyond the bounds of wartime munitions factories, the appropriation of someone else's clothing was a way of living out a short-term fantasy, or trying on a new or alternative sense of a gendered and sexualized self.[59] It must have been one way of making livable an existence of monotonous, grinding labour that stretched indefinitely ahead of them. For those who were caught and convicted, however, the sentences they abruptly faced included fines of several pounds, being dismissed from work and sent home to their parents, being put on probation, or even several months' imprisonment.[60]

Conclusion

Part of the purpose of this chapter has been to identify the simultaneously coexistent multiple cultural meanings of the clothing of this one cohort of women. I have shown how their clothes represented various meanings to the women themselves, to others who had vested interests in their gendered social status, and to wartime British culture generally. Clearly wartime is a moment when the fluidity of gendered roles opens up possibilities for multiplying gendered meanings of material artifacts, especially in the twentieth century which has seen a long-term radical shift in the gendered meanings of waging war through the gradual inclusion of women into the status of active belligerents.

But it is important to me as a historian also to identify the specific ways in which these multiple gendered meanings of women's clothing illuminate the particular historical developments of the First World War period. Before, during and after the First World War the Victorian system of gender relations was challenged and modified by feminism, suffrage and changes in women's employment among other factors. Looking at the cultural meanings of women's clothing allows us to read indicators of contemporary understandings of gender that were broadly pervasive; women workers' clothing, in this sense, can tell us about shifts in nuances of gender that focussing on, for example, feminist political organization cannot.[61]

The condemnation of women workers' taste for fancy clothes needs to be seen in the context of changing perceptions of women's social and sexual autonomy. To cast back to the longer-term historical context, the sexual segregation of work which occurred in the industrial revolution of the late eighteenth and nineteenth centuries was accompanied by increased gender differentiation in clothing.[62] The nineteenth-century equation of feminine respectability with domesticity, and the exclusion of women workers from skilled and better-paid areas of work, were both represented in the discourse over what was and was not appropriate dress for women of the working class. Women workers who dressed in bright colours or rich fabrics or wore ostentatious ornamentation were considered to have transgressed against respectability, to have become sexually and therefore socially unrespectable.[63] While First World War women munitions workers in uniforms, especially trousers, were a challenge to gender stability because they were invoking both masculine dress and the masculine role of belligerents, the public censure of women workers for their expenditure on street clothing harked back to this nineteenth-century discourse by calling women who earned high wages *un*respectable. This wartime attempt thus to exclude women from the social autonomy that accompanied men's work and men's wages, and thereby to exclude them from men's work itself in the postwar world, was soon echoed by the inter-war condemnation of young women workers who adopted lipstick, silk stockings and other adornments associated with Hollywood glamour. Sally Alexander (1989) has identified the misogyny within the socialist condemnation of inter-war young women's appropriation of some consumer goods, in the writings of Orwell, Priestley and others.[64]

The fact that young women workers chose to spend their wages on clothing, shoes and accessories in part reflects the fact that, especially since the creation of the ideology of the male breadwinner in the nineteenth century, sexual attractiveness and marriageability constituted women's strategies for survival and success. It was significant, however, that for the first time for some women, they were buying these items with their own money and at no one else's wish or favour; this was an important experience of autonomy.[65] But what most clearly reveals the shifts in the sex–gender system during and after the war is the rancour of the class- and gender-related condemnation of young women's choice of dress. Flaunting their relative and probably temporary autonomy from wartime jobs and post-war new occupations in light industry and service areas, young women were reminded that, while they could choose and define their clothing styles, others too could impose their own meanings on them.

Notes

I thank Carroll Pursell for generous help with the research for this essay, for being convinced I should write it and for coming up with the title; and Antoinette Burton for her typically insightful comments.

1. For example Wilson (1987), p. 47.
2. Wilson (1987), p. 117.
3. Roberts (1994), pp. 5–6.

4. By 1918 *The Sphere* was convinced that

> Quite half the feminine world must be in uniform now. Even the waitresses that have replaced men-servants at many of the London clubs and restaurants have been put into livery. ('The Feminine World in Uniform', 15 June 1918, p. iv)

5. Uniforms were believed by some to have the effect of social levelling. For example, an article in the 19 August 1916 issue of *Queen* stated of munitions uniforms that: 'Social distinctions are levelled in the democracy of overalls and caps.' The fact that the relatively small number of middle- and upper-class women who worked in munitions believed that their factory uniforms were emblems of their own patriotic contributions is shown by their accounts of their wartime work in which their 'blue overalls' are recurrent images. For example Brenda Girvin, 'Good-Bye, Munitions! What the Life Has Taught Me', Imperial War Museum [hereafter IWM], Women's Work Collection, Press Cuttings, vol. 2, Women in Munition Works, 1918–19.

6. A sergeant in the Royal Flying Corps, for example, commented bitterly that

> The days are so strange now when women are doing their best to become like men in dress, smoking and drinking, that one wonders where it will ever stop. I think that women would do best to keep all that men admire, which is a womanly woman. ('A Sergeant's Letter', *Our Own Gazette* [YWCA] vol. 36 (January 1918), p. 29)

7. An example of objection to women land workers wearing trousers in 1918 is recorded in Munson (1985), p. 250.

8. 'English Girl's Exploit', *The Birmingham Daily Mail* (22 August 1914), p. 3.

9. 'The Serbian "Jeanne D'Arc"– Sergeant-Major Flora Sandes', *The Tatler* (21 February 1917), p. 233; Bullough and Bullough (1993), p. 161.

10. A 'Welsh Girl's Escapade in London', may have been another; *The Times* (17 September 1917), p. 5.

11. 'Girl's Masquerade: Two Years as a Male Worker', *The Times* (21 January 1918), p. 3.

12. For example, women shipbuilders wore trousers buckled at the ankle, short tunics and matching tight-fitting cap. This outfit was said to permit 'perfect freedom of movement in confined spaces'. Yates L.K. (1918), pp. 34–50.

13. *Punch* (2 October 1918), p. 213; an example of women objecting to wearing trousers is 'No Alternative: Girl Munition Workers and Regulation Dress', *Sheffield Weekly Independent* (31 March 1917), p. 2.

14. IWM, Department of Documents, 78/31/1 T.G.F. Wilby (3 October 1918). Mrs Wilby, interviewed decades later about her work in WWI, remembered her then fiancé's strong objections to her wearing trousers and specifically his threat to pull them off her (a violent threat, from a man whose war record implied a degree of pacifism). IWM, Department of Sound Records, 9356/2.

15. According to one writer the munitions worker's overall was widely adopted by housewives as a 'delightfully practical and artistic garment' for doing housework in. 'Overall Revolution: Munition Girls' Aid to Our Dress Resources', *Sheffield Weekly Independent* (20 April 1918), p. 6.

The political symbolism of the munitions worker's uniform was illustrated by a cartoon in *The Tatler* on 11 April 1917 (when the likelihood of women's suffrage was becoming apparent). It depicts a woman in a munitions uniform using a key marked 'national work' to unlock the door to Parliament. She has just laid aside an axe marked 'militancy' and John Bull inside the door is admonishing her that it was no good 'axeing for it' but that now she had earned it she might enter. Thus the munitions uniform was represented as a direct symbol of national citizenship; in fact, it is represented as the price of that citizenship.

16. 'Bride in Overalls', *The Banbury Guardian* (21 December 1916).

17. *The Pioneer* (Woolwich) (20 September 1918), p. 5. In a similar way, Caroline Rennles remembered that she and her workmates would run down to Beresford Square from Woolwich Arsenal to show off their uniforms and 'think we were the cat's whiskers'. IWM, Department of Sound Records, 000566/07, 17.

18. Yates, for example (1918, p. 41), noted that in some factories the colour of women workers' caps designated their status as machine operators, setters-up, overlookers or inspectors.

19. 'Humanising Industry: Notable Experiments in Bradford', *Yorkshire Observer* (30 August 1917).

20. *Ibid.*

21. '[I]n many breasts are bunches of fresh primroses', *Daily Mail* (10 April 1918).

22. 'N.P.F.: A Working Example of the New Phenomenon', *Morning Post* (1 November 1916).

23. 'Press Pars S.F.F.', *Georgetown Gazette* (September 1918), p. 387, Public Record Office [hereafter PRO], MUN 5/154/1223/30. Another instance of group-specific adornment occurred at Woolwich Arsenal with a fashion of differently coloured ribbons being substituted for shoelaces. Foxwell (1917), pp. 43–4.

24. 'Arsenal Canaries', *Daily Express* (19 August 1918).

25. Wilson (1987), pp. 11–12.

26. Butler (1990), p. 136. *Gender Trouble: Feminism and the Subversion of identity (New York and London).*

27. Llewelyn Davies, M., 'Workers' Savings', *Daily News & Leader* (23 December 1915). One report stressed

> the better footwear given the children which obviates the constant chills, in winter, which cause countless disasters among the children of the poorer classes. ('British Women Earn Big Salaries in Wartime Work', *The Santa Maria Times* [California], 9 November 1918, p. 2).

28. 'Girl Munition Workers', *The Times* (19 October 1916). In a satirical response to complaints of women workers' big spending, the *Woman Worker* purported that: 'It was notorious ... that there was a connection between high wages and high-heeled boots', vol. 15 (March 1917), p. 3.

29. For example, the uniforms of the QMAAC patrols included high boots. 'Q.M.A.A.C. Patrols: A New Disciplinary Force', *The Times* (30 May 1918), p. 3.

30. Caroline Rennles remembered high-legged boots as too expensive for her and most of her workmates. IWM, Department of Sound Records, 000566/07, 39.

31. 'Ban on High Bots', *The Times* (7 December 1917), p. 5.

32. Loughnan (1917), p. 28.

33. Ring, C., 'Working Class Extravagance: An Apology', *The Common Cause* (28 January 1916), p. 564. Similar complaints included 'How Wages Are Wasted', *Sheffield Weekly Independent* (22 January 1916), p. 3. Other commentators referred to these accusations and rejected the 'foolish stories current about the munition workers extravagance etc. [sic]', 'The Health of the Girl Worker', *The Catholic Citizen* (15 July 1918), pp. 56–7; Harroden (1916), p. 10.

There is much contrary testimony that women workers did not commonly buy fur coats, and that those who did, did not buy real but imitation fur. For example, Pankhurst (1932), p. 163.

Elsie McIntyre remembered buying a rabbit fur coat that was supposed to pass as a fox fur. IWM, Department of Sound Records, 000673/09, 49.

34. For example, *Yorkshire Post* (1 March 1918); *Sunday Herald* (27 October 1918); '6,000 Women March to Whitehall', *The Times* (20 November 1918); 'London Women Protest', *The New York Times* (December 4 1918), p. 3; Munson (1985), p. 266; M.G. Carden, Hon. Secretary of the Women Patrols Committee of the National Union of Women Workers (19 November 1918), IWM, Women's Work Collection, Emp 42.4/50.

35. Commentators noted the irony of some of the middle and upper classes dressing shabbily to show wartime sacrifice, while workers were dressing better than they ever had. For example Peel (1929), p. 52.

36. 'Jewelry and Trimmings', *The War-Worker* I (July 1917). p. 28; 'Shoes and Stockings', *The War-Worker*, I (September 1917), p. 50. Even Mary Macarthur, leading trade union advocate of women workers, referred to the 'shoddy splendour' of women workers' clothing. *Woman's Life* (26 October 1918), p. 102.

37. 'The Sunday "Shift"', *The Times* (29 April 1916). Similarly middle-class munitions worker Brenda Girvin, for example, represented the class differences between herself and her working-class workmates through their choice of clothing and adornment: 'Flo with her fair hair fastened with several diamond combs, Gertie in a green velvet tam-o'-shanter, Harriet in a plush coat', 'Good-Bye, Munitions! What the Life Has Taught Me', IWM, Women's Work Collection, Press Cuttings, vol. 2, Women in Munitions Works, 1918–19.

38. Valverde (1989), pp. 169–88.

39. Steele (1985), pp. 8–9.

40. *Daily Express* (1 November 1917). Similarly 'a West-country shell girl' objected to the 'few disagreeable people grumbl[ing] because we turn out nicely dressed on a Sunday' when 'girls who work in munition factories deserve some little compensation for their long hours of work' and she herself could not 'spend much on pretty things' because she had to support her mother and 'the three children'. 'Managing Girls', *Empire News* (7 October 1917) The *Woman Worker* responded to the charges of extravagance with a satirical account of a munitions employer dreaming that women workers' complaints consisted of, for example, going 'for days without a box of chocolates'. 'The Employer's Dream', vol. 14 (February 1917), p. 2. See also the short story by Marion Phillips, 'Some Women War Workers', *The Labour Woman*, vol. 4 (November 1917), p. 220.

41. Munitions workers' wages varied greatly and not all had income left over from their living expenses or from supporting their families, but on average women's wages were about three times what they had been before the war. See Woollacott (1994), pp. 113–17.

42. Roberts (1994), Chapters 1–3.

43. Melman (1988), Chapter 1.

44. Shadwell, A. 'Ordeal by Fire', *The Nineteenth Century and After*, 81 (January 1917); p. 15. Sometimes the term 'the modern girl' was used in Britain and was also directly linked to changes in clothing style. K. Lyth Lofthouse, for example, claimed that: '[The modern girl's] body is much freer. Dress is a great exponent of personality. The modern girl has successfully burst the trammels of the flannel petticoat both physically and mentally. She leads a much more airy life'. 'The Personality of the Modern Girl', *The Newsletter* [YWCA] (June 1916), p. 62.

45. Steele (1985), pp. 222–36.

46. The cultural shift in perception of the ideal female body was related to the increasing participation of women in sports. Munitions workers took advantage

of opportunities to play sports which few women workers had previously enjoyed. Football teams and swimming clubs became part of the fabric of factory social life. See Woollacott (1994), pp. 135–8.

47. For example, Woolwich police court report, *The Pioneer* [Woolwich] (13 October 1916); 'The Canteen Spoon', *The Pioneer* (11 May 1917), p. 2; Woolwich police court report, *The Pioneer* (26 May 1916).

48. Cases of theft included, for example, a coat, *The Pioneer* (1 September 1916); two 'costumes' and a silk blouse, *The Pioneer* (28 September 1917), p. 3; undercloth-ing, *The Pioneer* (24 November 1916); and a pair of shoes, *The Pioneer* (3 August 1917), p. 3.

49. 'The Women Police Service', *The Common Cause* (2 February 1917), p. 561.

50. *Ibid*; Munson (1985), p. 227.

51. Joan Williams, a middle-class worker, called it 'an indescribable scrimmage'. IWM, Department of Printed Books, 'A Munition Workers' [*sic*] Career At Messrs. Gwynne's–Chiswick. 1915–1919', p. 7.

52. For example, case of Annie Nicholls, Woolwich police court record, *The Pioneer* (22 December 1916).

53. This may also be related to the fact that, apparently, at least some women muni-tions workers liked the opportunity to dress up in fancy dress. 'Ball for Munition Workers', *The Times* (17 November 1917), p. 3.

54. For example, Esther McKeown was caught wearing a coat, blouse, scarf and ring she had taken, 'Wearing Stolen Property', *The Pioneer* (20 December 1918) p. 6; Winnie Holden wore to work the coat she had taken from a cloak-room at Woolwich Arsenal, *The Pioneer* (27 July 1917), p. 3; Alice Lee wore to work a coat she had taken from the shifting-house some months earlier, *The Pioneer* (28 September 1917), p. 7. Most of my evidence about women stealing each other's clothes comes from the police court reports in *The Pioneer* (Woolwich).

55. The importance of clothing to women workers was evident in decades before the war through the widespread existence of young women factory workers' cloth-ing clubs. See for example Jones (1983), p. 199.

56. Steedman (1987), pp. 121, 123.

57. Elizabeth Fox-Genovese (1987, pp. 7–30) has insisted that fashion must espe-cially be seen this way.

58. Wilson (1987), pp.56–7, 244–7.

59. Sally Alexander has similarly contended that:

> Images and identifications acquired and rehearsed in play as she was growing up were elaborated and sustained in the imagination of the young woman with every new pair of shoes or special outfit. ('Becoming a woman in London in the 1920s and 1930s', in Feldman and Jones, 1989), p. 256.

60. Examples of such sentences were cases reported in *The Pioneer* (28 September 1917, p. 7; 27 July 1917, p. 3; 15 June 1917, p. 2; 8 February 1918; 30 November 1917, p. 6; 17 August 1917; 4 May 1917, p. 1; 3 November 1916).

61. For example, Roberts (1994), through her analysis of multiple cultural forms, takes a broader scope of the reconstruction of gender in post-war France than some other studies which have relied on feminists' discourse.

62. Wilson (1987), pp. 117–20.

63. See for example Valverde (1989), pp. 171–3.

64. Alexander (1989), pp. 245–9.

65. Hartley (1920), p. 42; Strachey (1936), pp. 249–50.

Bibliography

Alexander, S. (1989) 'Becoming a Woman in London in the 1920s and 1930s', in D. Feldman and G.S. Jones (eds), *Metropolis London: Histories and representations since 1800* (London and New York), pp. 245–71.

Barnes, R. and J.B. Eichler (eds) (1992) *Dress and Gender: Making and meaning in cultural contexts* (New York and Oxford).

Bullough, V.L. and B. Bullough (1993) *Cross Dressing, Sex, and Gender* (Philadelphia).

Butler, J. (1990) *Gender Trouble: Feminism and the subversion of identity* (New York and London).

Feldman, D. and G.S. Jones (eds) (1989) *Metropolis London: Histories and representations since 1800* (London and New York), p. 256.

Fox-Genovese, E. (1987) 'The Empress's New Clothes: The politics of fashion', *Socialist Review*, 91, pp. 7–30.

Foxwell, A.K. (1917) *Munition Lasses: Six months as principal overlooker in danger buildings* (London).

Garber, M. (1992) *Vested Interests: Cross-dressing & cultural anxiety* (New York and London).

Harroden, B. (1916) *Our Warrior Women* (London) p. 10.

Hartley, C.G. (1920) *Women's Wild Oats: Essays on the Refixing of Moral Standards* (London), p. 42.

Jones, G.S. (1983) *Languages of Class: Studies in English working class history 1832–1982* (Cambridge).

Loughnan, N. (1917) 'Munition Work', in G. Stone (ed.), *Women War Workers* (New York).

Melman, B. (1988) *Women and the Popular Imagination in the Twenties: Flappers and nymphs* (New York).

Munson, J. (ed.) (1985) *Echoes of the Great War: The Diary of the Reverend Andrew Clark 1914–1919* (Oxford).

Pankhurst, S. (1932) *The Home Front: A mirror to life in England during the World War* (London).

Peel, C.S. (1929) *How We Lived Then 1914–1918: A sketch of social and domestic life in England during the war* (London).

Roberts, M.L. (1994) *Civilization Without Sexes: Reconstructing gender in postwar France, 1917–1927* (Chicago).

Steedman, C.K. (1987) *Landscape for a Good Woman: A story of two lives* (New Brunswick).

Steele, V. (1985) *Fashion and Eroticism: ideals of feminine beauty from the Victorian era to the jazz age* (New York and Oxford).

Strachey, R. (ed.) (1936) *Our Freedom and Its Results* (London), pp. 249–50.

Valverde, M. (1989) 'The Love of Finery: Fashion and the fallen woman in nineteenth-century social discourse', *Victorian Studies*, 32, pp. 169–88.

Wilson, E. (1987) *Adorned in Dreams: Fashion and modernity* (Berkeley).

Wilson, E. and L. Taylor (1989) *Through the Looking Glass: A history of dress from 1860 to the present day* (London).

Woollacott, A. (1994) *On Her Their Lives Depend: Munitions workers in the Great War* (Berkeley).

Yates, L.K. (1918) *The Woman's part: A record of munitions work* (London).

14
Women under Austerity: Fashion in Britain during the 1940s*

Ina Zweiniger-Bargielowska

In September 1947 Sir Stafford Cripps, President of the Board of Trade declared in response to Dior's New Look with its long and wide skirt:

> the shorter the skirt the better ... The country ... [cannot] afford the great changes while we [are] so desperately short of material ... If we wasted any of our efforts ... we should be unable to effect the balance of imports against exports which [is] fundamental to the future possibility of our work and life.[1]

Regardless, women of all classes adopted the fashion with remarkable speed at a time of severe clothes rationing and the New Look dominated fashion well into the 1950s.[2]

The quotation illustrates the unusually political significance of fashion in the late 1940s. There are two reasons for this. On the one hand, the government took control of the entire clothing industry, including design, during the Second World War.[3] Fashion became subject to government decree and was effectively frozen for a number of years. The New Look challenged this state control of design of consumer goods which was accepted for the duration but became controversial after the cessation of hostilities. On the other, as a result of wartime dislocation of the economy the Labour government which was swept to power with a landslide majority in 1945 faced severe economic difficulties and particularly a balance of payments deficit.[4] Exports therefore acquired top priority and civilian consumption continued to be restricted after the war. In fact, shortages became worse and rations were lower and more volatile than during the war – for example, bread was rationed for the first time in 1946. During the crisis year of 1947 many food rations were cut and the government launched its menacing 'We work or want' campaign which raised the prospect of national collapse if export targets were not achieved.[5] Therefore a fashion which did not economize in materials was perceived as a threat to Britain's future prosperity by the government and adopting the fashion was a political statement indicating dissatisfaction with Labour's policy of austerity.

This chapter addresses Brewer and Porter's (1993) 'imperative that we investigate ... the links connecting ... material culture ... to the political and social systems with which it has become symbiotic'. Brewer and Porter emphasize the importance of consumerism and material culture as a key category of historical analysis and cite the recent history of Eastern and Central Europe to illustrate that 'the ultimate test of the viability of regimes rests in their capacity, in the literal sense, to "deliver the goods"'.[6] Britain experienced a rapid rise in consumption during the 1930s. The history of consumption during the 1940s is interesting because consumer spending was cut drastically during the war and held down for some years afterwards. The central purpose of this chapter is to examine the relationship between austerity and politics. More specifically it aims to explore how long a policy of reduced consumption can be sustained in a capitalist democracy and whether the continuation of shortages after the war damaged the Labour government's popularity.

During the 1940s the civilian population had to cope with extensive rationing of food and clothing as well as severe shortages of most other consumer goods. Food rationing was introduced in 1940 and continued until 1954 and clothes rationing lasted from 1941 until 1949. In 1942 total consumer spending was 15 per cent lower than in 1938. Spending was cut by more than one-third and household and miscellaneous goods by between one-quarter and three-quarters. Despite full employment, pre-war consumption levels of these domestic consumer goods were not reached until 1950 and surpassed only during the middle years of the decade.[7] This reduction in consumption, coupled with rigid controls of distribution and price, was unprecedented in British history in terms of extent and duration – during the First World War rationing had been confined to food, introduced late in the war and short-lived.[8]

These shortages of domestic consumer goods affected women to a greater extent than men since women were largely responsible for purchasing food, clothing and other household goods. The chapter examines the political significance of women's position as consumers, especially of clothes, during the 1940s. The transformation of women's attitudes towards fashion illustrates important changes in the relationship between state and society in war and peace. During the war women accepted sacrifice as a necessary part of the war effort, they made the most of limited supplies and morale remained high. By contrast after 1945 many women were fatigued and demoralized by the persistence of austerity. The success of the New Look indicated women's disillusionment with austerity and symbolized a reaction against excessive state interference in civil society. Austerity became a party-political issue after 1945; the debate revolved around the controversy between Labour's call for continued sacrifice and 'fair shares' and Conservative allegations of government mismanagement and demands for freedom and unrestricted consumption. This critique of austerity was directed particularly towards women and the Conservative strategy of establishing a coalition of consumer interests was central to their electoral success in the 1950s.

The chapter looks first at the importance of personal appearance to women and traces the emergence of the female mass consumer during the inter-war years. Secondly, it examines the transformation of fashion during the war as a result of a reduction in supplies, rationing, the utility scheme and austerity regulations. Post-war expectations centred on the desire for increased consumption as well as a return to 1930s' glamour. The final section assesses women's response to postwar austerity by focusing on the New Look controversy.

Beauty is not objective and universal but subjective and culturally constructed. There is no natural way for people to look and beauty – according to the fashion of the period – has been an aspiration for women and men from those social groups who could afford it for many centuries.[9] The visual image and the extent to which a socially prescribed ideal is achieved is central to defining a woman's worth or the 'exchange-value' of her body.[10] In the twentieth century magazines and advice manuals were increasingly explicit in their message addressed to women of a link between physical attractiveness through dress and make up and love and thereby happiness.[11] This emphasis on self-improvement and 'body maintenance' in which the body becomes a vehicle for pleasure and display is a key feature of the mass consumer culture which emerged during the inter-war years.[12] Evidence on the use of cosmetics shows that during the middle decades of the twentieth century female beauty-consciousness was no longer confined to the upper income groups but that the majority of women aspired towards the ideal beauty represented in magazines and the movies. According to a wartime Social Survey two-thirds of all women applied cosmetics. They were used by 90 per cent of the under-thirties but only 37 per cent of women over forty-five. Regular use of cosmetics was high among clerical and distributive workers (85 per cent), somewhat lower among factory workers (75 per cent) and lowest among housewives, the retired and unoccupied (55 per cent).[13] The Hulton Readership Survey after the war observed similar figures on the use of cosmetics which again declined with age. Lipstick and powder were used by 90 per cent of women under twenty-four and slightly more popular among working-class women. A more narrowly-defined 'beauty-conscious' woman who used a range of cosmetics accounted for over 70 per cent of all women in this age group.[14] During the 1940s age rather than class or income was a more important determinant in the use of make-up and it is not unreasonable to assume that women who spent a considerable amount of money on cosmetics were concerned about their clothes and aimed to follow fashion.

Of course there were differences in quality but the simpler styles of the twentieth century coupled with the general availability of sewing machines put fashionable clothes within reach even of the lower-income groups. The transformation in appearance especially among working-class women during the inter-war years was based on rising living standards and changes in demand as well as supply. Female demand for cosmetics and fashionable clothes was stimulated by a rapid rise in sales of women's magazines and cinema attendance, particularly among young and working-class women. Women's magazines, based on an editorial formula of fashion, romance, home and family were brimming with features and advertisements of cosmetics, clothing and household goods. Total sales of women's weekly magazines stood at 2.2 million and that of monthlies at 1.3 million at the end of the 1930s, 3.1 million and 1.9 million, respectively in 1946 and reached an all-time high of 11–12 million for the weeklies and 4.5 million for the monthlies during the second half of the 1950s.[15] The number of cinemas and cinema attendance increased rapidly during the inter-war years and particularly after the development of talkies and colour. On the eve of war 20 million tickets were sold each week and in 1949 four out of five people went to the cinema regularly with attendance highest among the young and the working class.[16] The convergence of a number of factors contributed towards satisfying this demand. Despite the image of the inter-war years as a period of mass unemployment and poverty, for the majority of the population (those in work) living standards were rising rapidly. As a result of economic growth and falling prices estimates put the rise of real wages at between 20 and 33 per cent.[17] The spread of mass production coupled with the expansion of multiple retailers placed cheap consumer goods including ready-made clothes and cosmetics increasingly within general reach.[18] In 1934 J.B. Priestley evocatively described this:

> ... new post-war England, belonging far more to the age itself than to this particular island. America, I supposed, was its real birthplace. This is the England of arterial and by-pass roads, of filling stations and factories that look like exhibition buildings, of giant cinemas and dance-halls and cafes, ... Woolworths, ... wireless, ... factory girls looking like actresses, ... and everything given away for cigarette coupons ... You need money in this England, but you do not need much money. It is a large-scale, mass-production job, with cut prices ... In this England, for the first time

in history, Jack and Jill are nearly as good as their master and mistress ... Jill beautifies herself exactly as her mistress does.[19]

This new England was not confined to the prosperous South East and George Orwell writing about depressed Lancashire in the late 1930s stressed the rise in consumption of cheap luxuries:

> The two things that have probably made the greatest difference of all [in helping people cope with the depression] are the movies and the mass-production of cheap smart clothes since the war. The youth who leaves school at fourteen and gets a blind-alley job is out of work at twenty, probably for life; but for two pounds ten on the hire-purchase system he can buy himself a suit which, for a little while and at a little distance, looks as though it had been tailored in Savile Row. The girl can look like a fashion plate at an even lower price. You may have three halfpence in your pocket and not a prospect in the world, ... but in your new clothes you can stand on the street corner, indulging in a private daydream of yourself as Clark Gable or Greta Garbo, which compensates for a great deal.[20]

These developments had an evident impact on fashion during the inter-war years. The youthful, boyish look of 1920s gave way to glamour and elegance during the 1930s (Figure 14.1). Chanel's simple styles and new

Figure 14.1   1930s' elegance: summer fashions, June 1939

Source: Drawn by S. Rouillard.

materials had been popular since the 1920s and Hollywood was influential, particularly in the 1930s. Lipstick and rouge were made respectable by the cinema, and one rising manufacturer, Max Factor, was a Hollywood firm. Fashionable clothes, including glamorous evening wear, were produced for the ready-to-wear market at a range of different prices.[21] Popular magazines such as *Woman* regularly featured fashionable patterns for home dressmaking and advice on how to alter clothes according to latest trends.[22] On the eve of war there had then been a striking transformation in female appearance compared with the Edwardian period. For the first time women of all classes could afford to look glamourous and fashionable with the help of mass-produced products, even if their make-up was bought for pennies at Woolworth and their clothes were made at home from a *Woman* pattern copying couture designs.

The Second World War altered fashion as a result of the reduction in supplies of clothing and cosmetics. Legislation intended to save raw materials, labour and factory space came into force in 1940 and output of consumer goods was restricted to two-thirds or less of the pre-war level at a time when demand was rising owing to increased female employment and spending power.[23] To enforce these reductions, the government gradually assumed complete control of consumer goods industries. This ranged from importing raw materials on government account and guidelines on output and quality to regulation of distribution by means of rationing and price controls. Clothes rationing was introduced in 1941. A Mass-Observation survey indicated that the initial public response was favourable, with 70 per cent approving of the policy and between 58 and 64 per cent claiming they were not affected by it. However, there were some notable gender and age differences: whereas 67 per cent of men thought they would be unaffected only 54 per cent of women felt this. Support was lowest among women under thirty (43 per cent) and highest among men under thirty (71 per cent). Women were also three times more likely to be critical; they anticipated difficulties in obtaining stockings and considered clothes rationing to be unfair to expectant mothers for whom no special provision was made.[24] Following ration cuts which gradually reduced the allowance by one-quarter, and the extension of rationing to household linen, clothes rationing became a persistent wartime grumble in Home Intelligence Morale reports. For instance, in autumn 1942 there was 'dissatisfaction' among housewives in nine out of 13 regions, '"Furnishing material on clothing coupons is reported to have been rather a sore point all along" but towels is "really a heavy blow"'.[25] A Mass-Observation report, based on surveys conducted in 1941 and 1943, concludes that the effect of clothes rationing was a 'tendency to wear older, shabbier clothes'. Women did not like the 'simpler, more informal clothes' and were 'very clear that, once restrictions are removed, they will return to buying clothes similar to those bought before the war'.[26] Wartime style was dominated by the utility scheme and austerity regulations with the unprecedented result that fashion became subject to government decree. Utility clothes, introduced in 1941, were produced according to strict guidelines, price-controlled and exempt from purchase tax (Figure 14.2). Soon 85 per cent of ready-made clothes were covered by the scheme which was intended to save labour and materials by encouraging long production runs while detailed specifications safeguarded quality.[27] The austerity regulations which applied to all ready-made clothes came into force in 1942 to ensure simple, economical styles by banning trimmings such as embroidery and restricting pleats, buttons and pockets along with the width of sleeves and collars.[28] In order to give utility clothing the best possible start, the Board of Trade chose top London fashion designers to create the prototypes and the initial response was favourable.[29] Utility clothing was made at every level of the market and at the lower end quality was often poor. Women frequently complained about the shoddiness of utility clothes and particularly stockings which were said 'to be shapeless and absolutely to be lacking in reasonable durability. The popular view is that they are just a waste of coupons'.[30] According to a Gallup poll, 80 per cent of the population had bought utility clothes by August 1944 but 67 per cent did not want the scheme to be continued after the war.[31] These measures coupled with the fact that more women than ever were in uniform led to a change in fashion from the elegance of the 1930s to a military look characterized by padded

Figure 14.2   Wartime styles: typical examples of utility clothing, 1942–3

Source: Drawn by S. Rouillard.

shoulders, short skirts and a severe, square silhouette. Clothes were plain, unadorned and functional and styles changed little throughout the war. Wartime fashion was also influenced by the needs of working women. With female employment high, turbans and headscarves became popular and trousers or dungarees were now socially acceptable as part of the female wardrobe. This does not mean that women renounced femininity. For instance, Doris White, a young, single engineering worker, did not forgo her dance on a Friday night even if she had to change at work after a 12-hour shift. She brought her dress and shoes, wore stockings under her trousers and curlers in her hair. At the end of the shift she was quickly transformed into a glamorous girl emulating one film star or another.[32]

Despite some grumbling, women accepted rationing and shortages as a necessary part of the war effort and female morale was of course maintained. Women developed a variety of strategies to cope with the shortages and keep up appearances. Elaborate make-up, frequently improvised or home-made, became more acceptable and inventive hairstyles and coupon-free accessories helped to counterbalance the drab and utilitarian clothes. Official propaganda such as the Board of Trade's 'Make do and mend' campaign instructed women on how to preserve and renovate clothes, and women's magazines aimed to help their readers cope with the shortages and keep up morale. The magazines became virtual propaganda tools, urging their readers to patriotic sacrifice and were fully committed to the war effort which affected every feature from fiction to fashion.[33] For example, stockings were treated with great care, rinsed in a variety of solutions, kept in air-tight containers and *Woman* advised buying two identical pairs and matching darning thread for instant repairs. Women used substitutes such as ankle socks (advocated even in *Vogue*) and stockingless cream was widely advertised.[34] An attractive appearance was not less, but more, important in wartime because it was perceived to be essential to female morale. As *Woman* put it, 'nowadays beauty is a duty, since it cheers and inspires both yourself and others'.[35] This duty was especially important during the Blitz. In 1940 *Woman's Own* advised on what to include in an 'air raid beauty make-up' kit and *Woman* recommended a miniature make-up set as the ideal Christmas gift to help women maintain morale during the Blitz.[36] The link between beauty, morale and the war effort was also reinforced by advertisements. To give just one example, the cosmetics firm Yardley coined the slogan 'Put your best face forward' and reminded women that

to yield to carelessness is to lower our standard to the enemy. There must be no surrender to circumstances, no giving ground to careless grooming. Now that we have less time and fewer beauty-aids, the greater our credit for good results. We must do our best to look our best always. Never should we forget that good looks and good morale go hand in hand.[37]

Post-war expectations focused on increased consumption and victory only served to reinforce the desire for spending. Mass-Observation noted the wish to 'buy new clothes in large quantities' among their mainly middle- and artisan-class sample. One woman maintained, 'After the war I hope to wear silk stockings again and to discard all my old clothes and have new very bright ones. I hope to buy a quantity of smart underclothes such as I have always had'.[38] There is some evidence that women expected restrictions to be lifted and that the plain, utilitarian wartime styles were not expected to continue indefinitely into the post-war era. A woman questioned by Mass-Observation about post-war clothes in 1944 dreamt of a 'decent costume with no restrictions on cut and pockets. I don't like utility costumes'.[39] In spring 1945, Paris, anxious to re-establish its leadership in fashion, promoted a more feminine, rounded silhouette which amounted to a return to where Paris had left off in 1939. This trend was picked up by *Vogue* as well as *Woman*, whose dressmaking patterns became more feminine and luxurious in 1945.[40] The symbolic importance of women's fashion was highlighted in a *Times* editorial on the day before the general election, 'Gay colours, beautiful frills, ... flowing lines are what every woman to-day is hoping soon to get'. However, the editor warned that 'if the right candidates are not chosen to-morrow, women must endure a disillusioned decade of universal beige'.[41]

Post-war expectations of unrestricted consumption were not fulfilled, shortages and controls persisted and in Paul Addison's words, 'it appeared as if the home front ran on without a war to sustain it'.[42] The clothes ration reached an all-time low during the first year after the war. There was some improvement in supplies of consumer goods but this was reversed after the fuel and financial crises of 1947 and the clothes ration, which had been raised in 1946, was cut again.[43] According to the editors of two popular women's magazines, initial optimism was soon replaced by low morale. Mary Grieve, *Woman's* editor, resented the imposition of postwar austerity 'upon a people sick of going without ... We were the victors, but he [Sir Stafford Cripps] refused us even modest spoils'. Similarly, James Drawbell, editor of *Woman's Own*, thought that women's post-war life was a 'drab and dreary let-down after ... high expectations'.[44] This pessimism was reflected in the magazines. Advertisements during the second half of 1945 adopted phrases such as 'Sorry ... not just yet' or 'Sorry! – but more to come' and the feminine clothes featured in *Woman* in March 1946 contrast with the reality of old-fashioned war-style coupon economy patterns in April.[45] Demand for clothes was certainly high and in October 1947 clothing topped the list as the first item women wanted to buy for their own use in Gallup polls. According to Social Surveys, over and above high levels of concern about food shortages, clothing difficulties scored between 10–13 per cent as the most important personal problem between December 1947 and May 1948. Again there are important gender differences and nearly twice as many women as men worried about clothes.[46] Since the need to win the war could no longer serve as a justification for sacrifice, shortages of consumer goods became increasingly controversial and politicized after 1945. For instance, the National Liberals opening a parliamentary debate in June 1947 highlighted the

> scarcity of many goods including clothing of every description, and especially nylons ... [whose] cumulative effect is very serious, both from the point of view of public morale and as a symptom of something wrong with the management of our affairs.

The National Liberals were supported by the Conservatives, who blamed socialist mismanagement as well as excessive controls and maintained that

> the people of this country would face anything – restrictions, controls ... – as long as they felt that they were necessary ... [but that] people are losing faith ... [because they] are not convinced that the continuation of these restrictions and shortages is really necessary.

Conversely, Sir Stafford Cripps defended government policy and claimed that the shortages were an inevitable consequence of post-war dislocation and Britain's balance of payments difficulties. He insisted that the government were doing all they could to redress the situation.[47] These arguments were repeated over and over in speeches, policy statements and party publications during the late 1940s. The critique of austerity and controls was taken up by the Conservatives in their attempt to reconstruct and electoral majority based on consumer interests while the Labour government stressed 'fair shares' and maintained that shortages were inevitable.[48] The New Look was unveiled by Dior in spring 1947 and public controversy about the fashion gathered pace during the autumn. The left-of-centre *Picture Post* captures both the absurdity and attraction of the fashion well.

> PARIS FORGETS THIS IS 1947: Straight from the indolent and wealthy years before the 1914 war come this year's much-discussed Paris fashions. They are launched upon a world which has not the material to copy them – and whose women have neither the money to buy, the leisure to enjoy, nor in some designs even the strength to support, these masses of elaborate material. ... The fact remains that these romantic frivolous clothes have such a seductive appeal that your eye is 'in' remarkably quickly. Their utter femininity recalls the splendour and elegance of the Avenue du Bois before the 1914 war ... But even if the many thousands of yards of material were available ... can anyone seriously contemplate ... doing housework, or sitting at a typewriter all

day, or working in a factory, tightly corseted, and encumbered and constricted with layers of hip-padding and petticoats?[49]

Fashion had been developing in the direction of the New Look since the end of the war and Dior's collection was essentially an extreme manifestation of the new female silhouette which emphasised curves rather than lines. The New Look in its most exaggerated forms was rarely worn but the influence of its essence – soft shoulders, a tight bodice, nipped-in waist and a very full, very long skirt – was far-reaching and lasted many years (Figure 14.3).[50] Paris had moved in this direction since 1945; there are many references in *Vogue* to more rounded, feminine lines, and *Woman* followed the trend from 1946 onwards. Softer, more feminine lines were highlighted in March, and in December the fashion editor decreed that 'the monstrous shoulder padding of a few years ago is completely out today'. The new line demanded longer skirts and women were advised to let down the hem which is 'a small operation but a vital one to present-day frocks'.[51]

The New Look was controversial not only because it was wasteful of material but also because it was launched when the clothing industry was controlled by the government. The austerity regulations were abolished in 1946 but rationing and the utility scheme continued and manufacturers

Figure 14.3   Dior's New Look

Source: Drawn by S. Rouillard.

were restricted by the scarcity of labour and raw materials. The government defined the clothing problem in terms of volume and the possibility of a radical change in fashion was apparently never considered by the Board of Trade. Clothes were seen essentially in utilitarian terms as mere coverings and the cultural and psychological significance of fashion was ignored. This approach was justifiable for the duration but could not be sustained indefinitely in peacetime in the face of public longing to return to the consumerism of the 1930s. The acceptability of wartime design was subverted by the gradual fashion changes since 1945 and openly challenged by the New Look. The continuation of wartime styles certainly tried the patience of the fashion-conscious who, as argued above, accounted for the majority, especially of younger women from all social backgrounds. In this context it is interesting to note that even the critics of the New Look acknowledged the fashion's aesthetic appeal. For example, Jill Craigie admitted that she 'like[d] the longer skirt' but she continued, 'Is not the question of taste, however, irrelevant to the main issue', namely Britain's economic crisis.[52] The aesthetic appeal of the new fashion transformed initial hostility into overwhelming support among Mass-Observation's observer panel. The New Look was

> said to be pleasing to look at, charming, graceful, more feminine, a welcome change after drab austerities ... This is the basis for the wide appreciation of 'the new womanly look' – the tight bodice and the billowing skirts that entrance the young and unmarried, the longer skirts that win over the older women ... [who] feel, with this housewife, that – 'the long skirt gives height and dignity and hides the ravages to her legs of age. The full skirt is always acceptable, as not only feminine but comfortable. It is a joy to the older woman ... I am glad to see the short, skimpy skirt which disclosed the backs of knees and thighs, when stooping, or sitting, disappear.'[53]

Public debate over the New Look clearly shows the division between government supporters and opponents and press coverage proceeded very much along party lines. Following the lead of Sir Stafford Cripps, Labour women urged British women not to adopt the fashion. In September 1947 Jill Craigie denounced the New Look as 'one of the most anti-social moves to have been made for some time' which would hopefully 'die a natural death'.[54] In an article in the trade-union-owned *Daily Herald* Labour MP Mabel Ridealgh condemned the fashion as

> Utterly ridiculous; stupidly exaggerated; waste of material and manpower; foisted on the average woman to the detriment of other, more normal, clothing ... The average housewife won't buy it. She can't afford the coupons let alone the price.

A request for readers' opinions showed that 92 per cent of correspondents to the paper endorsed these views.[55] By contrast, the fashion editor of the popular *Daily Express*, a paper with a Conservative editorial policy but read widely across the class and party divide, predicted in October 1947 that 'inside six months English women will be wearing clothes with this New Look'. Her answer to critics who held that women had neither coupons nor money was that the fashion-conscious woman 'will do what she has always done – use a lot of ingenuity and style-sense plus a little money and materials, to give last year's clothes next year's line'.[56] This settled the issue for the *Daily Express* and the regular fashion feature advised women on how to achieve the New Look. A similar stance was adopted by the Conservative *Daily Telegraph* and a male correspondent did 'not grudge [women] the extra yards of material' because he welcomed the return to femininity which symbolized the greater tranquillity and prosperity of the Edwardian era.[57] Women's magazines also supported the New Look. *Vogue*, an instant convert, declared, 'There are moments when fashion changes fundamentally. ... This is one of these moments'.[58] *Woman* was gradually converted. In October 1947 the magazine advocated a patriotic 'happy medium' but in February 1948 the editor maintained that 'it is possible to wear a moderately New Look on most occasions'.[59] Thus the commercial interests of ostensibly non-party political women's magazines coincided with Conservative criticism of Labour's austerity. The strength of the Conservatives' consumerist agenda was its ability to translate party politics into these ostensibly non-political areas of everyday life.

Despite clothes rationing there is general agreement among fashion writers and social historians that women adopted the New Look remarkably quickly. In 1948 ready-to-wear designs changed abruptly at all levels of the market. Wilson and Taylor cite the example of a sales assistant who coveted an expensive New Look dress and bought a cheap copy at C & A in the same season.[60] There is some quantitative evidence to confirm this change in demand. Rising stocks of women's made-up garments designed in the old style caused concern to Board of Trade officials in 1948 and skirts in particular became a 'high stock item'. The Board of Trade rejected suggestions to 'reduce the coupon values of these garments' and instead was 'assisting the trade to export surplus garments'.[61] In response to this pressure of market demand, even utility clothes were produced in the new style by 1949.[62] New clothes were only one element in this transformation of the female silhouette and women adopted the New Look largely by altering their existing clothes. Advice on how to achieve the new fashion by inserting waistbands, dropping hems or adding a contrast band was carried in newspapers as well as women's magazines (Figure 14.4).[63] Adaptation of clothes had always been necessary for working-class women and women of all classes used the dressmaking and renova-

Figure 14.4   Achieving the New Look: *Woman*, 17 April 1948

Source: Reproduced by kind permission of the Bodleian Library, Oxford.

tion skills developed during the war to acquire the New Look which was a 'symbol of a more decorative, more leisured [and] more feminine way of life'.[64]

Conclusion

Women's fashion during the 1940s illustrates the importance of austerity in the development of twentieth-century mass consumer culture in terms of both supply and demand. The shortages of raw materials and labour coupled with government controls, and above all the utility scheme, further accelerated the spread of mass-production techniques introduced into the clothing industry during the inter-war years. The combined effects of rationing, shortages and high taxation resulted in greater uniformity of consumption and helped to create a homogeneous mass market. The is illustrated well by the New Look which was more rapidly copied and more widely accessible than *haute couture* had ever been. Post-war demand for clothes and other consumer goods was high, if temporarily frustrated, but when the economic situation improved and austerity came to an end in the early 1950s the stage was set for the subsequent consumer boom. The transformation in women's attitudes from wartime acceptance of sacrifice to post-war disillusionment demonstrates the changing relationship between state and society in war and peace. The decision by many women to ignore government appeals for patriotic restraint and deferred gratification by adopting the New Look after 1947 is politically significant and can be interpreted as a symbol of female disaffection with Labour's policy of austerity. It is also a reaction against excessive interference in civil society which had been necessary for the war effort but was difficult to justify in peacetime. The New Look was much more than a media hype imposed from above on unwilling or passive women. Rather, the fashion's rapid success was largely based on women's ingenuity in adapting their clothes to the new style. This episode implies a popular rejection of government-sponsored design of consumer goods and thereby a turning-point in the battle to roll back the encroachments of the state into civil society after the war. The perpetuation of austerity, rationing and controls on consumption of clothes, food and other goods eroded support for the Labour government which, in Brewer and Porter's words, had failed to 'deliver the goods'. In 1945, social policy and social reform, areas where Labour could command strong female support, dominated the political agenda. Labour won the general election with a landslide majority and obtained a small majority of the female vote.[65] Labour's policy successes of maintaining full employment and introducing the welfare state remained popular but by the end of the 1940s the Conservatives had pushed the issue of consumption to the top of the political agenda. This was much more conducive to the traditional Conservative appeal to women and the party tried to harness, as well as exploit, female discontent with austerity. This strategy to win over frustrated female consumers was successful and the Conservative election victory of 1951 was based on a 12-point lead among women while the majority of men remained faithful to Labour. Of course, consumption was not the only issue deciding votes and the close result and high turnout during the 1951 general election indicate deep divisions within the electorate rather than a wholesale repudiation of the Labour government. Nevertheless, Labour's policy of attaching low priority to personal consumption had important electoral consequences, particularly in terms of the female vote and, conversely, the Conservative commitment to affluence is decisive in understanding the party's success in the 1950s.

Notes

* An earlier version of this chapter was presented at the Economic History Society Conference, Hull (April 1993). First and foremost, I want to thank Pat Thane who organized a session on 'fashion and design' which inspired me to write this chapter and who commented on various draft versions. I am grateful for comments and suggestions received in Hull, in Exeter and from my colleagues in Aberystwyth where I spoke on the topic of women's fashion at the staff research seminar. Special thanks are due to Avner Offer, Mike Roberts and Stana Nenadic for commenting on an earlier draft. The position of women under austerity and the wider impact of wartime and post-war shortages are discussed in my book *Austerity in Britain: Rationing and controls of consumption, 1939–1954* (forthcoming).

1. *The Times* (26 September 1947).
2. Howell (1975); Dorner (1975); Ewing (1986); Bond (1988); Wilson and Taylor (1989).
3. Hargreaves and Gowing (1952).
4. Morgan (1984); Pelling (1984); Cairncross (1985).
5. Zweiniger-Bargielowska (1993), (1994).
6. Brewer and Porter (1993), pp. 3, 1.
7. Hargreaves and Gowing (1952), Table 10; Worswick and Ady (1952), Table 7.
8. Beveridge (1928).
9. Porter (1991), pp. 206–32; Steele (1985), pp. 244–4; Banner (1992), pp. 4, 37–45; Liggett and Liggett (1989).
10. Featherstone (1982), pp. 21–2; Ferguson (1983), p. 42; Coward (1984), p. 75; Wolf (1990).
11. Steele (1985), pp. 214–16, 238; Ferguson (1983), pp. 44, 58–9; White (1970), pp. 147–8.
12. Featherstone (1982), pp. 18–19, 22–3.
13. Public Record Office, Kew (hereafter PRO), RG 23/17; Wartime Social Survey: Retail services and shortages, May 1942–March 1943 (Social Surveys are based on large and representative samples)
14. Nuffield College Library, Oxford, The Hulton Readership Survey, 1947, compiled by J.W. Hobson and H. Henry; Hulton (1950), pp. 60–2, 133–4 (this data is derived from the Hulton Readership Survey for 1949, based on a large and representative sample).
15. White (1970), Appendix, pp. iv–v.
16. Stevenson (1984), pp. 395–6; Hulton (1950), Table 63, p. 139.

17. Pollard (1992), p. 151.
18. Ewing (1986), pp. 118–38; Wilson and Taylor (1989), 75–86; Jefferys (1954); Rees (1969).
19. Priestley (1934), pp. 401–2.
20. Orwell (1957), p. 89.
21. Ewing (1986), pp. 122–7; see also Wilson and Taylor (1989); Howell (1975); Bond (1988).
22. *Woman*, the most popular women's magazine, was read primarily by lower-middle and working-class young women, see Hulton (1950), pp. 72–3, 77.
23. Hargreaves and Gowing (1952), pp. 92–115.
24. Mass-Observation, *Clothes rationing survey*, pp. 8, 61, 68–69 (this data is based on three small-scale surveys of 300 persons each conducted in London, Bolton and Worcester); PRO, INF 1/292, Home Intelligence Morale Reports, June 1941 (these weekly reports are based on a wide range of sources, including Ministry of Information's regional officers, police records, the BBC and voluntary organizations; while they are not representative in a strict quantitative sense they range considerably wider than Mass-Observation).
25. PRO, INF 1/292 (27 October–3 November 1942); discontent with clothes rationing persisted until the end of 1944 when reports were discontinued.
26. Mass-Observation (hereafter MO), File Report (hereafter FR) 1867, Rationing and changed clothing habits: men (July 1943); FR 1866, Rationing and changed clothing habits: women (July 1943); Mass-Observation extracts are reproduced with the permission of the trustees of the Mass-Observation Archive, University of Sussex.
27. Hargreaves and Gowing (1952), pp. 431–81; Wilson and Taylor (1989), pp. 118–22; Ewing (1986), pp. 139–44.
28. Hargreaves and Gowing (1952), pp. 436–7.
29. MO, FR, 1143, Utility clothing scheme (March 1942); MO, Topic Collection (hereafter TC), Personal Appearance and Clothes, Box 4/E, Utility clothes (March 1942); *Woman*, (7 March 1942); Howell (1975), pp. 96–7; Inner London Education Authority, CC41 (London, 1974), p. 33.
30. PRO, INF 1/292 (22–29 September 1942)(similar grievances are mentioned regularly in Home Intelligence Morale Reports); MO, FR, 2046, Women's clothes in Chester (March 1944).
31. Gallup (1976), pp. 93–4.
32. White (1980), pp. 14–15, 59, 63.
33. Grieve (1964), pp. 127–31 (Grieve was *Woman*'s editor from 1940–1962); Waller and Vaughan-Rees (1987).
34. *Woman* (1 February and 28 June 1941); Howell (1975), pp. 162–3; *Vogue*, the quintessential upmarket fashion magazine was read primarily by middle- and especially upper middle-class younger women, see Hulton (1950), pp. 72, 77; Waller and Vaughan-Rees (1987), p. 88; Wilson and Taylor (1989), p. 116.
35. *Woman* (23 December 1939).
36. Quoted in Waller and Vaughan-Rees (1987), p. 80; *Woman's Own* had roughly the same readership profile as *Woman*, but lower circulation, see Hulton (1950), pp. 72, 77; *Woman* (14 December 1940).
37. *Woman* (23 May 1942).
38. MO, FR, 1866, Rationing and changed clothing habits: women (July 1943).
39. MO, FR, 1046, Women's clothes in Chester (March 1944).
40. *Vogue* (March 1945); *Woman* (10 and 31 March and 5 May 1945).
41. *The Times* (4 July 1945).

42. Addison, P. (1985), p. 2.
43. *Board of Trade Journal* (25 August 1944, 23 February and 22 June 1946, 5 March, 12 April and 20 September 1947); special issue on 'Supplies of consumer goods to the Home Civilian Market' (7 May 1949) (the supplies situation improved again from 1948 onwards).
44. Grieve (1964), p. 131; Drawbell, J. (1968) p. 45; Sissons and French (1963), pp. 36–7, 133–4; Braybon and Summerfield (1987), p. 277.
45. *Woman* (4 August 1945, 2 March and 6 April 1946).
46. Gallup (1976), pp. 162–3; PRO, RG 23/92, pp. 94–6, 98, Survey of Knowledge and opinion about the economic situation (December 1947 until June 1948).
47. *Hansard*, fifth ser., 439 (26 June 1947), cols 688–9, 698–9, 704–13, 733–4, 769.
48. Zweiniger-Bargielowska (1994).
49. *Picture Post* (27 September 1947); *Picture Post* was read by nearly one-quarter of all women and popular among the higher income groups and younger women, see Hulton (1950), pp. 72, 77.
50. Wilson and Taylor (1989), pp. 145–6; Ewing (1986), pp. 155–60; Bond (1988), pp. 125–9.
51. *Vogue* (April and September, 1946, February 1947); *Woman* (2 March 1946 and 21 December 1946).
52. Correspondence, *The New Statesman and Nation* (4 October 1947).
53. MO, FR, 3095, New Look, panel reactions (March 1949)(based on surveys in September 1947 and September 1948).
54. *The Times* (25 September 1947).
55. *Daily Herald* (23 February 1948); readership was highest among older working-class women, see Hulton, (1950), pp. 72, 77.
56. *Daily Express* (8 October 1947).
57. *Daily Telegraph* (1 and 6 October 1947); this paper was read largely by the upper and middle class, see Hulton (1950), p. 72.
58. *Vogue* (October 1947).
59. *Woman* (25 October 1947 and 14 February, 1948).
60. Wilson and Taylor (1989), p. 153.
61. *Board of Trade Journal*, Wholesale stocks and sale of clothing (22 May, 12 June, 17 July, 18 September, 16 October, 13 November and 18 December 1948, 16 April 1949); *Hansard*, fifth ser., 448, 2 (March 1948), col. 55 (written answers), 450 (27 April 1948), col. 33 (written answers).
62. *Woman* (12 March 1949).
63. *Daily Telegraph* (6 October 1947); *Daily Express* (8 October 1947); *Vogue* (January 1948), *Picture Post* (14 February 1948); *Woman* (17 and 24 April 1948).
64. MO, FR, 3095, New Look: panel reactions (March 1949).
65. Charlot (1981), Figure 8–1, p. 245; Durant (1976), Table 2, p. 211; Hinton (1992), pp. 59–64, also analyzes the Gallup findings. Hinton rejects the argument that Labour's support among working-class women was eroded but his figures are different from those of other commentators and contradict a host of anecdotal evidence. See Zweiniger-Bargielowska (1996), pp. 194–223. See Craig (1971) for election results.

Bibliography

Addison, P. (1985) *Now the War is Over: A social history of Britain 1945–1951* (London).

Banner, L. (1992) 'The Fashionable Sex, 1100–1600', *History Today*, 42(4), pp. 37–45.

Beveridge, Sir William H. (1928) *British Food Control* (London).

Bond, D. (1988) *The Guiness Guide to Twentieth Century Fashion* (Enfield).

Braybon, G. and P. Summerfield (1987) *Out of the Cage: Women's experiences in two world wars* (London).

Brewer, J. and R. Porter (eds) (1993) *Consumption and the World of Goods* (London).

Cairncross, A. (1985) *Years of Recovery: British economic policy 1945–51* (London).

Charlot, M., 'Women and Elections in Britain', in H.R. Penniman (ed.), *Britain at the Poll, 1979* (Washington and London), pp. 241–62.

Coward, R. (1984) *Female Desire* (London).

Craig, F.W.S. (ed.) (1971) *British Parliamentary Election Statistics 1918–1970*, 2nd edn (Chichester).

Crofts, W. (1989) *Coercion or Persuasion? Propaganda in Britain after 1945* (London).

Dorner, J. (1975) *Fashion in the Forties and Fifties* (London).

Drawbell, J. (1968) *Time on my Hands* (London).

Durant, H. (1976) 'Voting Behaviour in Britain 1945–64', in R. Rose (ed.) *Studies in British Politics: A reader in Political Sociology*, 3rd edn (London).

Ewing, E. (1986) *History of Twentieth Century Fashion*, 3rd edn (London).

Featherstone, M. (1982) 'The Body in Consumer Culture', *Theory, Culture and Society*, 1, pp. 18–33.

Ferguson, M. (1983) *Forever Feminine: Women's magazines and the cult of femininity* (London).

Gallup, G.H. (ed.) (1976) *The Gallup International Public Opinion Polls: Great Britain, 1937–1975*, 1 (New York).

Gallup Poll (1976) 'Voting Behaviour in Britain, 1945–74', in R. Rose (ed.) *Studies in British politics: A reader in political sociology*, 3rd edn (London), pp. 204–15.

Grieve, M. (1964) *Millions Made my Story* (London).

Hargreaves, E.L. and M.M. Gowing (1952) *Civil Industry and Trade* (London).

Hinton, J. (1992) 'Women and the Labour Vote', *Labour History Review*, 57, (Winter), pp. 59–64.

Howell, G. (1975) *In Vogue: Six decades of fashion* (London).

Howell, G. (1991) *In Vogue: 75 years of style (London).*

Hulton, E. (Hulton Press) (1950) *Patterns of British Life* (London).

Inner London Education Authority (1974) *CC41: Utility furniture and fashion 1941–1951 (London).*

Jefferys, J.B. (1954) *Retail Trading in Britain 1850–1950* (Oxford).

Liggett, A. and J. Liggett (1989) *The Tyranny of Beauty* (London).

Mass-Observation (1941) *Clothes Rationing Survey* (London).

Morgan, K.O. (1984) *Labour in Power* (Oxford).

Orwell, G. (1957) *The Road to Wigan Pier* (London) (originally published, 1937).

Pelling, H. (1984) *The Labour Governments, 1945–51* (London).

Pollard, S. (1992) *The Development of the British Economy, 1914–1990*, 4th edn (London).

Porter, R. (1991) 'History of the Body', in P. Burke (ed.), *New Perspectives on Historical Writing* (Cambridge), pp. 206–32.

Priestley, J.B. (1968) *English Journey* (London) (originally published, 1934).

Rees, G. (1969) *St Michael: A history of Marks & Spencer* (London).

Sissons, M. and P. French (eds) (1963) *Age of Austerity* (London).

Steele, V. (1985) *Fashion and Eroticism: Ideals of feminine beauty from the Victorian era to the Jazz age* (Oxford).

Stevenson, J. (1984) *British Society 1914–1945* (London).

Waller, J. and M. Vaughan-Rees (1987) *Women in Wartime: the role of women's magazines 1939–1945* (London).

White, C.L. (1970) *Women's Magazines 1693–1968* (London).

White, D. (1980) *D for Doris, V for Victory* (Milton Keynes).

Wilson, E. and L. Taylor (1989) *Through the Looking Glass: A history of dress from 1860 to the present day* (London).

Wolf, N. (1990) *The Beauty Myth: how images of beauty are used against women* (London).

Worswick, G.D.N. and P.H. Ady (eds) (1952) *The British Economy 1945–1950* (Oxford).

Zweiniger-Bargielowska, I. (1993) 'Bread Rationing in Britain, July 1946–July 1948', *Twentieth Century British History*, 4, pp. 57–85.

Zweiniger-Bargielowska, I. (1994) 'Rationing, Austerity and the Conservative Party Recovery after 1945', *Historical Journal*, 37, pp. 173–97.

Zweiniger-Bargielowska, I. (forthcoming) *Austerity in Britain: Rationing and Controls of Consumption, 1939–1954* (Oxford).

Zweiniger-Bargielowska, I. (1996) 'Explaining the Gender Gap: The Conservative Party and the Women's Vote, 1945–1964', in M. Francis and I. Zweiniger-Bargielowska (eds), *The Conservatives and British Society 1880–1990* (Cardiff).

Index